Peacebuilding in the Balkans

Peacebuilding in the Balkans

The View from the Ground Floor

PAULA M. PICKERING

Cornell University Press ITHACA AND LONDON

First published 2007 by Cornell University Press

Printed in the United States of America

Library of Congress Cataloging-in-Publication Data

Pickering, Paula M. (Paula May), 1966–
   Peacebuilding in the Balkans : the view from the ground floor /
Paula M. Pickering.
     p. cm.
   Includes bibliographical references and index.
   ISBN 978-0-8014-4576-7 (cloth : alk. paper)
   1. Peace-building—Bosnia and Hercegovina. 2. Return migration—Bosnia and Hercegovina. 3. Bosnians—Ethnic identity. 4. Yugoslav War, 1991–1995—Refugees—Bosnia and Hercegovina. 5. Bosnia and Hercegovina—Politics and government—1992– 6. Bosnia and Hercegovina—Ethnic relations. I. Title.
   DR1750.P43 2007
   949.703—dc22

                  2007028873

Cornell University Press strives to use environmentally responsible suppliers and materials to the fullest extent possible in the publishing of its books. Such materials include vegetable-based, low-VOC inks and acid-free papers that are recycled, totally chlorine-free, or partly composed of nonwood fibers. For further information, visit our website at www.cornellpress.cornell.edu.

Cloth printing   10 9 8 7 6 5 4 3 2 1

Contents

Acknowledgments

I fell in love with Eastern Europe on the first day I set foot there in 1988. The people there drew me into the region. And it is the people of the former Yugoslavia to whom I owe the most. Without the willingness of those who have suffered so much to share their personal thoughts, their social lives, and their efforts to rebuild normal lives with me, I could not have written this book. I hope that my research does justice to them and their stories and helps contribute to an understanding that might make things better for them and their children.

I owe special thanks also to accomplished scholars who shared their vast wisdom about and passion for research with me. Zvi Gitelman has painstakingly mentored and challenged me to think, write, and conduct research in new and better ways about ethnicity, politics, and Eastern Europe. Kent Jennings has counseled me to reach beyond comparative politics and be more rigorous about the theory and methods I use. Martha Feldman has taught me to use qualitative methods to make better sense of everyday politics. John Fine has inspired and guided me by sharing on countless occasions his encyclopedic knowledge of the Balkans and his passion for its peoples.

I owe immense thanks to Katherine Cramer Walsh, Claudio Holzner, and Khristina Haddad for being my most critical and supportive readers and for consistently forcing me to think in innovative ways. Sherrill Stroschein and Kevin Deegan Krause have encouraged me to consider new literature and the comparative implications of my work. I also thank Sladjana Danković, Tone Bringa, Bob Donia, Bob Kaiser, Bill Zimmerman, Val Bunce, Amaney Jamal, Donna Parmalee, Lee Schwartz, Gary Crocker, Dina Smeltz, Janet Crayne, Patrick Patterson, Michael Ross, Chris Achen, Susan Woodward, Rob Franseze, Chip Gagnon, Pat Lynch, John Zerolis, Rod Mackler, Kim Gross, Kari Johnstone, Chris Nemachek, and Paul Manna for advice on key aspects of this research. This book has also benefited from comments by anonymous reviewers and from astute editorial assistance from Martin Schneider and Anita Holmes. I particularly appreciate Roger Haydon for his support of the book's ideas and for improving my writing about them.

My fieldwork owes a huge debt to those who took the time to help me learn and connect with people in the former Yugoslavia. For this, I am particularly indebted to Elissa Helms; scholars at the Institut za istoriju Sarajevo; Sonja Valtassari; Kathrine Biering; Jadranka, Nuna, Selma, and everyone at Žene Ženama; Majda, Azrija, and members of the Democratic Circle; Michael Sporluk; Centar za nenasilno rešavanje konflikata–Niš, Bill and Renata Steubner; Josie Lecraw; Luke Zahner; Karen Williams; and Mark Baskin. I am grateful for the generosity of staffers of many local and international organizations across Bosnia, including those with the UNHCR, the OSCE Mission, the Office of the High Representative (OHR); the International Organization for Migration (IOM); the International Rescue Committee, Edinburgh Direct Aid, CARE, Orthodox Relief, Hilswerk; Open Broadcast Network's (OBN) "povratak" team, the Property Commission; Pax Christi; Merhamet, Banja Luka; Through Heart to Peace; the Center for Democracy–Konjic; International Forum Bosnia; and Žene u crnom, Belgrade.

Several organizations and individuals assisted me with data, resources, and artwork for this book. I appreciate the IOM's permission to use the data it collected on refugees returning to Bosnia-Herzegovina. Dina Smeltz provided in-depth analysis of data collected by the U.S. Department of State's Office of Research. Randy Hodson shared data contained in the Consortium of Institutes for Social Science in Yugoslavia, Survey on National Tolerance, 1989. Predrag Pajic guided me to resources at the Library of Congress. And Leo Dillon and Will Armstrong produced this book's map and illustrations, respectively.

I am deeply indebted for the financial support of my research provided by the U.S. Institute of Peace's Jennings Randolph Peace Scholar Fellowship, the Fulbright-Hays Doctoral Dissertation Research Abroad Fellowship, the Social Science Research Council's International Field Dissertation Research Fellowship; the University of Michigan's Department of Political Science, the Wallenberg Endowment Grant, Foreign Languages and Area Studies Fellowships; Margaret Dow Towsley Scholarship at the University of Michigan, University of Michigan's International Institute and the Working Group on War and Peace in Southeastern Europe, the South East European Studies Association, and The College of William and Mary's Reves Center for International Studies and Arts and Sciences.

My family, Margaret, Richard, Andy, and Kristin Pickering, has provided unwavering support. I dedicate this book to my parents, who encouraged me to pursue my dreams, and to the memory of Blanche Coles, who taught me early that love penetrates cultural boundaries.

Peacebuilding in the Balkans

Introduction
The View from Below

> *Nela*[1] [a middle-aged teacher of Serb background from Sarajevo]: When I decided to return [in 1998 to Sarajevo from Serbia], and when I realized that I'm Bosnian—from here [Sarajevo]—my colleagues in Sarajevo helped me [reclaim my job]. But telling the refugees [in Serbia] that we were leaving created problems. They couldn't comprehend that I just wanted to live a normal life.

THE international community has spent billions of dollars encouraging ordinary people, particularly those like Nela, now tendentiously considered a member of a "minority," to return to their homes of origin so that they can integrate into postwar Bosnia and help create a democratic and multiethnic state. Bosnia is just one of a group of states that includes Rwanda, East Timor, Afghanistan, Iraq, Tajikistan, not to mention other former Yugoslav territories of Croatia, Macedonia, and Kosovo, where international actors are directing multifaceted reconstruction[2] and democratization projects. These regions have in common several traits: They are all recovering from war, they all lack a democratic tradition, and they are all poor, weak, and culturally splintered (Bunce 2005). The strategies of the international community focus on reforming political institutions at the top and supporting nongovernmental organizations (NGOs) at the bottom. If international reconstruction programs do not resonate among ordinary people, however, they will alienate citizens, compelling them to emigrate or leaving them susceptible to mobilization by extremist elites willing to send them back into war, both of which threaten the project of bringing about peace and multiethnic democracy. Political scientists and

---

1. All names of people observed and interviewed have been changed to protect their confidentiality. For their demographic backgrounds, see appendix B.

2. Unless otherwise specified, this book uses the term *reconstruction* to refer to broad efforts to rebuild political institutions and communities, as well as the economy and physical infrastructure of war-torn states.

practitioners must understand how ordinary people—people other than politicians and community leaders—interpret and react to peacebuilding programs; ignoring their input can result in the exclusion of ordinary citizens, particularly minorities, and spell defeat for institutional reforms.

For an example of how ordinary people face the dilemma of reintegration, we need look no further than the epigraph of this chapter: Nela chose to defy nationalists by returning to an area where she was in the minority, but she found neither the local government nor internationally financed local NGOs useful in her arduous quest to rebuild a normal life in postwar Bosnia. She shared the opinion of most citizens of Bosnia that the local government, which had prevented her from reclaiming her prewar apartment for four years, was corrupt and that it discriminated against minorities. At the same time, she viewed local NGOs advocating for the rights of minorities as too weak to be helpful. So she did what anyone would do: She ignored these formal institutions and developed her own strategy. Her idea was to reach out to members of the majority group, such as her colleagues, who could help her in an environment otherwise hostile to minorities. Nela's case demonstrates how the everyday actions of ordinary people influence the reconstruction process by contesting both the nationalists' efforts to solidify ethnically homogeneous regions and the international community's goals of fostering democratic and multiethnic formal institutions. Nela continues to this day the struggle she began in 1998 to rebuild her own life and that of her teenaged son in Sarajevo (see chapters 3 and 4).

Frustrated by the categories, roles, and formal institutions that domestic elites and international officials built, ordinary people, duly labeled minorities by outside groups, tend to ignore them and rely instead on strategies that match the more nuanced and complex circumstances they encounter every day. Armed only with a confidence that they understand their situation better than international observers or domestic politicians, they forge unexpected, informal social networks that often cross ethnic lines to carve out their own place in postconflict Bosnia. This process of quietly contesting and resisting formal structures for integration or homogenization is a time-honored tradition for common citizens in post-Communist societies used to thwarting the institutionalization of political projects that fail to gain their trust (Rose, Haerpfer, and Mishler 1997) or meet their needs (Drakulić 1993). Grassroots participation in the Velvet Revolution that toppled Czechoslovakia's unpopular Communist government demonstrates the power of ordinary people.

Enough has been written about international engineers and domestic elites. What of the choices made by ordinary people facing difficult (some might say impossible) circumstances? What of their reactions to programs that seek, in good faith although often with insufficient attention to the needs of ordinary citizens, to build viable states and sustainable peace? *Peacebuilding* describes broad efforts to consolidate peace and prevent a recurrence of fighting (Paris 2004, 38), a process that includes *statebuilding*, or reconstructing an effective indigenous government (Caplan 2004, 53). This book features extensive fieldwork that highlights firsthand observation of how ordinary people respond to postwar institutions in *natural settings*, including neighborhoods, workplaces, informal groups at cafés, voluntary associations, and municipality offices. It is an attempt to reconcile some obvious shortcomings in the literature focused on formidable power elites and new institutions, based on the actual behavior of ordinary people I witnessed, their interpretations of peacebuilding, which I heard about in intensive interviews, as well as statistical analysis I conducted on mass survey data.

Even though local political elites set the official terms of citizenship, it is ordinary people in the postwar period who interpret official constraints and decide what to do about them. So it is ordinary people on whom I focus my research.

To understand the reconstruction process better, I investigate explanations for three phenomena: (a) the decisionmaking processes of minorities about where to rebuild their lives, (b) the sites they select to develop bridging strategies for social reintegration, and (c) the shape of their political participation. Ultimately, processes underlying all these phenomena influence the nature of the statebuilding project.

My central argument is that ordinary people influence the implementation of peacebuilding programs through their everyday reactions to these projects. The case of postwar reconstruction in Bosnia shows that the everyday reactions of common people to a central goal of reconstruction—reintegration into more or less diverse communities—are not simply determined by elites, institutions, interests, or resources from on high—quite the contrary. Instead, even the most cursory focus on everyday life reveals an obvious component often absent in the literature—that the responses of ordinary people are guided by their own particularistic understandings of self and of their social location. It is through the social processes of daily life that people understand themselves and their social connections (Brubaker and Cooper 2000). Armed with these notions, people cope with one statebuilding project after another, all of which fail to gain their confidence and instead make them feel like lab rats in scientific experiments. The experience of reconstruction in Bosnia shows that internationally designed institutions often do not help popular efforts to reintegrate and rebuild normal lives.

Consider Jasna's reaction to the discrimination she encountered for speaking Croatian in her workplace in the Muslim- or Bošnjak-dominated[3] town of Bihać. Her own self-understanding and social connections guided her response to the nationalists' culturally exclusive statebuilding project:

> Ordinary people don't have a problem with my language. It's the government who has the problem; it is trying to make me go. [If I left Bihać,] I would betray the people who supported me during the worst times [when I was fired]. Then, I had acquaintances stop me on the street. They didn't lose their faith [in me].

Jasna suggests that the Croatian language is critical to her self-understanding, yet so are the weak (she uses the term *acquaintances*) but important connections that she has to segments of the broader community in this town in northwestern Bosnia. Together, her sense of who she was and how she fit into the social milieu led her to decide not only to stay in a nominally diverse local community but also to build on those informal social networks. Studies of domestic elites and the ample incentives that political institutions provide for them to privilege the majority group would accentuate the difficulties Jasna would have; they are not capable of anticipating her strategy for coping with her treatment as a minority.

Divided Postconflict Societies

This book seeks to identify the factors that influence the opportunities for coexistence among different ethnic groups after years of violence and coercion directed against those who, whether culturally different or ideologically opposed, threaten efforts by powerful domestic elites to create culturally exclusive states. The Bosnian case of peacebuilding and minorities' roles in that process struck me in both an intellectual and an emotional way. Years of experiences with remarkable people in terrible circumstances in Bosnia impressed upon me what international officials often missed: the capacity of ordinary people to develop their own strate-

3. The Congress of Bošnjak Intellectuals in 1993 voted to use "Bošnjak" for the Bosnian Muslim nation (Filandra 1998). This was done largely to reinforce national—rather than merely religious—distinctiveness of Slavic peoples of Muslim heritage (Bringa 1995). I use terms (Bošnjak or Muslim) that my contacts use. Otherwise, I use the term *Bošnjak*. I found that Serbs and Croats rarely used the term Bošnjak for Muslims.

gies for rebuilding their lives. Bosnia has lessons to offer students of peacebuilding because it shares key attributes of other ongoing cases of peacebuilding, including societies seeking both to recover from war that occurred largely between cultural groups and to overcome a lack of experience with democracy, poverty, weak institutions, and covetous neighboring countries. Furthermore, the conglomeration of international organizations dispatched to implement the Bosnian peace agreement represented one of the international community's first multifaceted efforts at postconflict statebuilding after the end of the Cold War. Intergovernmental and nongovernmental organizations have struggled for more than ten years to repair not just the physical infrastructure but also the economic system and the political institutions—indeed, the very society—of this postconflict state. The ambitious "central premise" of the General Framework Agreement for Peace in Bosnia and Herzegovina, commonly referred to as the Dayton Peace Agreement, that ended the war was the "re-construction of Bosnia as a single multiethnic country" (Holbrooke 1998, 362). If we can understand how ordinary people responded to the postconflict statebuilding process, that will help us see how the external investment of billions of dollars (Sumka 2003) influenced the democratization and reintegration of the Bosnian state.

Specifically, much of that assistance has been targeted to support the unprecedented right of displaced persons to return to their homes of origin, rather than just to their homelands. For many, returning to their prewar homes means living in areas where their ethnic group is in the minority. The decade-old process of reintegrating minorities in Bosnia has much to tell us about which institutions and resources minorities found helpful in mediating the interethnic interaction necessary for navigating even a modestly diverse environment, and which ones they found useless or worse, counterproductive. Looking at this process also uncovers how ordinary people with varying backgrounds and wartime experiences—including those who stayed and suffered sieges lasting years—react to minority return and how they influence reintegration at the communal level. Observing the regular person's reaction can help us assess what it was external intervention accomplished. It can also reveal whether internationally imposed goals relate to what people really needed. The answers to these questions will help guide the international community's responses to peacebuilding in places such as Kosovo, Macedonia, Croatia, Tajikistan, Rwanda, and Afghanistan.

This investigation makes four primary contributions to scholarly theory and to practice.

1. It calls for more attention to the ways that ordinary people interact with elites, public policy, and institutions to influence the implementation of reconstruction projects.
2. It argues that interests and resources cannot alone explain why ordinary people arrive at different conclusions about the supposedly objective incentives for reintegration. Close attention to ordinary people and their actions shows that particularistic understandings of self and social location largely govern their behavior. This observation runs counter both to rationalist explanations of behavior and to primordialist arguments that all persons placed into cultural categories such as "Serb" have uniform attitudes about nationbuilding.
3. It suggests that scholars and practitioners who emphasize the potential of civil society to assist integration should recognize the obstacles to the development of ethnically diverse civic organizations that a deeply divided society with an intrusive authoritarian legacy presents. In the Balkan context, for example, bottom-up approaches to statebuilding would be better off adopting a broader notion of civil society that incorporates not just Western-favored NGOs but also informal social networks rooted in tradition. In many ways the local tradition-based networks are a better guide than solutions imposed from without.
4. Field research suggests that reconstruction efforts could significantly assist reintegration by generating nondiscriminatory employment, which allows ordinary people to develop both the financial security and the social networks needed to bridge differences.

The Problems of Minorities

The perceptions and actions of ordinary people who live as minorities deserve particular attention because their hearts and minds are the primary focus of a battle between domestic elites and international officials over the nature of the postconflict Bosnian state. Consistent with use of the term by international practitioners in Bosnia, I consider *minorities* to be persons who belong to ethnic groups other than the one that now dominates their prewar municipality of residence (UNHCR 2005).[4]

How did minorities become such an Achilles' heel for statebuilding projects in the Balkans and beyond? Prominent scholars and politicians

---

4. This book discusses both minorities who returned to their prewar localities after the war and those who relocated to new localities where they are now in the majority.

have long viewed the ethnic diversity characterized by minorities who maintain strong attachments to subcultures and territory as a problem that undermines democracy and stability (Dahl 1989). Such minorities resist assimilation, robbing political elites of the chance to mold a cohesive, culturally based nation theorized by advocates of the nation-state as a prerequisite for a building a viable state (Gellner 1983). Many of the troubled, ethnically diverse areas that are the focus of international reconstruction and democratization efforts arose out of empires whose key achievement was constructing and then politicizing diversity (Bunce 2005). For example, imperialists introduced the idea of the cultural-based nation into settings where cultural communities were often territorially concentrated (Donia and Fine 1994; Toft 2003) and then used the policy of "divide and rule" to dominate the indigenous populations. Belgian rule over Rwanda provides a vivid example of this strategy. The colonizers created the cultural categories of Tutsi and Hutu in very broad strokes out of the economic strata existing in local communities and then favored the Tutsis, fomenting the resentment that the Hutu extremists would mobilize during the 1994 genocide (Berry and Berry 1995).

This imperial construction and politicization of diversity in the Balkans is also crystal clear. Simply put, Ottoman rulers favored Muslims. Confronted with ethnocentric authoritarianism in the interwar period, ethnic minorities in Eastern Europe then felt destined to remain second-class citizens forever unless they redrew the borders (Rothschild and Wingfield 2001, 8). During World War II, Croatian fascists waged genocide against Serbs in areas where Serbs were in the minority. Socialist Yugoslavia adopted a system of shared sovereignty that attempted to remove the fears of minorities (Woodward 1995a). Between 1945 and the first multiparty elections in 1991, Bosnia's inhabitants of Muslim, Serb, and Croat background were treated as the founding (constituent) nations of both the republic of Bosnia and of the Socialist Federation of Yugoslavia (*Ustav* 1991) and coexisted peacefully.[5] But when the nationalist parties who won the 1991 elections began to implement their exclusive agendas, many ordinary persons of Serb and Croat background—still legally classified as constituent nations in Bosnia—felt relegated in practice to the vulnerable status of minority.

Minority activists in the Balkans who participated in the wars of the 1990s resurrected and manipulated past instances of violence against mi-

5. Socialist Yugoslavia reserved the label "minorities" for groups whose homelands exist outside of Yugoslavia. These included Hungarians, Roma, Albanians, and Slovaks. Socialist Yugoslavia invested constituent nations—Croats, Macedonians, Montenegrins, Serbs, Slovenes, and Muslims—with greater rights than minorities.

norities (Bugajski 1993). Even in the twenty-first century, elites in multi-ethnic Macedonia—considered a relative success story in the Balkans—have threatened to obstruct implementation of the internationally brokered peace plan by charging that "the majority cannot protect . . . minorit[ies] . . . living in ethnically mixed municipalities" (Stojanovska 2005). Self-interested elites today continue to voice the mantra of minority vulnerability, a strategy also embraced by ethnic entrepreneurs in divided post-Soviet states (Kolsto 2002) and beyond (Horowitz 2001).

The particularly troubling record of minorities in the Balkans has complicated intervention by the international community, whose most powerful members have advocated the "protection of minority rights." In general, use of the term *minority* implies the right of the majority group to control the state (Wilmer 2002, 253; Gagnon 2005). Several scholars of the region have pointed out the grave consequences of imposing the status of "minority" on peoples who just a short time earlier had been considered "constituent nations" (Bringa 1993; Hayden 1993; Mertus 2000). Susan Woodward (1996, 339) argues that a call by European Community officials to "guarantee minority rights" ironically actually stoked the conflict. In an interview in 1991 with the U.S. ambassador to Yugoslavia, Bosnian Serb leader Radovan Karadžić asserted that it was the prospect that Serbs would become a national *minority* and thus "lose their basic rights" that fueled the Bosnian Serb drive for "national self-determination" (Zimmermann 1996, 176).

In the early 1990s, extremists waged violent campaigns of ethnic cleansing[6] that targeted heterogeneous local communities for elimination (Dimitrijevic and Kovac 2004). By recognizing new postwar demographic "realities"—in effect, codifying the subordination of minorities—internationally designed political institutions for postconflict Bosnia also contributed to the problem of minority status. The territorial division of Bosnia into two entities—the Serb-dominated Republika Srpska and the Bošnjak- and Croat-dominated Federation of Bosnia-Herzegovina—is one manifestation of this. Another is the way that Russian peacekeepers in 1996 "resolved" a dispute about the location of the interentity boundary line running straight through a hamlet in Bosnia's northeast corner. I observed a peacekeeper point to the ground on the eastern side of the boundary line (territory included in the Republika Srpska) and then point to the "representative" of the Serb population and declare, "This is yours."

---

6. *Ethnic cleansing* is a campaign in which authorities, acting according to a premeditated plan, capture or consolidate control over territory by forcibly displacing or killing members of opposing ethnic groups (Human Rights Watch/Helsinki 1996, 6).

He then repeated the process on the western side of the line, pointing to the "representative" of the Bošnjak population. It goes without saying that this solution, blithely imposed from without, did not take into account the pattern of settlement in the hamlet. Given the war and the international acquiescence to partition that immediately followed, it is not difficult to understand that the hamlet's inhabitants felt compelled to uproot themselves rather than remain a minority in territory deemed to belong to "somebody else" by the fiat of a random interloper.

Boško, an informant of Serb background, summed up this dynamic in 1998, during the intensive efforts by international implementers to encourage refugees to return to prewar homes. He predicted that people would not return after the war to reconstructed homes located in areas dominated by another ethnic group:

> They don't want to be a minority, because everywhere in Bosnia, minorities have experienced oppression. Everywhere. It's better to live elsewhere, in worse conditions, than to return to a place where you're insecure, don't have a social circle or friends, and there is discrimination in jobs and schooling. All public policies are designed to create fear for minorities.

Confronted with such policies during and after the war, many shared Boško's inability to fathom how the international community would reconstruct a multiethnic Bosnia.

Nonetheless, minorities remain the intended beneficiaries of recent international efforts to reverse the consequences of wartime ethnic cleansing. Partly as a result, of the more than one million refugees who have returned to their homes of origins, some 400,000 have returned to areas where they are now in the minority—at least temporarily. How can minorities who returned after war and minorities who stayed throughout the war work toward reintegration into local communities? Doesn't Boško's analysis have it right?

Focusing on behaviors at the individual level provides clues to this puzzle. Take the experiences and views of Davor, a Croat cobbler who endured the war in Sarajevo. He was just as disconcerted in 2002 as he was in 1998 that his town was dominated, both politically and economically, by Muslims whom he believed privileged their own nation. Despite this, Davor had mostly positive experiences with ordinary people of Muslim background, particularly his customers. Davor opposed calls by Bosnian Croat officials to create a separate Croat entity within the Federation, asserting, "I'm not *that* kind of Croat." Davor's attachment to his ethnic community and his social experiences and relationships led him to contest efforts by Croatian nationalists to define what it means to be a Croat and to pursue a nationbuilding project of monoethnic territories.

A Fresh Approach

These interpretations of cultural categories challenge the assumptions of scholars of ethnic conflict who have assumed that there is no difference between the notions of self, social belonging, and interests held by ordinary people and those espoused by nationalist political elites (Hayden 1996).[7] The traditional view of ethnicity as both given and stable fails to account for the variation in decisions made by people of the same ethnic group (Snow et al. 1986; Somers 1994). Macro-level forces, such as the political system that all citizens of Bosnia share, also cannot explain these differing choices. Why have individuals who share the same ethnic background and similar socioeconomic characteristics reacted in different ways to international humanitarian programs and the postwar social and political environment?

Interests and identity offer two competing explanations. Interest-based arguments of behavior see human action as instrumental, seeking to maximize goals—typically money and power, but also social status—that are largely determined by others (Laitin 1998). For example, Dragan, a twenty-something refugee who returned in 1999 from Serbia to Sarajevo, reclaimed his family's prewar home. The financial benefits of recovering private property clearly influenced his decision to return to Sarajevo after the war. But my research suggests that the interest-based framework is overly simplistic.

An alternative explanation for individual-level behavior is rooted in identity or one's sense of self and social location (Tilly 2002; Brubaker and Cooper 2000). Self-understanding is constructed through a process of social comparison during which one solidifies one's identification and social connections. That internally generated self-understanding then filters future information and guides behavior. Reconsider Dragan. I asked him to describe his nationality. He first answered, "Serb," and then added a set of increasingly inclusive, *nested* identifications: "I am a Sarajevan, a Bosnian, a European, and a member of planet Earth, in that order." As an expression of his identification as a Sarajevan, Dragan told me that at the beginning of the war, he made it through multiple checkpoints manned

7. Following Gellner, I define nationalists as those who argue that the political and ethnic-based national unit should be congruent (1983, p. 1). Smith defines a nation as a named population sharing an historic territory, common myths and historical memories, a public culture, and a common economy and legal rights (1991, 14).

by extremists on both sides in order to see his friends in the capital. After Bosnian Serb irregulars told him he had to fight, he fled to Serbia. Dragan's self-understanding involves affiliation to multiple social groups. This connection to a rich informal network clashes with the efforts of extremists to force him to choose one identity and allegiance over another. As a result, he fled during the war and returned when he felt that he could take advantage of international assistance and an environment he hoped would allow him to express his self-understanding by depending on his accustomed social networks. Nela's self-understanding as a citizen of Bosnia also guided her return to Bosnia and her turn to colleagues in Sarajevo for help.

I argue that understanding the anomalies of minorities in postwar Bosnia requires observing ordinary persons—most of all listening to their accounts of their own actions. After all, they usually know best. The subjective dimension of ethnicity makes this approach particularly important. Marc Ross (2001, 161) argues that individuals' interpretations of events matter more to the dynamic of ethnic conflict than the "objective" events themselves. Stuffing people into cultural or socioeconomic categories can only go so far in explaining responses to nationbuilding efforts because what those categories *mean* to people varies. What influences how regular people make sense of laws, policies, and high-pitched rhetoric about diversity? But even attending to subjective expressions is not enough. Context is also crucial.

By taking a micro-level approach, I hope to fill a gap in the study of ethnic politics in postconflict societies: how individuals labeled as minorities settle on strategies to rebuild their lives and how they approach integration in the context of the political constraints imposed by the peace plan, international implementers, and nationalist policies. This perspective builds on the approach of David Laitin (1998), who concentrates on how minorities in the "near abroad" develop strategies to cope with the constraints imposed by history and elites. My approach is also influenced by studies that rely on participant observation in natural social settings. Katherine Cramer Walsh (2004) demonstrated how retirees in Ann Arbor used both their own everyday experiences and elite-driven public opinion to develop their own interpretations of public affairs, which then guide their actions. Jonathan Rieder (1985) investigated how ordinary white Brooklynites experienced racial integration and, in turn, influenced that process. Participant observation is a critical method used in this book because the role played by subjective understanding and social contexts in deeply divided postconflict areas is essential.

Any focus on integration will necessarily be a long-term process involving many twists and turns, requiring an in-depth approach that follows individuals over time. I followed particular individuals and families for more than eight years (1996 through 2004), which offered insight into how the evolution of nationbuilding projects influences ordinary people and how they in turn influence nationbuilding. This design also allowed me to look at the dynamic social processes within which people understand and locate themselves. To identify mechanisms for reintegration, I lived with six local families in apartment buildings that housed a mix of ethnicities and observed their everyday interaction with different ethnic groups for fourteen months in the calendar years 1999, 2002, and 2004. My deep conviction in the contribution of systematic, long-term field research is influenced by the complex nature of the research question and my professional experiences. These experiences include four often frustrating years in the early 1990s of generating analyses on Yugoslavia from the confines of a desk at the State Department in Washington, D.C.; a rich and in obvious ways painful learning experience as a human rights field officer in Bosnia throughout 1996; and a highly rewarding three years of living among and learning from Bosnians.

Why have political scientists overlooked the importance of grassroots reactions to reconstruction in deeply divided postconflict societies? Most scholars of ethnic politics view elites and the institutions they design and manipulate as creating the overriding incentives and constraints that determine interethnic relations, both in general (Horowitz 1985; McGarry and O'Leary 1993; Wilkinson 2004) and in Bosnia particularly (Cohen 1995; Burg and Shoup 1999; Bieber 2004). Building on this tradition, scholars of the Balkans have depicted how international policies (Chandler 2000; Cousins and Cater 2001; Papić 2001; Bose 2002) have failed to convince domestic elites to reconstruct Bosnia into a stable, self-sufficient, and plural democratic state. Another example is the body of research by human rights groups (Human Rights Ombudsperson 1997; Human Rights Watch/Helsinki 1997; Federation Ombudsmen 1997, 1999; Human Rights Department 1999) who focus on the state's treatment of its minorities.

Ashutosh Varshney (2002) is one of the few scholars of ethnic politics who advocates a shift away from the study of political institutions and elites; he argues that civic networks forged in formal organizations in mixed cities in India explain variations of interethnic relations. Some scholars of Bosnia have taken up this midlevel approach, digging below the surface of politicians and institutions and scrutinizing local activists instead (DeMichelis 1998; Dahlman and Toal 2005). Other than a few notable exceptions in the social sciences (Bringa 2003; Stefansson 2004; Kollind 2005), studies of grassroots perspectives take the form of public opinion polls (Bell and Smeltz 2001; UN Development Programme 2000–2005) or focus groups (Cushman 1998; Poggi et al. 2002), techniques rooted in manufactured settings.

Such research on elites, political institutions, policies, NGOs, and mass opinion is important in understanding why Bosnia remains divided, why so many minorities feel threatened, and why minorities in Bosnia and other postconflict areas continue to face tremendous constraints. But it's only part of the story. Simply put, this way of approaching the subject cannot help us anticipate how minorities will react to these programs in real life. Understanding the reconstruction process requires considerable and careful effort—effort that must be concentrated not in parliaments or in research institutions but in ordinary shops and restaurants, not with political candidates but with mechanics and teachers, on the ground with ordinary persons. This ground-level approach is needed because ordinary people are aware of David Chandler's (2000) observation that reintegration becomes more difficult when it is politicized and highly scrutinized in the media. In response, common citizens logically deploy strategies intended to dip below the radar screens of international and domestic elites, not to mention scholars. Any analytical strategy that does not take into account these evasive strategies risks looking nonsensical in the years to follow.

Outline of the Book

This introduction has described the research questions that motivate the book. Chapter 1 presents the interactive multilevel network that shapes the behavior of ordinary minorities. This model consists of the nationalizing state, putative external homelands, transnational actors, local minority activists, and ordinary minorities themselves. Chapter 2 considers whether interest-based or identity-based theories of grassroots behavior better predict the reactions of ordinary Bosnians to peacebuilding projects. It also introduces the design of the investigation and its comparative sites of focus. Chapter 3 draws on testimony from intensive interviews to find out how minorities understand the decisions they make about where to call home, how to rebuild their lives. When ordinary people talk about their choices, they cite more than just money or the instructions of political elites, they constantly stress their desire to live in a community that accords with their notion of who they are and where they fit socially. The strategies that minorities use to reintegrate and the factors that influence the development and success of those strategies are the subject of chapter 4. Fieldwork reveals that ordinary people almost instinctively distrust the newly crafted postconflict institutions that have arisen to assist them, and this distrust has undermined peacebuilding efforts. Chapter 5 compares the process of minority reintegration in the investigation's primary sites to the reintegration process in areas of varying levels of urbanization and ethnic dominance. A look at voting and other forms of political participation reveals why ordinary people—particularly minorities—even as they favor political reintegration, are so disaffected by the political system that they remain largely outside it. The final chapter spells out some implications of this study for other peacebuilding projects in Eurasia: Kosovo, Croatia, Macedonia, Tajikistan, and Afghanistan. I also clarify the contribution of my investigation to the comparative literature on postconflict reconstruction and interethnic relations and suggest some ideas for further research.

1

Below the Surface

Anica [a middle-aged professional of Serb background]:
It's a very complex issue and one must get below the surface.

There is no simple flow of ideas or attitudes from elites to regular people; any depiction that presents the process as a monolithic or unidirectional one will inevitably fall short. Indeed, minorities, like anyone else, interact with the environment around them in many ways, and it is these interactions that shape their attitudes toward reconstruction. If we are to understand the strategies that such people use, we have to place them within a larger dynamic context, a context that both imposes limits on them and provides opportunities for them. Robert Kaiser and Elena Nikiforova (2006) have expanded on the work of Rogers Brubaker (1995) and Graham Smith (1999) in developing a comprehensive model for understanding the environment within which minorities take such action. Their multitiered model has the virtue of incorporating *nonactivists*, previously excluded from so much of the literature on national minorities, and allowing its components to interact. In other words, the model represents an improvement because it includes regular people and does not insist on a static role for each component. In this model, nonactivists (aka ordinary people) and local minority activists in the post-Soviet region interact with national-level minority leaders, nationalizing states, putative external homelands, and transnational actors to refine their identities and carve out a home (figure 1.1).

A state becomes an external national "homeland" for its ethnic diaspora when political or cultural elites define ethnic kin in other states as members of the same nation and claim that they "belong" to one state. After Yugoslavia collapsed, Serbia and Croatia each became at once a nationalizing state within its own borders, attempting to build a cohesive nation out of its ethnically diverse citizenry, and a putative or assumed homeland state that claimed its own respective co-ethnics living as mi-

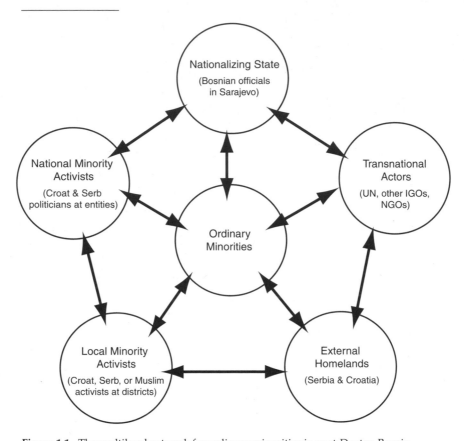

Figure 1.1. The multilevel network for ordinary minorities in post-Dayton Bosnia.

norities in Bosnia and other states of the former Yugoslavia.[1] For example, throughout the 1990s, Serbia's dominant political elites claimed Serbs who live in Croatia, Bosnia, Montenegro, and Macedonia. Against the claims of the putative homeland states of Serbia and Croatia, the nationalizing state of Bosnia is attempting to build a cohesive nation out of its varied peoples and a viable state within its internationally recognized borders (see figure 1.1).

The multilevel model for understanding minority behavior is especially appropriate for Bosnia since local minority political activists, whose autonomy is encouraged by a decentralized political system, sometimes

1. Just before its disintegration in 1991, Yugoslavia consisted of the republics of Slovenia, Croatia, Serbia (including its provinces of Vojvodina and Kosovo), Bosnia-Herzegovina, Montenegro, and Macedonia.

employ strategies that diverge from those of national-level minority activists (Toal and Dahlman 2005). Furthermore, the near-protectorate status that the international community now exerts over Bosnia also points to the critical role—one much greater than in the post-Soviet space—played by transnational actors, such as the United Nations (UN), North Atlantic Treaty Organization (NATO), the European Union (EU), and international NGOs (Knaus and Martin 2003). The actors in the network model react to one another, but the relative power of each actor varies according to resources, domestic political structures, and the regional and global strategic environment. Transnational actors today play a formidable role in Bosnia, but even their power depends on how much influence domestic political structures grant them, the political will of transnational actors and indigenous elites, and the receptiveness of ordinary people, including minorities.

In this chapter, I illustrate the usefulness of the multilevel network model by discussing how the interaction of network actors in key historical periods has influenced statebuilding projects in the Balkans. The intention is not to provide a comprehensive account of interethnic relations and statebuilding during Ottoman rule, Socialist Yugoslavia, newly independent Bosnia, and wartime Bosnia. Rather, I hope to depict the benefits gained from applying the multilevel, interactive network model. I also describe the network in the postwar period to depict the setting for grassroots influence detailed in the rest of the book on the current peacebuilding process.

Historical Multilevel Networks

The regimes that have ruled over Bosnia have largely determined the policies for ethnic diversity in Bosnia, policies that have ranged from attempts to wipe out difference through genocide (World War II) and assimilation (Royal Yugoslavia) to favoritism toward one religion but tolerance of others (the Ottoman Empire) to one-party control and the promotion of cross-communal cooperation (Socialist Yugoslavia). Through their responses to these official policies, ordinary people and local activists have formulated their own self-understandings and managed to alter programs crafted by transnational actors or putative homelands.

The Ottoman Multilevel Network

The Ottomans ruled over Bosnia for hundreds of years, leaving an indelible imprint on the region. The interactive multilevel framework illustrates how the behavior of those ordinary people who would now be labeled minorities contradicts the preferences of transnational actors, leaders of external homelands, and national-level minority activists.

Ottoman rulers acted as a transnational actor in Bosnia. The Ottoman's millet system of governance struck a delicate balance by privileging Muslims while tolerating non-Muslims, who were granted some degree of autonomy (Itzkowitz 1977; Andrić 1990). In the nineteenth century, local Franciscan and Orthodox priests in parochial school systems in Bosnia, influenced by co-religionists in their putative homelands of Croatia and Serbia respectively, spread nationalist ideas that encouraged their communities to consider themselves Croats and Serbs (Donia and Fine 1994, 65–66). In the mid-1840s, putative homeland elites advocated "Greater Serbia" and "Greater Croatia," projects that claimed much of the peoples and territory of Bosnia (Banac 1984, 82).

While the Ottomans and the putative homelands pushed particular collective identities, ordinary people often resisted being boxed in. For example, religious conversions among the Slavic peoples at the beginning of Ottoman rule in 1463 occurred as a gradual, multidirectional process, an illustration of the fluidity of religious identities in Bosnia at that time (Fine 1975, 35–39). For example, it was not uncommon for brothers to choose different religions. In daily life, ordinary people often blended religious traditions into shared local practices (Donia and Fine 1994). Clear distinctions among Islam, Orthodoxy, and Catholicism that the Ottoman state and religious leaders emphasized were far less pronounced in daily life, where shared local practices were more significant (Mazower 2002, 62). These cases show that ordinary people's social interactions with those of different backgrounds failed to conform to the agendas of powerful elites. It was in the chaotic dusk of the empire that ordinary people began to express frustration at the abuses of their rulers, which resulted in increasingly large social uprisings, generally on the part of Christian peasants against the local Muslim landlords (Jelavich 1977, 141).

The Socialist Multilevel Network

Though they ruled hundreds of years later, the Socialists shared with the Ottomans the notion that successful rule over the South Slavic peoples required recognizing the differences among those peoples. To attract fighters to his Communist Partisans in World War II, Josip Broz Tito promised to end the mass suffering from the ethnic violence waged by occupiers and domestic extremists and to establish a Yugoslav state that would treat all nationalities equally (Denitch 1976; Burg and Shoup 1999, 39). After the Partisan victory, Tito established a Socialist Yugoslavia that, far from repressing national identities, institutionalized them (Burg 1983;

Woodward 1995, 45). Tito's "brotherhood and unity" policy of managing ethnicity included simultaneous affirmation of ethnic identity and Yugoslav patriotism, territorial organization into a federation with extensive decentralization to republics (including Bosnia), the defusion of ethnic tensions through local self-management, and opposition to the ideas of both separatism and unitarism (Ramet 1992, 54).[2] As part of their strategy of balancing peoples, the Communists even cultivated an ethnonational identity among smaller groups such as Muslims (Baskin 1984). The evolution of the census status of "Muslim" illustrates this process. Censuses beginning in 1948 allowed for the declaration only of "muslim, undetermined," then "Muslim (ethnic belonging)" in 1961, "Muslim in the sense of nationality" in 1971, and finally "Muslim" beginning in 1981 (Statistički godišnjak 1991, 9). Raising the status of Muslims granted them a greater slice of political, economic, and cultural power in Yugoslavia. By manipulating census categories, institutionalizing power-sharing among ethnic groups (e.g., forming federal units around ethnicity and enforcing ethnic quotas in the Federal and Bosnian collective presidencies), the Communists politicized ethnicity. Throughout most of Socialist Yugoslavia's existence, policies ensured that ethnicity was the strongest institution after Socialism.

Anthropologist Tone Bringa argues that Socialist Yugoslavia's republic of Bosnia offered three different paradigms for mixing.[3] The first was intermixture, which occurred in some cities. In the Bosnian cities of Sarajevo and Tuzla, for example, one-quarter of all marriages were ethnically mixed.[4] After the war, it would be common to hear urbanites wax nostalgic: "Before the war, I didn't know what my ethnicity was," a remark that was not intended to be taken literally but rather emphasized the relative unimportance of ethnic affiliation at that time, in such stark contrast to the present. The second paradigm was "living side-by-side," which occurred in some mixed villages in central Bosnia; most neighborhoods were separate with little intermarriage, but there still was interethnic interaction. For example, female villagers of different backgrounds frequently engaged in coffee visiting, an interaction that allowed for the expression of both differences (religious affiliation) and commonalities

---

2. In the 1970s, the Communists imprisoned nationalists, including future Bosnian president Alija Izetbegović, who advocated a re-Islamicization of Muslims. During the early 1990s, Serb and Croat politicians charged that Izetbegović's "Islamic Declaration" (1983) mandated creation of an Islamic state in Bosnia.

3. Personal communication, Washington D.C., January 2000.

4. Ten percent of marriages in Bosnia in 1990 were ethnically mixed. I calculated figures for mixed marriages using 1991 census data (Republika Bosna i Hercegovina 1994).

(co-villagers and hostesses valuing hospitality) (Bringa 1995). The third paradigm was "living separately," which occurred in many rural areas, where a Muslim hamlet would exist next to a Serb hamlet, for example; inhabitants, usually with modest levels of education, rarely engaged in interethnic contact. Those rare contacts that did occur—for example, at the town market—were too superficial to break down ethnocentrism (Lockwood 1975, 197–98).

So for ordinary people, different local residential settings in Bosnia afforded a fairly wide range of possibilities for interethnic interaction. People constructed a sense of who they were and what it meant to be a Croat, for example, based on their experiences and interactions with neighboring groups and people of other official categories (Bringa 1995). As an example of the influence of the nationalizing state's elites on intercommunal relations, an increase in ethnic conflict between politicians at the republic and national levels (accompanied by a deterioration in standards of living) contributed to a general increase in ethnic distance at the grassroots level (Bertsch 1976; Baćević et al. 1991, 8).[5] That is, citizens of Bosnia were less willing to accept someone of a different ethnicity for varying levels of intimate contact in 1986 than they were in 1966. While that demonstrates the impact that elites and macro-level forces had on ordinary people, citizens from the mid-1970s onward judged interethnic relations at the local level as better than those at the regional or national level.

Sociological data throughout the Socialist period strongly suggest that citizens in Bosnia and its fellow Yugoslav republics were neither consumed by ethnic hatred nor free of ethnic prejudices. In light of the subsequent horrific violence, it is shocking that two separate surveys taken in the late 1980s and early 1990s, just before the violence began, revealed that citizens in Bosnia expressed the highest levels of ethnic tolerance of all of the Yugoslav republics (Pantić 1991; Hodson, Sekulić, and Massey 1994, 1548).[6] On a five-point scale with five propositions about tolerance toward other nations, with a five representing the highest level of toler-

5. *Ethnic distance* is measured using the Bogardus scale of social distance, which involves degrees of willingness to accept someone of a different social background as a spouse, friend, coworker, neighbor, fellow citizen, or tourist. Pantić (1991, 170) uses ethnicity as the salient social cleavage.

6. In late 1989 and early 1990, the Consortium of Social Research Institutes of Yugoslavia conducted door-to-door interviews in all the republics of Yugoslavia, utilizing a random sample of households. The full sample consisted of 13,422 adults and was distributed across republics in accordance with their populations. Bosnia's sample contained 2,312 respondents; I calculated the figures in the following sentences using the raw data that Randy Hodson graciously agreed to share with me.

ance, Bosnia's inhabitants scored an average of 3.88 while Slovenia's inhabitants scored an average of 2.67.[7] To illustrate better sentiment within Bosnia, 32 percent of respondents in Bosnia believed that ethnicity should be a central factor in choosing a marriage partner, and one-quarter believed that mixed marriages were unstable. Just 11 percent agreed with the proposition that people can feel completely safe only when the majority of people belong to their nation. An even lower level—7 percent—agreed that every nation should have its own state. The diversity of Bosnia, which offered repeated opportunities for interethnic connections, helped increase tolerance among its peoples. Socialist Yugoslavia's system of shared sovereignties among its nations (Woodward 1995) and the state's commitment to interethnic cooperation undoubtedly encouraged these views. In other words, the state did not compel Bosnia's Serbs and Croats to choose between their putative homelands and the nationalizing "state" of Bosnia, which was encompassed by Yugoslavia. Reflecting limits to positive views about cross-national relations, particularly at the macro level, 41 percent agreed that "among [ethnic-based] nations, it is possible to create cooperation but not full trust."

Even in mid-1990, on the verge of mass violence, assessments of interethnic relations were not generally negative. Many—38 percent of Bosnians—viewed interethnic relations in the workplace as good, 28 percent as satisfactory, and 6 percent as bad (Obserchall 2000, 988). Opinion about interethnic relations in the neighborhood was even better, with 57 percent assessing them as good, 28 percent as satisfactory, and 12 percent as bad. These opinions on interethnic relations, demographic figures, and voting preferences cannot be inferred from the policy of any one actor in the multilevel network. As it happens, a look only at the nationalizing state's (the Communist Party's) policies would have predicted even better relations among ordinary people of different background in the 1960s and early 1970s, but worse relations in the mid-1970s into the 1980s. As the multilevel network model reveals, however, these views are more dependent on local situations, where ordinary minorities interact with local minority activists and local authorities to create a sense of self-understanding and to assess the quality of interethnic relations.

7. The scale recorded disagreement with the following propositions: "nationality should be a central factor in choosing a marriage partner; nationally mixed marriages are more unstable than other marriages; every nation should have its own state; people can feel completely safe only when the majority belong to their nation; and among nations it is possible to create cooperation but not full trust" (Hodson, Sekulić, and Massey 1994, 1544, 1548).

The Post-Socialist Multilevel Network

By the mid-1980s, all the factors that were holding Yugoslavia to-gether—a balancing act in the international arena and a mixed economy and political system that provided protections of social and economic equality and of shared sovereignty among its nationalities—began to be threatened (Woodward 1995, 22). Given the elements of the Yugoslav so-cialist policy for managing ethnicity, it is logical that its inability to resolve political conflict among ethnic elites over decentralization and the econ-omy in the 1980s resulted in the emergence of ethnicity as the most pow-erful organizational principle for political parties.[8] That is, once it became clear that the various parties were not going to agree on these issues, eth-nicity emerged as the salient trait that each party emphasized. The old ideology of communism and the new ideology of nationalism may not have had much in common, but they did share a belief in the importance of a one-dimensional, unwavering identity that glorifies "us," demonizes "them" (Verdery 1993, 192–93), and justifies a monopoly of power. In the devolution of power to the republics, the elites of each nation saw a springboard for pursuing their own aims at the expense of shared sover-eignty and the country of Yugoslavia as a whole (Cohen 1995; Bunce 1999). Nationalist elites in Yugoslavia skillfully propagated a "crisis" frame of hostile interethnic relations that resurrected painful collective memories that had lain dormant since World War II. Invoking fear of the "other" is a time-honored strategy for communal entrepreneurs in deeply divided societies, including the U.S. South (Key 1950) and Northern Ire-land (Mitchell 1994). It is a strategy that reduces all issues to communal ones. In elevating the crisis frame, Yugoslav leaders also had to relegate the "normal" frame of cooperative interethnic relations to an aberrant condition seen only during Socialism, an outright false statement (Ob-serschall 2000). That the crisis frame resonated with so many ordinary people even before the violence began is a puzzle that deserves further research.[9]

8. Lipset and Rokkan (1967) demonstrated that political parties in Europe formed out of the most important social cleavages at the time. Building on their findings, Horowitz (1985) and Tull (1994) argue that in divided societies undergoing democratization, new political parties tend to form around the most prominent social cleavages—such as ethnicity.

9. Milivojević (1994) uses survey data of Serbs who fled Croatia to argue that a sub-ject, or passive, political culture (Almond and Verba 1963) helps explain the readiness of common people to accept messages of fear despite their generally positive direct in-terethnic relationships. Gagnon (2004) argues that incumbent politicians resorted to vio-lence to change the positive lived experiences of Yugoslavia's diverse peoples and to convince them to acquiesce to their hold on power.

Serbia's Communist Party leader Slobodan Milošević systematically undermined power-sharing arrangements, spurring Slovenian and then Croatian elites to accelerate their own moves toward independence. The dismantling of the system of shared sovereignty reframed the republics' relationships into more starkly conflictual ones. Leaders of the dominant group in each republic (e.g., Croat elites in Croatia) sought to create nationalizing states that were now oriented against the putative homeland (Serbia) over its Serb minority and territory. At the same time, a nationalizing state like Croatia also asserted itself as a putative external homeland for Croats living in Bosnia (see figure 1.1).

In the chaos of the disintegration of the Yugoslav state, new nationalizing states—Yugoslavia's republics—and republic-level minority activists saw that it was to their benefit to try, quite artificially, to harden ordinary peoples' identities into ones defined by ethnicity (Bringa 1993). This process unfolded in the first multiparty elections. About 76 percent of Bosnian voters threw their support to ethnic-based political parties in the 1990 elections (Arnautović 1996, 118). Even so, nearly a quarter of the Bosnian electorate voted for parties that were not ethnically defined. The multilevel model offers a more sophisticated framework for understanding the results of the 1990 Bosnian elections than the conventional frame of viewing them as a direct reflection of a widespread embrace of ethnic identity and of parties that claim to represent the interests of their ethnic group (Hayden 1999; but see Gagnon 2004). The multilevel model calls attention to the influence of the institutions that the nationalizing state's elites created to constrain the political options of ordinary voters, the strategies of minority activists, and the complex reactions of ordinary people to these forces.

One key institution of the nationalizing state that influenced the election was Bosnia's Constitutional Court, which in February 1990 struck down as unconstitutional a law banning ethnic parties (Burg 1997, 127), or parties that derive their support from and appeal to a single ethnic group exclusively.[10] In Bosnia, the dominant ethnic parties are the (Muslim) Party of Democratic Action (SDA), the Bosnian branches of the Serbian Democratic Party (SDS), and the Croatian Democratic Community (HDZ).

The newly adopted Bosnian electoral law, which required that each ethnic group receive assembly seats equal to within 15 percent of their portion of the republic's population, also helped ethnic parties dominate the elections.[11] By guaranteeing slots for ethnic groups and discouraging ide-

10. See Horowitz (1985) for in-depth analysis of ethnic parties in developing countries.
11. Article 19 of the "Constitutional law on the implementation of amendements LIX

ologically based parties, Bosnia's collective, rotating presidency provided additional incentives for voters to turn to ethnic parties. The presidency was comprised of two representatives each from the Muslim, Serb, and Croat communities, but only one representative from among members of smaller nations, minorities, or those who did not declare a nationality.[12]

The multilevel framework allows voters to be more than mere followers of state incentives or ethnic elites. Ordinary people are more likely to have complex motivations for voting and to interpret—rather than swallow—politicians' rhetoric. Testimony suggests that voters believed that they had to counterbalance the expected nationalist voting of other ethnic groups. Mirsada, a middle-aged homemaker from Bihać, explained that her vote for the Muslim SDA was compelled by her anticipation that Serbs and Croats would support their ethnic-based parties.

> In 1990, I didn't feel like a Muslim. I knew I was, but . . . they [Serbs and Croats] were lining up with [the Serb] SDS and [the Croat] HDZ. I had no choice; for survival, I had to vote for SDA. It wasn't out of love.

It is clear that Mirsada's Muslim background did not lead her to vote automatically or enthusiastically for the Muslim nationalist SDA.

Many voters may have engaged in another type of "negative voting," or voting against incumbents—in this case against the Communists. Surveys conducted in Croatia found that many voters viewed their first opportunity to participate in multiparty elections as a chance to vote *against* Communist Party rule rather than to choose among parties with different platforms.[13] The most prominent alternatives to the Communist Party were ethnic parties. Given the bankruptcy of the Communist Party, Socialist Yugoslavia's reinforcement of ethnicity, the turmoil of brand-new political pluralism, the ready availability of ethnicity to serve as an organizing principle for new political parties, and institutional rules, it is not surprising that the results of the 1990 elections closely matched Bosnia's ethnic distribution. The evidence, however, does not support the contention that voters threw their support to ethnic parties in the hopes that they would ethnically partition the country.

Indeed, the three victorious ethnic parties formed a coalition government and agreed to establish a system in which critical political decisions,

---

through LXXIX to the Constitution of the Communist Republic of Bosnia and Hercegovina," as cited in National Republican Institute for International Affairs, 1991.

12. Article 1 of the "Law on the election and recall of members of the presidency of the Communist Republic of Bosnia and Hercegovina," as cited in National Republican Institute for International Affairs, 1991.

13. Šiber (1992) interprets the 1990 elections in Croatia this way.

especially those dealing with ethnic issues and constitutional amendments, required consensus (Seroka 1993). They also continued to use ethnicity to bolster their political power by applying ethnic quotas to divide up ministerial positions, municipal-level government appointments, and leadership spots in public organizations (Burg 1997). Simply put, nationalist parties took over previously Communist-controlled organizations by establishing separate but parallel monopolistic patronage networks (Donia 2000, 3). In this atmosphere, Zlata, a Serb who temporarily returned to Sarajevo, feared the subordination of Serbs and Croats in the state. Her fears were stoked when a neighbor approached her after the 1990 elections and boasted, "Now we have our state!" Zlata was disturbed that "we" appeared to refer narrowly to Muslims rather than to all of Bosnia's citizens.

Just after the elections, the governing parties agreed that a sovereign Bosnia should remain within Yugoslavia (Andrejevich 1990, 22). At the same time, the putative external homelands of Bosnia's minorities—Serbia and Croatia—more aggressively pursued claims on co-ethnics in Bosnia. In particular, Belgrade used its domination of the media to demonize ethnic "others" (Thompson 1994). Serbian media painted Bosnian Muslims as religious radicals intent on establishing an Islamic state and plotting to conduct genocide against Serbs. Milošević and Croatian President Franjo Tudjman discussed partition of Bosnia along ethnic lines in 1991, conjuring up the partition of the Bosnian province in 1939 by Serb and Croat nationalists. Belgrade and Zagreb's ruling elites orchestrated leadership coups of their ethnic parties in Bosnia (SDS and HDZ, respectively), replacing moderates with hardline nationalists dedicated to the goals of their external homelands (Gagnon 2004).

Lacking the glue of genuine agreement about the future of the country, the parties in the multiethnic coalition quickly deadlocked governance in Bosnia, setting the stage for minority activists to take control. At the national level, SDS and HDZ elites were merely minorities unable to exert control over state politics. But each minority group dominated certain municipalities, and they quickly transformed themselves into powerful majorities seeking to establish separate states, or "nationalizing parastates" within Bosnia (Bieber 2000, 274). At the local level, SDS leaders controlled local government and police, purging non-Serbs (Donia 2000). SDS proclaimed "Serb autonomous regions," secured with the help of the Serb-dominated Yugoslav army (Andrejevich 1992).

The secession of Slovenia and Croatia from Yugoslavia in June 1991 also fueled political fragmentation in Bosnia by forcing the parties to take positions on Bosnia's relationship with a Serb-dominated rump Yugoslavia.

While Bosnian Muslim and Croat leaders supported Bosnian independence, Bosnian Serbs adamantly rejected Bosnia's exit from what was left of Yugoslavia, asserting that they would not be a minority.

Aware that Bosnia's peoples were divided on the future configuration of the state and that Slovenia's and Croatia's secession would only make Bosnia more fragile, Bosnian leaders joined with Macedonian leaders in advocating a reconfiguration of Yugoslavia into a looser confederation. SDA leaders, however, rejected calls by Serbs for federalization of Bosnia. This decision exacerbated fears of a "tyranny of the majority." Knowing that they represented Bosnia's largest group and that Muslims were dispersed throughout Bosnia, SDA argued for a whole, unitary, and ethnically mixed Bosnia. In the face of hostile alliances between putative homelands and minority activists, war in neighboring Croatia, and the willingness of the EU's predecessor, the European Community (EC), to consider Yugoslav republics' bids for international recognition, Bosnian Muslim and Croat leaders in October 1991 adopted a memorandum on Bosnia's "sovereignty and neutrality" (Bugajski 1993, 14). In protest, Bosnian Serb leaders walked out of the republic's assembly, declaring the memorandum a violation of consensus decisionmaking rules. A month later, Bosnian Croat leaders proclaimed the creation of "Herceg-Bosna" in territory adjacent to Croatia as a distinct Croat entity within Bosnia that would recognize Sarajevo only if the Bosnian government maintained Bosnian independence (Zagreb Radio 1991).

Minority activists took practical steps on the ground to partition the republic along ethnic lines. Because Muslims were interspersed with Croats and Serbs, partition of Bosnia into Serb and Croat "republics" would require the destruction of multiethnic life and the separation of peoples (Gjelten 1995, 132; Burg and Shoup 1999). By January 1992, Bosnian Serb leaders declared that Bosnia no longer existed and that Bosnian Serbs were entitled to 60 percent of Bosnia (Bugajski 1993, 16).

Transnational actors hastened the partition of Bosnia. The UN refused a request by the Bosnian government in 1991 to deploy preventive monitors or peacekeepers (UNSYG 1992). The EC precipitated violent disintegration by encouraging Bosnia to hold a referendum on independence, the success of which was a prerequisite for recognition by EC member states. With Serbs boycotting the plebiscite, the majority of Bosnians (99.7 percent of the 63.4 percent of the electorate that turned out) voted in a March 1992 referendum to "support the sovereign and independent state of equal citizens, the peoples of Bosnia and Hercegovina—the Muslims, Serbs, Croats and members of other nations living in it" (Andrejevich 1992a). The referendum sparked immediate violence, and Bosnian Serb activists set up barricades in Sarajevo to close it off (Radio Beograd 1992). On April 6, 1992, the EC recognized Bosnia as an independent state. The next day, the Bosnian Serbs established a "Serbian Republic of Bosnia-Hercegovina" and withdrew from all Bosnian state institutions (*Tanjug* 1992; "Politika" 1992.) Aiming to consolidate control over a separate Serb territory, Bosnian Serb leaders launched a war with the assistance of the army and paramilitaries from its putative external homeland (Bugajski 1993).

War

So it was that putative external homelands teamed up with minority activists to dominate weaker actors in the multilevel network—transnational actors feuding over how to respond, the nationalizing state desperately trying to cobble together an army, and most of all, ordinary people disempowered by overwhelming force. Putative external homelands and minority activists worked to transform their peoples into the majority group of their nationalizing parastates. This required ethnically cleansing the territories they coveted. The UN Secretary General wrote in 1992 that "all international observers" agree that the Bosnian Serbs, with support from the Yugoslav army, were working to create "ethnically pure" regions through the seizure of territory by military force and intimidation of the non-Serb population (UNSYG 1992, 2). Within sixty days, Serb forces captured much of eastern Bosnia, expelling an estimated one million persons and killing tens of thousands of people, most of them Muslims (UNSYG 1999, 7). For nine months, the mainly Muslim forces of the Bosnian government fought against Bosnian Croat forces over control of ethnically mixed territory in central Bosnia. After moving in 1992 to seize power in municipalities with significant numbers of Croats, the military wing of HDZ in Bosnia, the Croatian Defense Council (HVO), in April 1993 initiated attacks to ethnically cleanse central Bosnia's Lašva valley of Muslims (ICTY 2001).[14] Croat forces also expelled Serbs from areas in Herzegovina (UN Economic and Social Council 1993). Abetted by the Muslim-led Bosnian government army, Muslim gangs terrorized Serbs in Sarajevo between 1992 and 1993 (Slatina 1998; Dizdarević 1998) and expelled Croats from areas of central Bosnia (Burg and Shoup 1999, 177). Belying labels of the war as ethnic in nature and emphasizing power

---

14. The International Criminal Tribunal for former Yugoslavia (ICTY; 2001) noted that these attacks involved the destruction and plunder of towns and villages; the killing, injury, and detention of the Muslim population; and the deliberate targeting of mosques and other religious and educational institutions.

struggles, the Muslim-led Bosnian army for years battled the autonomist forces of Muslim Fikret Abdić in northwest Bosnia.

The manner and extent of ethnic cleansing not only determined the number of minorities remaining but also influenced the prospects for reconstruction of local communities after the war. The cleansing varied partly according to the ethnicity dominating the army and settlement types. In the two towns that served as the base for my investigation, Sarajevo and Bihać, extremist minority forces—Serb—besieged the town to try to strangle their populations and pound them into capitulation. Towns such as Mostar and Banja Luka, however, also suffered house-by-house violence, with Mostar violently partitioned between its Croat and Muslim inhabitants and Banja Luka cleansed of its non-Serb population.

The rural areas suffered the most intimate violence. Nationalists sought to destroy the longstanding tradition of neighborly relations and to make ethnic belonging the only basis for safety and identity. This targeting demonstrates how seriously nationalists took the capacity of the neighborhood to facilitate positive interethnic relationships among common citizens (Zimmerman 1992). Sometimes outsiders—from neighboring areas of Bosnia or from putative homelands—would descend on a village and move from house to house forcing minorities from their homes. Expulsion was particularly painful for rural Bosnians because many of them had spent years building their homes with their own two hands. At other times, elites fomented distrust and fear of those ethnically different, and the creativity they needed to do it undercuts the argument that such hysteria was always there, easily accessible, waiting to be exploited. In some cases extremists had to spread false rumors and stage incidents carried out by troublemakers from outside to mobilize people within a community along ethnic lines (Christie and Bringa 1993; Oberschall 2000). The mantra of nationalists—that an individual must protect his home from other ethnic groups—often successfully convinced locals of one group to engage in "preemptive" violence against neighbors of a different ethnicity. Violence conducted by known covillagers helped accelerate separation, spread the violence, and ingrain distrust of those ethnically different. The process largely destroyed multiethnic life in the countryside (Beguiler 1996, 13) and seriously damaged any possibility of future return and reintegration.

Confronted with such powerful organs of propaganda and violence, ordinary people had little choice. Throughout Bosnia, military groups targeted common people living as minorities in their locality. Some minorities who acted early fled to putative external homelands, either to avoid becoming targets or to dodge the draft. At the end of the war, more than

Table 1.1. Demographic changes during the Bosnian War

Minorities in each of the three ethnically controlled areas	Prewar population	Population at end of the war	Wartime loss of minorities	Percentage of that minority who stayed (%)
Minorities in what is now Serb-controlled Bosnia:				
Croats	149,763	15,000	134,763	10.0
Bošnjaks	450,382	32,000	418,382	7.1
Others	116,169	60,000	56,169	51.6
Minorities in what is now Croat-controlled Bosnia:				
Serbs	83,807	11,000	72,807	13.1
Bošnjaks	120,704	20,000	100,704	16.6
Others	28,206	18,500	9,706	65.6
Minorities in what is now Bošnjaks-controlled Bosnia:				
Serbs	397,383	133,000	264,383	33.5
Croats	255,081	65,000	190,081	25.5
Others	196,041	164,500	31,541	83.9

Source: Medjunarodni Forum Bosna 1999.

half of Bosnia's population—2.5 million people—had been displaced. Of these, 1.2 million became refugees, fleeing Bosnia entirely; another 1.3 million were internally displaced within Bosnia.[15] Reflecting the varying intensities of the ethnic-cleansing campaigns, a lower percentage of minorities remained in Serb- and then Croat-controlled areas than in Bošnjak-controlled areas (table 1.1).

In an effort to erase signs of minority culture and discourage the return of minorities, Bosnian Serb forces destroyed every one of the hundreds of mosques that existed in territory they controlled (Burg and Shoup 1999, 174). Most Orthodox and Catholic churches remain in Bošnjak-controlled territory, though some have been targeted by Bošnjak extremists.

The Postwar Multilevel Network

What to do about minorities—particularly displaced minorities—has been a major dilemma for transnational actors in the Balkans since the end of the war. The postwar multilevel network has been important in shaping the reaction of ordinary minorities to aspects of the peacebuilding process. At the end of the war, transnational actors went from being

15. The term *internally displaced persons* refers to persons displaced inside their country. *Refugees* are persons recognized to be outside their country of nationality for reasons that make them of direct concern to UN High Commissioner for Refugees (UNHCR 1998, 8).

weak actors in the multilevel network to powerful ones. Initially, transnational actors played an agenda-setting role by mediating the peace agreement, setting up international organizations to implement it, and writing Bosnia's postwar constitution. But then other actors in the multilevel network became more important in how postwar politics was conducted. Transnational actors evolved from aggressive institutional engineers to reactive policymakers and then to international governors.

Transnational Actors as Institutional Designers

In the wake of the Bosnian Serb military's massacre in Srebrenica in July 1995[16] and the deterioration of the military situation in Bosnia, which threatened to draw in U.S. forces to extricate UN peacekeepers, NATO bombed Bosnian Serb military targets and infrastructure. In November 1995 international mediators compelled regional leaders to sign on to the agreement they had hashed out with the guidance of U.S. mediation in Dayton, Ohio. That agreement was signed by the presidents of Bosnia, Croatia, and Serbia; the latter two were instructed by the U.S.–led negotiators of the Contact Group[17] to ensure the cooperation of Bosnian Croat and Bosnian Serb leaders, respectively.

Each side interpreted the Dayton Peace Agreement and its implications for statebuilding differently. American negotiator Richard Holbrooke asserted that the goals were "first, to turn the sixty-day cease-fire into a permanent peace and, second, to gain agreement for a multiethnic state" (1998, 232). Bošnjak leaders portrayed Dayton as a reaffirmation of the sovereignty of Bosnia as a unified, multiethnic state and as reinforcement of the right of displaced persons to return to their prewar homes. Serb politicians, however, emphasized that the agreement allowed for a separate Serb entity, complete with its own army and police force; in effect they saw it "as a way station on the path to partition" along ethnic lines (Holbrooke 1998, 352). Bosnian Croat leaders, too, anticipated that it would lead to partition. Clearly Holbrooke's hopes for an effective multiethnic state were dashed almost from the start. The Dayton Peace Agreement proclaimed no winner and satisfied no one.

The political system that transnational actors imposed on Bosnia at Dayton complicated an already difficult situation for ordinary people

16. Serb extremists massacred an estimated seven thousand Muslim males in Srebrenica, a campaign that led the International Criminal Tribunal to convict Bosnian Serb General Krstić of genocide (ICTY 2001).

17. The United States proposed formation of the "Contact Group," comprising the United States, Russia, France, the United Kingdom, and Spain, in May 1994 to end the fighting in Bosnia (Burg and Shoup 1999, 265).

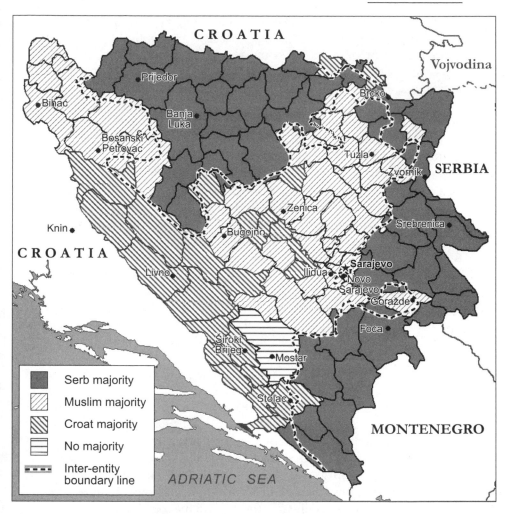

Figure 1.2. Bosnia after Dayton. Leo Dillon 2006. Data Source: UNHCR 1997.

from areas where their ethnic group after the war was now in the minority. This is because the Dayton constitution's provisions for ethnic separation and multiethnicity are irreconcilable. First of all, Bosnia consists of two entities: the Croat-Muslim Federation of Bosnia and the Republika Srpska (figure 1.2). Its postwar political system is modeled on consociationalism, which guarantees major ethnic groups a role in governing. Advocates of such power-sharing recipes insist that states recognize their major ethnic groups, isolate them at the mass level, and constrain interethnic contact to the elite level in order to transform ethnic groups into

constructive elements of stable democracy (Lijphart 1975; Nordlinger 1972; Burg and Berbaum 1989). This is because this political prescription views the mixing of ordinary people as contributing to conflict. Accordingly, the Bosnian political system features several mechanisms that institutionalize Bošnjak, Serb, and Croat cleavages: the grand coalition (a triethnic collective presidency), ethnic-based federalism, a vital interest veto, and ethnic quotas in public institutions. Even scholars of consociationalism have recognized that the Dayton constitution's rigid power-sharing arrangements do not create enough incentives for interethnic cooperation among elites and instead encourage political conflict—at best, isolation—along ethnic lines (Burg and Shoup 1999).[18] For instance, an ambiguous vital interest veto paralyzes decisionmaking on the national level; since each group can block national-level activity, in practice nothing gets done (European Commission 2005). The veto interacts with the significant powers allocated below the national level to federal, regional, and local assemblies; the lower the level of government, the more likely it is that one ethnic group can predominate, making it far better situated to control institutions than at the national level. The problem is that increased authority on the local level is an additional incentive for nationalist parties in Bosnia to block national governance (Hayden 1999; Bose 2002; Caspersen 2004).[19] Why should a group compromise at the national level when it can do what it wants within its own territory at no cost?

The Dayton constitution codifies group rights, with Bošnjaks, Croats, and Serbs named as the constituent nations of Bosnia. Immediately after the war, the Federation granted constituent nation status only to Bošnjaks and Croats, while Republika Srpska conferred constituent nation status only on Serbs.[20] But in 2000, Bosnia's constitutional court mandated that each of the three groups be treated as constituent nations throughout the country, a decision made only with the votes of the court's foreign judges. In practice, even after 2000, ordinary people of the "wrong background" in Bosnia's entities—Serbs in the Federation, for example—feel relegated to minority status. The Bosnia-wide collective presidency has the unfor-

18. At the local level, less formal systems of power-sharing, such as those adopted in Brčko, better promote interethnic cooperation for governance than more rigid and complex power-sharing arrangements, such as those adopted in Mostar (Bieber 2005).

19. The central government lacked the authority even for a united military until international pressure compelled reform in 2004.

20. "Constitution of Bosnia and Hercegovina" 1995; "Constitution of the Federation of Bosnia and Hercegovina" 1994; "Constitution of the Serbian Republic of Bosnia-Hercegovina" 1992.

tunate effect of disenfranchising those Bosnians belonging to a group in the minority in the entities because the presidency members consist of three persons: one Bošnjak and one Croat, each directly elected from the Federation, and one Serb, directly elected from Republika Srpska (Annex IV, Article 5). For instance, a Serb or a Jew living in the Federation must vote for either a Croat or a Bošnjak presidency member.

Alongside these provisions for division, there were more integrative measures in the constitution. But they relied on institutions not strong enough to enforce them. Dayton's formal political institutions do not cultivate a strong enough constituency for inclusiveness and the overall state; instead they create many opportunities for activists to fight for a particular ethnic group. The Dayton constitution guarantees internationally recognized human rights and fundamental freedoms for all persons within Bosnia and establishes oversight institutions, such as an Ombudsman and a Human Rights Chamber, all partly staffed by internationals (Annex VI). In practice, these semidomestic institutions are too weak, while solely domestic ones, such as the police, are too politicized to back them up on the ground.

In what would prove a very troublesome provision to implement, the constitution grants refugees and displaced persons the unprecedented right to return to their "homes of origin" and to regain lost property or, failing that, "just compensation" (Annex VII).[21] Yet curiously, the accord does not specify an agent for enforcing these rights, even though refugee return would do so much to overturn the ethnic homogenization elsewhere enshrined in the accord. Remember, this homogenization is so critical in empowering the nationalist leaders who had prosecuted the war and are still very much in power. By reinforcing ethnic divisions and failing to create institutions capable of protecting the impressive array of individual rights guaranteed, Dayton essentially sold out people who are ethnically mixed or do not define themselves ethnically by severely restricting their protection and ability to express themselves politically (Woodward 1999).[22] The power-sharing arrangements that transnational actors saw as so necessary to convince elites to end violence later worked against the crucial transition to an effective government, which in turn undermined sustainable democracy and peace. Bosnia is far from the

---

21. The "right of return" enunciated in the Universal Declaration of Human Rights has been interpreted as the right to return to one's country. However, the Dayton Peace Agreement provides refugees and displaced persons a broader right to return to their home of origin and repossess property illegally taken during the war (Rosand 1998, 5).

22. The clearest case of constraints on the political choices of those ethnically mixed or those who do not define themselves ethnically is the triethnic collective presidency.

only example of such a fate; a cross-national study of statebuilding in war-torn areas like Lebanon, found that the very power-sharing arrangements that facilitate the end of the war later hinder the building of good governance and sustainable peace (Roeder and Rothchild 2005).

Minority Activists as Nationalizing Parastates

Not surprisingly, elites who used violence to try to create homogeneous areas turned to other means for achieving the same goal after war. Devolution and the power vacuum at the center of the postwar political system benefited minority activists most because they were the ones who could exercise considerable power at lower levels of the political system and through the parallel informal political, security, and economic networks that were strengthened during the war. Though the Dayton Peace Agreement helped end the massive violence in Bosnia, minority activists continue to wage subtle campaigns of ethnic engineering to achieve the same ethnically exclusive statebuilding projects that would effectively turn the areas they dominated into homogeneous mini-states where they are in the majority. Ethnic engineering involves promoting or compelling co-ethnics to relocate from areas where they are in the minority to areas within Bosnia where they are in the majority. An example would be the movement of Serbs from a Bošnjak-dominated town to an area within Republika Srpska. It also works to privilege the majority group by implementing discriminatory property legislation, employment practices, educational programs, and social policy (Ombudsmen of the Federation 1999, 10). Weak integrative measures in Dayton, the nationalizing state, and entrenched minority activists favoring separation create a powerful logic for minorities to relocate.

Immediately after the war, minority activists favoring partition compelled their own people to leave areas that the peace plan had bestowed on one of the "other" groups, partly by threatening those who considered staying among Bošnjaks and partly by offering them incentives to resettle in strategic areas under their control. One important case of ethnic engineering occurred in the first few months of 1996, when Serb nationalists, with the help of rhetoric by Bošnjak nationalists, orchestrated the exodus of sixty thousand Serbs from several suburbs of Sarajevo that had been controlled by Serbs during the war but were designated at Dayton for reintegration into the Bošnjak-dominated capital. Serb activists steered these peoples into areas of Republika Srpska where they sought to increase Serb demographic dominance (Sell 2000). A UN High Commissioner for Refugees (UNHCR) protection officer told me of another case of in-group policing in central Bosnia in which nationalist leaders vilified those Serbs and Croats displaced from central Bosnia who had expressed an interest in returning to their prewar homes. They labeled them traitors or threatened to evict their family members, to have them fired, and to remove their children from school.[23] Local Serb activists sent death threats to three co-ethnic municipality officers in charge of returns and stabbed another for daring to do their job: facilitating the return of minorities displaced by the war.[24] The Croatian Democratic Community (HDZ) distributed leaflets and dangled economic incentives among displaced Croats in central Bosnia and Croat refugees in Germany, calling on them to relocate to Croat-majority Herzegovina (ICG 1998, 8). Humanitarian workers found handouts in Croat-majority areas imploring Croats not to associate with returning Serb neighbors.

Minority activists and the Bošnjak-controlled nationalizing state also used institutions to further their goals, particularly discouraging sustainable minority returns. They have stacked administrative bodies that control local housing with individuals opposed to the return of refugees to their prewar homes. Such minority return may threaten their own jobs and housing as well the nationalists' constituency. By rewarding those opposed to return with jobs, nationalists use mechanisms Dayton intended for encouraging return to instead obstruct minority return. Nationalists also funded supposedly nongovernmental organizations that advocate relocation. One such organization is "Remain" (*Ostanak*), which offers displaced Serbs money, housing (often illegal occupation of a Muslim or Croat home), or land if they stay in Republika Srpska.[25] Transnational actors failed to grasp early on how the nationalist grip on the administration and the economy would overpower weak integrative institutions created by Dayton and half hearted efforts to foster minority return.

The most common incentive offered to relocatees was housing, which nationalists used to solidify their demographic and ideological domination over territory. Faced with the need to accommodate increasingly large numbers of displaced persons, nationalist authorities allocated housing that had been abandoned during the war. Emergency conditions were one thing; eager to cement the effects of ethnic cleansing, nationalist authorities also misappropriated property and promoted illegal occupancy during the war and afterward (Cox 1998, 38). Under wartime laws concerning abandoned property, tens of thousands of socially owned

23. Interview with UNHCR protection officer, Konjic, July 1999.
24. Interviews, OSCE, Sarajevo, and Office of the High Representative, Bihać 2002.
25. Interview with Serb Civic Council official, Bihać, August 1999.

apartments were taken away from their original occupants because they were no longer there.[26] After canceling the rights of the original occupants, the authorities reallocated the apartments—not surprisingly, this process was often arbitrary and illegal ("Decisions on Property Laws" 1999). Many apartments were allocated to displaced persons on a temporary basis; others were permanently reallocated to individuals as a blatant form of patronage. The latter was common in major cities such as Sarajevo, Mostar, and Banja Luka.

As a result, minority return to urban areas has been difficult, since the housing to which minorities would return is often occupied by members of the majority group. This means that local authorities must undertake several politically painful steps, including eviction, before minorities can return. This dilemma was painted clearly by one observer (ESI 1999, 10):

> SDA wants to keep control of the housing stock [in Sarajevo], so that it can control the population. . . . SDA-led institutions [will resist] . . . evict[ing] persons whom they've rewarded with apartments, [because] that will decrease the support among the population for SDA.

Though the political costs of allowing minorities to return are universal, the dynamic of the return process has been different in rural areas, where housing is more likely to be privately owned than in towns. Nationalist authorities in rural areas did allow for the illegal occupation of private homes and sometimes destroyed property records or forcibly compelled minorities to "waive" their ownership rights (Pickering and Jenness 1996). These barriers made reestablishing property rights a challenging and slow process (Das 2004). At least as often, however, extremist forces razed or significantly damaged minority homes. This left displaced persons seeking to return to rural areas desperately in need of reconstruction assistance, given their lack of personal resources needed to rebuild their homes (figure 1.3).

Even if nationalists grudgingly allowed displaced persons to return to their original homes, they often blocked minorities and returnees regardless of background from finding jobs in order to undermine the sustainability of returns (UNHCR 1997; Federation Ombudsmen 1999, 21). These strategies built on the discriminatory employment practices of local Serb, Croat, and to a lesser extent Bošnjak authorities who had indiscriminately fired minorities at the beginning of the war (Human Rights Department 1999). To make matters worse for peacebuilding, Bosnia's al-

---

26. *Socially owned property* was a status in between ownership and tenancy (Pickering and Jenness 1996).

Figure 1.3. Return and reconstruction in rural areas of Bosnia.

ready struggling economy was devastated by the war. Many companies and employers disappeared altogether. At the end of 1998, the World Bank estimated the unemployment rate to be 33 percent in the Federation and between 36 and 47 percent in Republika Srpska (Bukvić 1998, 11, 19), even though many people earned some cash on the black market.

Competition over the few jobs available in the domestic economy has been fierce for all Bosnians. But some of the steps taken during the war to meet economic needs put those displaced by the war at a distinct disadvantage in the postwar economy. Many firms dismissed or initially put on waiting lists personnel who were absent during the war and then reassigned those positions to others. In addition, state companies have generally given priority to demobilized soldiers, war invalids, and war-widow family members of the majority group; returnees—particularly minorities—are always the lowest priority (UNHCR 1997, 3). Nationalists also saw to it that the voucher privatization process was turned into an "ethnic privatization" in which wealthy individuals of the majority group with strong connections to the nationalist parties gained control of the most productive companies (Cousins and Cater 2001; Stojanov 2002, 55).

The education system is another potent tool that the nationalizing state and parastate builders have used to promote ethnic separation. Texts in public schools are important in inculcating nationalist ideology and intimidating minorities. During the bulk of my research, each of the three nationalist parties used its own textbook: Bošnjaks used ones written in Sarajevo during the 1992–95 war, Bosnian Croats used textbooks written in Croatia, and Bosnian Serbs used textbooks written in Serbia.[27] School texts function primarily to socialize students into the "comprehensive world-view of the ruling parties" (Donia 2000, 42).

In portraying the 1992–95 war, textbooks informed students that members of their own group were primary victims of collective violence and that other groups were the principal perpetrators (Donia 2000, 45). Comparing each group's treatment of the war in Bosnia reveals their common logic:[28]

> *For students in Bosnian Serb–controlled areas:* "Muslims, with the help of mujahedeen fighters from Pakistan, Iraq, and Iran, launched a campaign of genocide against the Serbs that almost succeeded."
>
> *For students in Bosnian Croat-controlled areas:* "Croatian forces in the 'homeland war' fought off 'Serbian and Muslim aggressors.'"
>
> *For students in Bošnjak-controlled areas:* "The Serbs attacked our country. . . . The aggressor's intent was to entirely cleanse the territory of Bosnia-Hercegovina of the non-Serb population, especially the Bošnjaks, in order to create an ethnically pure Serb territory. . . . The četniks have driven a huge number of the population into the camps. . . . In their huge predicament, people drank their own urine. Mothers and daughters were raped, children impaled on long knives, and men beaten to death."[29]

The texts suggest the collective guilt of the other ethnic group(s) and fail to acknowledge crimes committed by those within their own ethnic

---

27. An important exception occurs in the special district of Brčko, where international administrators, who possess more power over local affairs than elsewhere in Bosnia, have successfully worked to unify the schools and the curriculum for all but national subjects such as history and culture (Bieber 2005).

28. As cited in Hedges 1997, A4.

29. "UNESCO Interim Report. Annex 3," "Textbook analysis of 'Nature and Society' grades? 1-4," 18, as cited in Donia 2000, 46–47.

group. Furthermore, the vivid descriptions of the Bošnjaks' desperation and the methods of violence used against them seem intended to horrify Bošnjaks, instill a sense of victimhood, and elicit hatred against Serbs. The textbooks even attacked those who had fled during the war, accusing them of committing treason (Donia 2000, 47).

While most schools were ethnically homogeneous immediately after the war, minority return to rural areas and small towns after 2000 created the polarizing situations of "two schools under one roof." When minorities reach 10 percent of the population of a municipality, they have the right to education in their own language. In areas with relatively small populations, the community, having only one school, would then segregate the minority group. This was often accomplished by establishing a separate entrance, which ushered minority students directly into classes taught by minority teachers in their language using their own textbooks. The opportunity to educate their children under their own programs acts as an incentive for families to return and to educate their children in local schools rather than send them to schools in areas where they would be in the majority. Separating students by ethnicity and language and preventing interaction in the classroom, however, clearly harms reintegration efforts.

While manipulation of the educational system has discouraged younger generations of minorities, exploitation of social services has similarly deterred older generations of minorities. During the war, nationalists developed parallel systems of social services. For example, authorities in what is now Republika Srpska distributed retirement checks and controlled health care benefits for Serbs living in their territory—whether they were domicile or displaced. Those who fled from Bošnjak- or Croat-dominated areas often lost access to their retirement funds from there (Stubbs 2001). Minorities who returned then faced discrimination in their attempts to resume receiving social services from the region of origin rather than from the region to where they temporarily fled during the war. The financial difficulties of the nationalizing state increased its hostility toward supporting minority returnees.

External National Homelands

The manipulation of the educational system illustrates the disruptive role that the putative external homelands have played in the postwar reconstruction of Bosnia. Up until 2000, the leaders of Serbia and Croatia provided support to their co-ethnic activists in Bosnia—SDS and HDZ Bosnia and Herzegovina (BiH), respectively—to carve out separate spaces in the country (Friedman 2004). These co-ethnic activists received funds (and moral support) to reject their de facto minority status in

Bosnia and to maintain parallel structures of power with closer ties to the putative homelands than to the nationalizing state of Bosnia (Bose 2002). Croatia offered many perquisites: special opportunities for higher education, voting rights and representatives in Croatia, highly coveted passports to Bosnians who could prove Croatian background, and material for socialization such as textbooks and media programs (Bieber 2001). Serbia offered similar enticements (Cousins and Cater 2001).

But these strategies were not monolithically supported; not everyone in the putative homelands agreed with the tactic. As evidence, look no further than the change in these policies after the death of Tudjman, the fall of Milošević, and the election of new governments that excluded Tudjman's and Milošević's parties. The new governments in Croatia and Serbia cut off funding to their co-ethnic national minority activists in Bosnia; at the same time, the rhetoric that earlier had rejected any possibility that Bosnia's Croat and Serb communities might have futures in the Bosnian state became less strident. Zagreb's withholding of funds for Croat activists in central Bosnia weakened the ability of HDZ leaders in Bosnia to resist minority return (Bringa 2003). However, it also seemed to spur a siege mentality among the most die-hard HDZ separatists in Herzegovina, who temporarily withdrew their soldiers from the Federation army and mounted a campaign to create a third entity for Croats in Bosnia under the slogan, "There is no identity without an entity" (*nema identiteta bez entiteta*) (figure 1.4). Only concerted intervention by transnational actors managed to stop this crisis—at least temporarily.

Despite the official lines from the post-Milošević and -Tudjman governments that recognize Bosnia's sovereignty, actions by prominent politicians in both putative homeland countries have raised questions about the depth and breadth of support for such policies. The Serbian government's rhetoric about its co-ethnics in Bosnia has been less consistent than that in Zagreb, as illustrated by former president and current prime minister Vojislav Kostunica's pronouncement during the 2002 election campaign in Bosnia that the Republika Sprska was "part of the family that is temporarily separated from Serbia" ("Bura" 2002). Furthermore, right-wing parties in Croatia and particularly in Serbia have never wavered in their support of co-ethnic separatists in Bosnia.

Nationalizing State

Minority activists in Bosnia, who prefer secession and still receive support from elements of their putative homelands, encourage Bošnjak nationalists to work toward building Bosnia as a state primarily for Bošnjaks. After all, these "friends" have emphasized, unlike Bosnia's

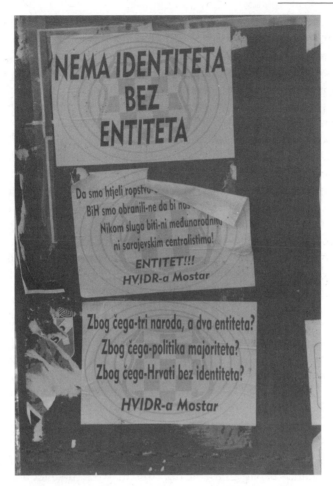

Figure 1.4. Croatian nationalist sentiment: There is no identity without an entity!

Croats and Serbs, Bošnjaks have no homeland other than Bosnia. From their privileged position as the majority group in the nationalizing state, Bošnjak texts promote an ideology that supports SDA's agenda of a unitary, multiethnic state. The high-school history textbook used in the latter part of the 1990s paints a rosy picture of modern Bosnian society:

> Instead of being tied by ethnic roots or religious belonging, Bošnjaks, Croats, Serbs and Jews in Bosnia-Hercegovina restored the cult of the neighborhood [*komšiluk*]. There was a wider understanding that the neighborhood laws were stronger than those of kin. On this fundamental basis, people were bound together. (Relidija and Isaković 1994, 169)

This description emphasizes the commonality of those living in Bosnia and their traditions of coexistence, preconditions for Bosnia's reunification. One-sided portrayals of the war and the intrusion of religion into public schools have made a mockery of Bošnjak authorities' so-called commitment to the cult of the neighborhood. While religion is not officially required, Cantonal education ministers—appointed by the ruling nationalists—have encouraged it behind the scenes. In practice, religion has become a prominent subject of study in some areas' public schools. When I lived in Bihać in 1999, students attended classes in Islamic religion unless the parents contacted the school and filled out a form specifying why their child should not attend them. Bosnians of mixed background, Bošnjaks who were secular, and officials with the Federation Ombudsmen in Bihać all acknowledged that there was significant pressure to accept the religion classes, with ostracism the likely reproach from the community.[30] Such policies of the nationalizing state challenge the statebuilding project of transnational actors and non-nationalists that envisions Bosnia as a civic state for all its citizens.

Influence of Local Activists

Minorities across Bosnia are uncomfortable. But just as local minority activists contributed to varying patterns of wartime violence, they also contributed to varying opportunities for postwar reconstruction. As bad as the environment for minorities was in the Bošnjak-dominated urban areas, it was still largely better than it was in rural areas throughout Bosnia and in comparison to Serbian-dominated and Croatian-dominated areas of Bosnia (Kukić 1998).

While it was easier after the war for minorities to return to rural areas in Bosnia than to urban areas, the opposite may be true over the long run. In rural areas, minorities' homes may have been empty or partly destroyed, but they are still privately owned, making it easier for returning minorities to reassert ownership rights, move back into the home, and begin to reestablish roots there. Furthermore, returnees to rural areas have been better able to support their own needs through farming, which they cannot do in urban areas. The paucity of nonagricultural jobs, transportation links, social services, and schools in rural areas, however, has discouraged the return of younger generations, who during the war fled to towns where they realized the benefits of urban life. In this way, the war accelerated urbanization (Walsh 1997, 9; Doughten 1998, 13). In fact, the expectation that those minorities seeking to return to rural areas

---

30. Interviews with Bošnjak parents and the Federation Ombudsmen, Bihać, August 1999.

would be older and would soon die off with no family members willing to take their place probably encouraged nationalists to acquiesce to such returns in the first place. Human rights officials acknowledge that local authorities have often deflected minority return to nonstrategic areas, such as isolated hamlets.[31] Furthermore, local authorities may spark more fear in returnees to rural areas, particularly those who experienced intimate ethnic cleansing conducted by people they know during the war. This is because rural areas are often isolated from international observers and peacekeepers—they are small communities where everybody knows everybody else and their business.[32] Jovan, a Serb who lived part-time in Sarajevo, explained that he felt safer in a town because of the density of the population, the presence of transnational actors, and the higher educational level of urbanites.[33]

Local authorities across Bosnia have discouraged minorities from staying or returning, but those in Republika Srpska have made the environment for minorities the most difficult (ESI 1999, 2). Fewer minorities have returned to Republika Srpska than to Bošnjak and even Croat-dominated areas even though numerous polls indicate that a higher percentage of Bošnjak displaced persons said they want to return to their original homes (in areas where they would be in the minority) than do Croats and Serbs. Early rates of resolution of property disputes in the three areas, albeit uniformly dismal, have tended to substantiate this. By the end of my first round of fieldwork in 1999, housing authorities in Republika Srpska had resolved only 1.6 percent of the registered claims on property, many housing authorities in Croat-ruled areas of Bosnia had *failed to resolve a single claim,* and housing authorities in Bošnjak-dominated areas had resolved about 15 percent of claims (ESI 1999, 11). This miserable record improved only with relentless pressure from the international implementers. While employment discrimination persists throughout Bosnia, authorities in Serb- and Croat-dominated areas have taken no steps to rectify summary wartime firings of minority employees (Human Rights Department 1999).

Media outlets in Serb- and Croat-dominated areas have tended to express views supportive of the builders of Serb and Croat parastates, and media in Bošnjak-dominated areas have likewise often expressed skepticism of transnational actors' goal of building a multiethnic Bosnian state.

31. Interview with Federation Ombudsmen, Bihać, July 1999.

32. This was particularly true for young people, who lacked opportunities, and for women, who bear most of the responsibility for farming in Bosnia (Bringa 1995; Edwards 2000).

33. A UNHCR protection officer for Sarajevo confirmed that this sentiment was common in an interview in Sarajevo, 1998.

Table 1.2. Levels of safety expressed by returnees, by entity

	Federation (N = 500)		Republika Srpska (N = 500)	
	Majority returnee (%)	Minority returnee (%)	Majority returnee (%)	Minority returnee (%)
Very safe	78	60	92	10
Somewhat safe	20	32	7	74
Not very safe	1	7	1	14
Not at all safe	1	1	—	1

Source: U.S. Department of State 2001.

Note: The State Department data (2001, 3) were gathered from face-to-face interviews with samples of adult refugees and internally displaced persons who returned to their original city/town/village in the Federation (500) and Republika Srpska (500). A list of municipalities known to have sizeable communities of returnees was compiled, and sampling points were randomly selected from it. Samples of this size differ by no more than about 6 percentage points. Sampling error is larger for subgroups.

A popular journalist in Bihać warned Bošnjaks against trusting those Serbs and Croats who returned to the town and pleaded to resume the neighborly relations that existed before "that hellish war" (Bejdić 1999, 5). She portrayed such returns as merely temporary stops driven by a strategy of reclaiming prewar property in order to rent or sell it to fund permanent relocation to Serb- or Croat-dominated areas. Such rhetoric made minorities across Bosnia feel uncomfortable. As a reflection of local variation in the intensity of campaigns against minorities, however, a survey conducted in 1999 indicated that minority returnees felt safer in the Federation than in Republika Srpska (table 1.2).[34]

Another sign of the different atmospheres for minorities in the region is the varying attitudes about diversity expressed by ordinary people who belong to the majority group in their locality. In areas where they are in the majority, Bošnjaks expressed more toleration of difference than did Croats or Serbs (table 1.3). This may be explained partly by the overwhelming support of Bošnjaks for Bosnia as their homeland (USIA 1999) and the recognition that a viable Bosnia relies on the return of Bošnjaks to areas now dominated by Serbs and Croats. A greater tolerance among Bošnjaks is also consistent with the higher level of support among Bošnjaks than among Serbs and Croats for a Bosnian state that is ethnically mixed (USIA 1999).

34. The survey did not break down the Federation into areas controlled by Croats and by Bošnjaks. Other evidence, however, strongly suggests that minority returnees would feel less secure in Croat-controlled than in Bošnjak-controlled areas.

Table 1.3. Majority groups' attitudes on ethnic relations, by ethnicity

Proposition	Bosnian Serbs as a majority (%) (N = 944)	Bosnian Croats as a majority (%) (N = 939)	Bošnjaks as a majority (%) (N = 921)
I believe Croats, Muslims, and Serbs can live peacefully together in the country	17.4	36.2	85.1
I disagree that people can feel completely safe only when they are the majority nationality in their country	12.6	20.2	34.1
I would not mind if my son or daughter married someone of another ethnicity	7.1	7.6	21.6
I support the return of minorities to my own village/town	42.0	63.0	93.0

Source: U.S. Information Agency (USIA) 1999.

Note: The USIA survey is based on face-to-face interviews with a representative sample (2,925 total respondents) of the principal nationality in each of Bosnia's three ethnically predominant regions. For the full survey, the sampling error is 4 percentage points.

Though all groups in Bosnia have become increasingly tolerant of difference since the end of the war, Bošnjaks remain the most tolerant and Serbs are the least tolerant (UNDP 2000, 2001, 2002, 2003a, 2004b, 2005).

However, attitudes toward difference in hypothetical situations often diverge from views and actions in everyday life. Bošnjaks often reluctantly received those who fled during the war and returned afterward, particularly minorities, viewing the mere fact that they escaped the war as enough reason to perceive them as evaders or traitors (UNHCR 1997, 2). Halid, a Bošnjak informant who stayed in Sarajevo, perhaps unconsciously paraphrased sentiment contained in the Bošnjak history text, "No matter what your ethnicity, if you fled your town when it was under attack and then later returned, you cannot expect to be heartily welcomed." Furthermore, surveys indicate that Bosnians resent the better job marketability of recent returnees from Europe who received training abroad.[35]

35. One study found that 50 percent of Bosnian Muslims, 32 percent of Bosnian Croats, and 26 percent of Bosnian Serbs felt that returnees were given greater opportunities than those who stayed in Bosnia (USIA 1998, 51).

If the returnees belonged to a minority group, Bošnjaks tended to add an additional dimension of hostility toward them. Again, Halid's reaction to minority returnees was a common response. He distinguished between male minorities who fled beyond Bosnia to Serbia and those who were "starving us and shooting at us," the group toward whom he focused his anger. He rejected, however, the possibility of forgiving minorities who claim to have been "swept up" in the fighting, maintaining that they should have fled into Serbia, where they would have more easily dodged the draft.

Edin, a Bošnjak who stayed in Bihać, took a more strategic view. He both distrusted Serbs who left and tolerated their return because he believed that it would enable the return of Muslims to their homes in Serb- and Croat-dominated areas of Bosnia. Less common was the view expressed by Elvadin. When asked if he knew whether his neighbors in Bihać who fled had fought in the Republika Srpska's army, Elvadin shrugged off the question.

> It's not important to me. They had to fight, just like we did. That is, I didn't want to fight. I had to go into the military police. I think only a small percentage of Serbs knew [about Serb activists' preparations for war]. The rest are victims of narrow ideology, like our [Bošnjak] people.[36]

For Elvadin the most important division was not ethnicity but that between "those who fell victim to nationalism" and those who resisted it. It is the attitude of people like Elvadin, as well as the variation of views about difference expressed by common citizens, that contributes to the judgment of Serb returnee Nikola that "the return of trust will happen faster between ordinary people" than between elites involved in the power structure. The development of interethnic trust even at the grassroots level, however, will continue to be a slow process. Echoing the Bihać journalist's cynical perspective, most locals I encountered expressed skepticism about the interest of minorities in returning permanently. In addition, the low levels of support for mixed marriages across the three groups (see table 1.3) indicate that few Bosnians of any background embrace difference.

---

36. Elvadin may have offered socially desirable answers to my questions, but several indications suggested that he did not. First, I asked many of the same questions to Edin, who also worked for an international organization (IO), and received different answers. Second, Elvadin's answers seemed well argued, not trite like those I heard from Bošnjak elites.

The Oscillating Role of Transnational Actors

Confronted with the concerted efforts of domestic and regional forces for ethnic separation that dominate the multilevel network and the relative ambivalence of ordinary people on the same subject, transnational actors seeking to promote integration have had their work cut out for them. Although they took the initiative by designing the state and deploying international organizations to implement the peace agreement, transnational actors failed to follow through in the first postwar years to push for reintegration. Instead they reacted haphazardly to developments on the ground. While transnational actors were dawdling over the deployment of the various field missions, in effect wasting the unprecedented network of international organizations tasked with implementation, nationalists were using any means at their disposal (war was not) to solidify their hold on power and nudge the geopolitical map in the direction they wanted. The International Enforcement Force (IFOR) lacked the political support needed to protect vulnerable populations and capture indicted war criminals, and the consequence was that minorities were slow to return. In the first few years after the war, there were negligible minority returns.

The international strategy of *electoralism*—the idea that holding elections will jump-start democracy and stability (Pugh and Cobble 2001; Bose 2002; Friedman 2004)—failed to promote the parties most committed to the democratic process and governance for all citizens. This adversely affected subsequent political developments as well as the grassroots attitudes toward politics (see chapter 5). Domestic politics in the United States also drove the unproductive U.S. policy of insisting on elections nine months after Dayton despite the widespread judgment of human rights monitors—including the author—that the lack of freedom of movement, the nationalist control over resources, and the high levels of insecurity meant that the conditions necessary for free and fair elections were conspicuously absent. Conducting elections in postconflict societies before indigenous institutions have established at least minimal competence has been counterproductive for peacebuilding (Lyons 2002). The main product of the frequent election campaigns in Bosnia have been heightened tensions (UNHCR 2005). Given these conditions, it is not surprising that the first postwar elections only reinforced the power of nationalist parties.

The paucity of minority returns in the first postwar years and the failure of electoralism to strengthen domestic elites who shared the transnational actors' multiethnic statebuilding goals eventually helped convince key transnational actors to go on the offensive in Bosnia. The international community almost certainly contributed to palpable lack of resolution of the Bosnian conflict by frittering away valuable months while partitionists accumulated power; when in 1999 the international community finally did something decisive, the resultant policy was a heavy-handed imposition of ill-considered policies that served only to undermine domestic accountability and democracy (Cousins and Cater 2001). At a meeting of the Peace Implementation Committee in Bonn in December 1997, the UN High Representative won extraordinary powers enabling him to override Bosnian institutions to pass legislation and to remove from office domestic officials obstructing implementation of the peace plan. After Bosnian politicians failed to agree on basic decisions—such as a common currency or property laws that comply with international standards—the High Representative decreed the necessary legislation. By one count, the UN High Representative had imposed by fiat more than five hundred decisions between 1997 and the end of 2003 (Knaus and Martin 2003).

Whether such decisiveness on the part of transnational actors harms or promotes reintegration and a stable peace is open to debate. Most observers agree that promoting democracy through undemocratic means seems unlikely to work (Cox 1997; Cousins and Cater 2001; Knaus and Martin 2003). In particular, observers have criticized the UN High Representative's removal of high-level elected officials.

Other types of international intervention have been more effective. A more productive, but still controversial, type of intervention cultivates the rule of law and, with it, space for democratic-minded forces to grow. One example is the common license plate, which significantly increased freedom of movement. Another is the imposition of property legislation and the removal of indicted war criminals from governmental and police positions in several areas such as Prijedor, both of which made the return of refugees more likely.

Implementation of the more integrative aspects of Dayton has increased since 2000 (Caspersen 2004). Assistance by transnational actors has played a key role in this shift by promoting return. Donors largely dedicate reconstruction funds to schemes for persuading minorities to return home.[37] International assistance to local governments often remains contingent—at least in theory—on their willingness to accept minority returnees. This has encouraged opponents of return to get more creative

---

37. Critics of the priority given to minority return argue that it has undercut the reconstruction of Bosnia as a viable state by sapping funds for economic development.

about undermining return, imposing bureaucratic hurdles and reallocating confiscated land to those displaced persons who seek to relocate to live among their co-ethnics rather than return to their home of origin. A concerted international effort launched in 1999 helped overcome some key obstacles thrown up by minority activists opposed to return. To plan and coordinate programs for return, the Office of the High Representative and the UNHCR created several interagency programs, including the Return and Reconstruction Task Force (RRTF) and the Property Legislation Implementation Plan (PLIP). The RRTF regularly brought together local authorities, intergovernmental organizations, international NGOs, and local NGOs, including associations of displaced persons, in practice, to broker the exchange of groups of displaced persons. The PLIP program moved away from the RRTF's strategy to enforce individual property rights programs for returnees (Dahlman and Tuathail 2005). PLIP placed international pressure on local authorities to make decisions about contested property, using monthly reports delivered to transnational donors and implementers as sticks. This process was slow at first, but by 2005, 93 percent of claims made on property in the Federation and the Republika Srpska had been settled (UNHCR 2005). This coordinated international pressure was instrumental in allowing for more than a million displaced persons to return to their homes of origin, at least temporarily (UNHCR 2004). Of these, perhaps 400,000 were minorities.

Accurate figures of returnees, however, are elusive. A look only at policies of the transnational actors implementing Dayton would lead to overly optimistic conclusions about the prospects for return. International implementers have found it difficult to verify if a given return is permanent or involves the entire family that originally applied for aid. I gained an appreciation for this challenge when I accompanied humanitarian officials to newly reconstructed homes in villages. They traipsed from door to door to try to verify occupation, in the end sometimes relying on the word of a neighbor or a single member of the household. Indeed, a portion of reconstructed homes and repossessed apartments are clearly not reoccupied by their prewar owners (Cox 1998, 31; Srskpo Gradjansko Vijece 2002). This suggests that some beneficiaries of reconstruction may have later decided that their return was not sustainable, due to feelings of physical insecurity as well as discrimination in employment, social services, and schools (UNHCR 1998a). Recalling our Bihać journalist, returnees may never have intended to reoccupy reconstructed homes but instead to rent or sell them later to facilitate their relocation. After 2000 the international community tried to improve occupancy rates of reconstructed property. Assistance involved the provision of materials and limited funds to the returnees rather than hiring a local contractor to rebuild homes. This change sought to identify those most committed to returning permanently by putting more onus on recipients of aid themselves for reconstructing their homes.

The nationalizing state and minority activists have both endeavored to undermine the policies of international implementers. All have benefited from Dayton's enshrining of ethnicity as the central cleavage permeating politics, the economy, and society. For example, the nationalizing state has pressed implementers to focus assistance on the return of those displaced rather than on providing the displaced with options to decide *whether* to return or relocate. In addition, local minority activists who favor return are encouraged to invoke their lowly minority status as Serbs or Croats to justify their own slice of the reconstruction pie.

The Power of a Better Model

The multilevel networks depicted at key points in Bosnia's past and present emphasize the dynamic nature of the relationships among actors who influence the behavior of ordinary minorities. The networks especially uncover the role of local-level players, so often overlooked. The multilevel network active in the current postwar period significantly constrains the space within which ordinary minorities can work toward rebuilding normal lives. It does not, however, control their views and actions. Instead of waiting for the other actors in this network to dictate their lives, ordinary minorities, in the mere acts of living their daily lives and formulating opinions on the events affecting them, interact with members of the network to influence the reconstruction process in unexpected ways. I demonstrate how in the next four chapters.

2

Self-Understandings versus Power

Interviewer: Do you feel you have a sense of community with a specific group of people?

Davor: Long-term residents [of Sarajevo]. I have lived with these people, not with Croats there [in Croat-dominated Herzegovina]. The local community leader [a Muslim] comes to say hello to me every day.

Davor's account of his positive interactions with other ethnic groups confounds the picture anticipated by prominent theories on identity and behavior in deeply divided societies. How can this be? One virtue of the multilevel network model for the postwar period is that it clarifies the forces with which ordinary minorities interact to form their sense of self. These forces also help determine both where they fit within a radically altered society and what institutions they find helpful for reintegration. Interviews and observations of Bosnians living in two towns reveal how ordinary people generate their self-understandings and then refine them through discourse, everyday social interaction, and contact with actors in the multilevel network. Ultimately, it is this interactive process that influences the outcome of reconstruction programs. International actors may have the best of intentions and the ability to draw on extraordinary resources. But if the people on the ground trying to implement the Peace Accord do not consider these local nuances, it will all come to naught .

Interests versus Identity

Theories seeking to explain how ordinary persons react to social categories and behave in divided societies can themselves be divided into two broad groups: those emphasizing self-interest and those emphasizing identity. The two groups differ both on the nature of identity and on the direction of influence between identity and interest: Interest-based theories view social identity as arising out of common interests, while identity-based theories view identity as shaping perceptions of interests (Ross 2001, 159) as well as social and political attitudes and behavior (Turner 1982, 19).

One important example of the interest-based approach is David Laitin's (1998) investigation of the formation of social identity of Russian speakers in the panoply of former Soviet states other than Russia ("the near abroad"). He argues that the decisions of Russians to stay in the near abroad and learn a new language—his proxy for social identity—are based on a combination of three factors: (1) the expected economic returns (less the costs of learning a new language), (2) the loss of in-group status that a Russian might experience if his co-ethnics consider the choice as betrayal, and (3) the potential gain in status if members of the majority group fully accept linguistic assimilants into their community (p. 29).

Laitin's approach raises several issues. He does not investigate the *basis* for an individual's in-group, a group consisting of people considered similar to the self. He assumes that it is ethnicity, an assumption challenged by Edwin Poppe and Lou Hagedoorn's (2001) finding of diverse types of identifications of Russians living in the near abroad. In addition, using language choice as the chief indicator of identity ignores the varying bases for collective identity (Smith 1981). Learning and using a language need not indicate a choice about identity but may merely be a strategy for adapting to a deeply divided society, a conclusion suggested by Lowell Barrington's (2001) study of Russian speakers other than Russians in the near abroad, which showed that speaking Russian did not undermine attachment to non-Russian ethnic identities, such as Ukrainian.

Interest-based scholars rarely stop to consider the following questions: Who forms the in-group (Smith 2004)? Who decides about its content and boundaries? Cultural elites from the nationalizing state? Minority groups? Common citizens? All of the above? Even an interest-based investigation into the politics in divided societies ought to consider these factors.

Other aspects of Laitin's interest-based theory have not always held up well against the empirical record. For example, his argument that Russians in Estonia stay there because they are better off there than if they moved to Russia flies in the face of high levels of ethnocentrism among ethnic Estonians, employment discrimination, and economic segmentation of Russians into blue-collar work in unproductive Soviet-era industries. These factors combine to create high "costs": Estonia's Russians must contend with high levels of unemployment and significant social exclusion, both of which are significant (Kolsto 2002).[1] These shortcomings of Laitin's interest-based theory suggest the need for a complementary or alternative explanation.

Enter identity-based theory. The term *identity* can be confusing because the conventional notion of identity invokes immutability. Building on this conception, some scholars and many journalists of the recent Balkan wars have embraced essentialist notions of identity: the idea that individuals are born into a cultural identity that remains with them throughout their lives and determines their behavior (Kaplan 1993; Erlanger 2001). Social scientists, however, generally reject this deterministic assertion (Chandra 2001; Smith 2004; Hale 2005), instead viewing identities as constructed through social interaction. Drawing on extensive empirical evidence, scholars of the Balkans such as Franke Wilmer (2002) and V. P. Gagnon (2004) convincingly debunk explanations for the wars of the mid-1990s that rest on an unwavering ethnic identity inherently hating those ethnically different.

Identity-based theory does not assume that the significance of cultural categories is the same for each individual or that cultural categories are necessarily more important than other categories. It *does* argue that how individuals conceive of their sense of self matters for their social and political behavior. It views identity as formed through a social comparison process whereby persons who are similar to the self are categorized with the self and labeled as the "in-group," and persons considered different are dumped into the "out-group" category (Stets and Burke 2000, 225). The pervasiveness of nationalist rhetoric, the political structure, and the raw memories of the war encourage Bosnians to elevate group categories—particularly ethnic ones—and downplay their sense of individual self.

This postwar Bosnian environment makes social identity salient. *Social identity* is "that part of an individual's self-concept which derives from his knowledge of his membership in a social group (or groups) together with the value and emotional significance attached to that membership" (Tajfel 1978, 63). How strongly an individual feels an attachment to a social group affects his or her views on social relations and politics. The

1. Estonia's citizenship law treats those who settled in Estonia after its forcible incorporation into the Soviet Union in 1940—overwhelmingly Russians—as illegal immigrants. Naturalization requirements feature mastery of the Estonian language. Despite the progress of Russians in learning Estonian (by 1998, 15 percent spoke Estonian fluently), there is no evidence that Estonians have allowed their integration, much less assimilation (Kolsto 2002).

more strongly individuals identify with their own group, the more they will attempt to achieve intergroup differentiation, a process that helps them feel good about themselves (Gibson and Gouws 2000, 280). For example, in the Netherlands, immigrant youth who strongly identify with their ethnic group were more likely to restrict their socializing to members of that ethnic group (Verkuyten 1991), a process that can complicate integration. Jewish immigrants from the former Soviet Union with the highest levels of ethnoreligious consciousness were also the most ethnocentric (Gitelman 1983, 45).

Those who feel strong attachments to a particular social group are likely to think and behave politically in ways that are distinct (Campbell et al. 1960). In South Africa, Gibson and Gouws (2000, 291) found that as cultural identity becomes more important to citizens, they will increasingly emphasize group solidarity, which correlates with intolerance toward the political activities of out-groups. Strong attachments to subnational identities, in this example Afrikaner over South African, hinder democratization in heterogeneous polities. Kinder and Winter (2001) found that a strong attachment to one's racially defined in-group, distance from out-groups, and racial resentment helped influence attitudes on racial policies, such as affirmative action.

What these studies emphasize is the *variability* of meanings attached to ethnicity. Simply because individuals have been labeled by official categories such as ethnicity does not mean that they equally value these categories, much less share or act on the expected interests arising from these categories. As Tone Bringa's (1995) work in Bosnia suggests, the citizens who chose "Croat" among official categories for nationality on the 1990 census probably derived different meanings from that category, a product both of their personal experiences and interactions with neighboring groups and of their perceived relation to them.

Consider Goran, a twenty-something war veteran. One morning, Goran puzzled over his recent visit to Livno, a predominantly Croat area of Bosnia that experienced fighting between Bošnjaks and Croats. He could not understand why Croat officials in Livno refused to accept his documents, which had not been translated from the Bosnian language into the Croatian language, which are mutually intelligible. After working with him for months, I learned that his positive interactions with Bošnjaks both during and after the war resulted in his identifying both as a Croat and a Bisčani (a person who lives in Bihać). He felt he had more in common with members of the local Bihać community than he did with his co-ethnics in Livno, who viewed mere Croat background as enough to necessitate conflict with Bošnjaks. The meanings that Goran and the

Livno officials assigned to the label *Croat* have radically different conse-quences for their behavior toward Bošnjaks and politics in Bosnia.

That Goran's self-understanding is rooted in attachment to several col-lective groups is far from unique. Theorists agree that most people have social identities that include attachments to multiple groups (Smith 1991; Ross 2001). But the importance of those group identifications partly varies over time, in reaction to elite rhetoric and policies (Tajfel 1982, 3; Malkki 1995). What is rare in Goran's case is that these multiple identifications survived the war. When leaders of the groups to which individuals ex-press affinity—local Croat activists in Livno and Bosnian state authori-ties in Sarajevo—make competing demands, the ability of individuals to manage these multiple identifications becomes very difficult (Brewer 2001, 123). Like the officials in Livno, many Croat activists demand that people of Goran's background express their preeminent affiliation to Croats and distance themselves from those ethnically different. Fueled by the war, the totalistic rhetoric of nationalists exerts powerful pressure on individuals to reduce their identities to one dimension—in this case, eth-nicity (Drakulić 1993b). Meanwhile, another group, Bosnian state au-thorities, exerts competing pressure on people like Goran to express loyalty to Bosnian and local communities, to accept being a de facto mi-nority, and to cooperate with his fellow citizens of all backgrounds. If in-dividuals feel more passionate about one collective identity (say, Croat) than another (Bisčani or Bosanski [a Bosnian, citizen of Bosnia]), they are likely to limit the boundaries of their in-group to one exclusive group (e.g., only Croat), thus reducing possibilities of compromise.

Anyone whose social identity involves strong attachments to several groups (e.g., both Croat and Bisčani), however, is likely to seek a com-promise between these competing demands (Brewer 2001). Goran con-siders his identification as a Croat to be compatible with his identification with Bihać, a town which is dominated by Bošnjaks. His approach to lan-guage bridges these communities; he speaks Croatian but also under-stands Bosnian and feels no need for translation. Varying attachments to multiple social groups help us understand why ordinary people of Croat background—even ones from the same municipality—have made differ-ent decisions about where to call home and how to interact with those ethnically different. Goran's emotional ties to several collective groups are strong; they encourage him to stay in Bihać. The supraethnic group to which Goran feels the most attachment is the *local* community (Bihać), not the state citizenry (Bosnian). This is enough for him to remain in his home in Bosnia. His views and behavior do not satisfy the statebuilding proj-ects of either minority activists or those of the nationalizing state.

While an attachment to social groups influences views and actions, it is not static. For adults like my respondents who have reached stages of life where they have already forged their basic outlooks on ethnicity,[2] social groups generally help them refine, not reinvent, their identities. Studies in the United States have shown that adults clarify their self-understandings through social interaction. Katherine Cramer Walsh (2004) argues that the more time a person spends in a social group that holds views that resonate with one's prior sense of self, the more likely those social interactions will help that person clarify his or her sense of self. In this way, prior identities act as reference points for interpreting new information.

The disintegration of Yugoslavia, the war, and the postconflict setting —where actors in the multilevel network are still battling through other means over how to define the state—induce ordinary people to continue to refine their sense of self and their attachments to social groups. The nationalizing state and minority activists have rewritten history texts, altered languages, renamed cities and streets, engineered demographic changes, resurrected ancient symbols, crafted new political institutions, propagated new visions of the nation, and proposed new roles for the state, both in the region and in the rest of Europe. The atmosphere that Goran encountered in Livno compelled him to reflect on who he is and where he belongs.

Identity-based theory appears to offer a better framework for understanding behavior in postconflict societies than interest-based theory. That said, scholars have criticized the ambiguity of the concept of "identity" (Somers 1994; Smith 2004). For instance, Rogers Brubaker and Frederick Cooper (2000) advocate replacing "identity" with more specific terms since scholars have failed to devise a concept of identity flexible enough to be constructed through social interaction but robust enough to help explain attitudes and behavior. They contend that the term "self-understanding" best captures explanations for actions that are not driven by interests. "Self-understanding designates one's sense of who one is, of one's social location, and of how, given the first two, one is prepared to act" (Brubaker and Cooper 2000, 17). Compared with social identity theory, self-understanding places the locus of power for the refining process more with the individuals themselves than with the groups they enter. Nonetheless, social interaction also plays an important role in updating self-understandings. Recall from the introduction that Dragan's

2. Miller and Sears (1986) and Neimi and Hepburn (1995) argue that, by the young adult stage, individuals have already formed views on race and ethnicity.

sense of self—his attachments to a nested set of identifications—emerged both as a reaction to the policies of the nationalizing state and minority activists and as a product of interactions with ordinary people living in Sarajevo, each of whom was advocating categories, which he then tried to resist.

The influence of self-understandings on the behavior of ordinary people can help us understand the rebuilding process in Bosnia, including possibilities that hold out hope for coexistence. It can also help us understand mechanisms to manage ethnic diversity constructively. Marc Howard Ross (2001) illustrated the ability of people to transform a confrontational event that tried to force individuals to choose among identities into an inclusive one that allowed them to acknowledge their attachments to several groups. This occurred when local leaders in Northern Ireland toned down their threatening postures over a proposed Protestant parade through a mixed city by organizing a more inclusive event of a Protestant parade that would be embedded in a cultural festival celebrating the whole city's history. Taking into account attachments to social groups helps scholars and practitioners understand what kind of institutions are needed in postconflict societies for the expression of these identifications and for the pursuit of interests shaped by those identifications.

Uncovering Self-Understandings

To understand the impact that self-understandings have on reconstruction in Bosnia, we first have to understand the conceptions themselves. That process of refining self-understandings, which hinges on the interaction of ordinary people with members in the multilevel network, demands an approach that allows for depth and time. Goran was able to express how he fits in the mixed society of Bihać only after his interaction with co-ethnic Croats who live in a region where interethnic relations were hostile. But in both Bihać and Livno, the environment for interethnic relations changed over the eight years of my investigation. To tease out the complex dynamics of the multilevel network, I use a comparative case-study design centered on Bihać and Novo Sarajevo,[3] two towns in the Bošnjak-dominated area of Bosnia (see figure 1.2). The Bosnian state-building project envisioned by transnational actors is likely to bear fruit first in the prewar strongholds of interethnic cooperation—urban areas that did not experience intimate interethnic violence. I focus initially on

---

3. Novo Sarajevo municipality includes some areas occupied by Serbs during the war.

towns in the Bošnjak-dominated area because, of the three ethnically dominated areas of postwar Bosnia, it is the most diverse, with at least 10 percent of its population consisting of minorities (UNHCR 1997; Medju-narodni Forum Bosna 1999).

I highlight the views and actions of a segment of Bosnia's population that is critical to the outcome of the reconstruction process: middle-class urbanites living among the state's predominant group, Bošnjaks. The self-understandings and reactions to postwar institutions of persons of Serb, Croat, and other non-Bošnjak backgrounds will be very important in shaping what kind of state Bosnia will become and how stable it will be. Furthermore, the skills they possess are needed for economic reconstruc-tion. Because of their importance to the statebuilding process, there is great pressure on middle-class citizens of cultural backgrounds other than Bošnjak. Transnational actors want them to stay in or return to their prewar homes and help rebuild a culturally diverse state rather than con-tribute to a weak patchwork state of ethnically homogeneous areas. Imag-ine that you are a police officer of Serb background in Bošnjak-dominated Sarajevo. Minority activists and parastate leaders want you to leave Sara-jevo for Serb-controlled Republika Srpska. Putative homeland elites in Serbia also dangle opportunities for you to relocate to the Republika Srp-ska or Serbia so that you are among the majority. At the same time, local activists and transnational and nationalizing state officials would like you to stay in your home and act as a loyal minority.

The reintegration process in urban areas is particularly important be-cause it also involves people displaced from villages, a social group cre-ated by the war that significantly influences statebuilding. In chapter 4, I expand my investigation beyond Bihać and Novo Sarajevo to rural areas in the Federation and to the Republika Srpska. If we are to grasp the pro-ject of reconstruction across the entire country, we must attend to the poignant situation of refugees returning to their original homes in areas dominated by another ethnic group. These refugees are like the canary in the coalmine—if they can successfully realize their goals of returning home (indeed, if they can be convinced that they should return home), then that bodes well for the overall reintegration project. The news on this front has been promising: The number of Bosnians who returned to areas in which they are minorities jumped from an estimated 96,500 at the end of 1999 to 400,000 at the end of 2004 (UNHCR 2005).[4]

---

4. Estimates of persons who return permanently are notoriously difficult to verify (see chapter 3). The UN High Commissioner for Refugees estimates that 800,000 Bosnian dis-placed persons and refugees still seek a durable residential solution (UNHCR 2005).

A comparative case study such as this one helps generate theory (Lijphart 1971), all the more important given the dearth of attention paid to politically relevant grassroots processes in postconflict areas. By focusing on several municipalities, I can apply different methods to uncover how the multilevel network model shapes the reactions of minorities in different places. This design helps illuminate the impact of local minority activists on variation in the reconstruction process.

Between Bihać and Novo Sarajevo, minorities would be expected to have a more difficult time in Bihać. First, residents of Novo Sarajevo are more tolerant toward those ethnically different than residents of Bihać. Novo Sarajevo is embedded in Sarajevo, the capital city of Bosnia, known for its tradition of cosmopolitanism,[5] while Bihać is a small town nestled in a rural pocket of northwestern Bosnia. Novo Sarajevo's residents have more education, greater opportunities for employment, and higher incomes than the residents of Bihać. Novo Sarajevo also provides more access to local NGOs,[6] which can be crucial in assisting reintegration and preventing interethnic violence (Bugajski 1993; Varshney 2001; see discussion in chapter 4). The political environment in Novo Sarajevo should also be more favorable toward minorities, since nationalists in Bihać exert more influence. Finally, Novo Sarajevo is more diverse than Bihać (table 2.1), which may contribute to tolerance. Diversity in localities did lead to increased tolerance before the war (Hodson, Sekulić, and Massey 1994), overriding its potential to heighten fear.[7]

Local experiences with violence also shape self-understandings and, more specifically, prospects for reintegration. In Sarajevo and Bihać, extremists who encircled the cities inflicted most of the war's violence. Serb extremists besieged both towns, terrorizing urban citizens by firing mortars and artillery from afar and trying to starve out the population by blockading the city. As a result of the silent exodus of much of the city's Serb population prior to the violence and the subsequent attacks by Serb extremists, Bošnjaks from Sarajevo and Bihać grew to distrust Serbs more than Croats and "mixed" persons.

While Novo Sarajevo and Bihać share these key characteristics of com-

5. Ulf Hannerz (1990, as cited in Baubock and Rundell 1998, 335) describes *cosmopolitanism* as a perspective "toward the co-existence of cultures in the individual experience."
6. There is no breakdown of the number of NGOs per municipality of Sarajevo.
7. Diversity is more threatening in Bosnia after the war than before (see Pickering and Schwartz 1998; Caspersen 2004). It may now play a role similar to "racial threat" in U.S. urban areas, in which majority group elites express fear when the percentage of minorities in their locality reaches above a nominal level to a level perceived to threaten majority power (Key 1950; Oliver and Mendelberg 2000; Sigelman et al. 1996).

Table 2.1. Demographic and socioeconomic characteristics of my sites and Bosnia

	Novo Sarajevo	*Bihać*	*Bosnia–Herzegovina (BiH)*
Prewar population	95,225	70,896	4,364,574
Prewar ethnic breakdown			
	36% Muslim	67% Muslim	43.7% Muslim
	34% Serb	18% Serb	31.3% Serb
	9% Croat	8% Croat	17.3% Croat
	21% Others	7% Others	7.7% Others
Postwar population	58,548	49,590	3,364,825
Non-Bošnjaks as a percentage of the postwar population (%)	23	3	51
Education[a]	0.71	0.40	—
Per capita income (Euro/month)	335	118	—
Persons seeking employment in 1999	7,166	6,744	411,787

Sources: UN High Commissioner for Refugees (UNHCR) 1997b; *Statistički godišnjak* 1990, 1998.
[a]This figure is a ratio of the number of students in secondary education in 1990 to the number of students in primary education in the same year (*Statistički godišnjak* 1990).

munal conflict, the local social dynamics differ. Bošnjak–Serb relations were worsened in Sarajevo by ethnic cleansing conducted by Serb extremists in the suburbs and by Muslim gangs, who killed approximately one thousand Serbs in the city during the war (Burg and Shoup 1999, 177). Bihać's predominantly Bošnjak population, on the other hand, also suffered attacks from co-ethnic rebels: Bošnjaks loyal to the Bošnjak autonomist Fikret Abdić, a businessman and politician based just north of Bihać, participated in the siege of Bihać. This assault expanded the conception of enemies held by Bošnjaks in Bihać to include co-ethnic autonomists as well as Serbs (O'Shea 1998). Bihać is an important case for postwar social relations because divisions among Bošnjak activists may have created greater possibilities for ethnic minorities to reintegrate and influence reconstruction.

The main benefit of "soaking and poking" (Fenno 1978)—that is, spending time listening to and observing Bosnians as they engaged in everyday social interaction over eight years—was that I could uncover the dynamic mechanisms of the multilevel network model in a way that would not have been possible with surveys. I lived with local families— five minority and one Bošnjak—in apartment buildings in Novo Sarajevo and Bihać that house a mix of ethnicities because I wanted to study up close their interaction with postconflict citizens and institutions (see

Figure 2.1. Neighborhood site in Sarajevo.

appendix C). As a precaution against neighborhood idiosyncrasies, I lived in different neighborhoods in each city. Of the people I formally interviewed, I observed nearly half (25 of 52) in at least one natural setting outside of the interview. Attention to the Balkan tradition of good neighborliness, including coffee visits and the use of barter networks, provided me with unique opportunities to view interethnic relations in nearly natural settings.[8] My base in neighborhoods allowed me to explore the role of neighborhood networks in providing practical help and camaraderie, both so important in molding self-understandings and assisting reintegration. Neighborhood-oriented venues for interethnic interaction included cafés, playgrounds, markets, and farms (figures 2.1, 2.2, and 2.3). The return of minorities, even if temporary, provided opportunities for me to listen to residents debate the place of these returnees. I talked with

8. My Bosnian hosts were always aware that I am a foreigner. Over time, however, my presence appeared to become less and less disruptive, a pattern found also by other ethnographers (Dewalt and Dewalt 1998, 288; Fetterman 1989, 46). See appendix A for further discussion.

Figure 2.2. Neighborhood market in Sarajevo

and observed 130 Bosnians of diverse backgrounds in widely different social contexts (see appendix B).

Basing myself in apartment buildings afforded a close look at actual, rather than merely reported, interethnic exchanges in real life. This avoids overreliance on social views offered in surveys, whose relationship with actual social behavior is ambiguous (Romann and Weingrod 1991; Walsh 2004).

Combining intensive interviews with participant observation rather than using a survey questionnaire with fixed responses gives us a much better chance of understanding how Bosnians sort out where they belong and how they perceive postwar institutions. Intensive interviewing allows Bosnians to discuss motivations and to offer explanations different from those derived from scholars' preconceived theories.[9] Using my apartment building as a base, I interviewed minority neighbors toward the end of my stay (each of which lasted at least several months) at each site. The strategy of rooting myself in local communities helped me de-

9. See appendix D for the interview protocol.

Figure 2.3. Neighborhood site in Bihać.

velop trust and concentrate on the "quiet" segment of minorities who do not employ attention-getting public strategies for integration and thus often stay hidden to outsiders.

To locate minorities beyond my circle of neighbors, I used *snowball sampling*, a process whereby interviewees suggest additional persons for questioning. It was necessary for me to use this sampling method because there is no postwar census, and it is impossible to identify minorities by sight. To prevent systematic confinement of the sample to one faction of minorities, I relied on local activists with varied backgrounds and social networks to suggest other Bosnians.[10]

While I focused on Serbs and Croats who had stayed in or returned to Bošnjak towns, I also talked with Serbs and Croats who had relocated to regions where they are now in the majority. Other marginalized persons

10. Activists included leaders of local voluntary organizations and prominent persons in the neighborhood. Humanitarians also helped. Because I focused on urban areas, the sample includes a higher percentage of university-educated persons than exists in the general Bosnian population. In chapters 3–5, I discuss how education influences attitudes about home, interethnic relations, and politics.

who shared their experiences included supporters of the Bošnjak autonomists, as well as displaced persons and female heads of household of all backgrounds. I also spent time examining the perspectives and choices of people who belonged to the *majority* group. Talking with and observing Bošnjaks was essential to understanding both the obstacles they confronted in rebuilding their lives and their reactions to minorities. Only a holistic approach can accurately portray the postwar reintegration process.

Because I use an in-depth approach and because local peculiarities influence interethnic relations, I seek to make an analytical generalization (Yin 1994). My research suggests ways that ordinary minorities in Bošnjak-dominated towns that escaped intimate violence influence reconstruction. The dynamics I found in Bihać and Novo Sarajevo cannot be extended to cities such as Mostar or Banja Luka, which experienced ethnic cleansing; I look at them separately in chapters 4 and 5. Quantitative analysis of more than thirty nationwide surveys helps describe and explain regional and Bosnian-wide patterns.

Interpreting Official Nationality Categories

I tried to assess whether interest-based or identity-based theory is better at explaining how Bosnians react to official categories supplied by the nationalizing state. I asked Bosnians to specify their "nationality according to the census" and whether they had "declared themselves differently before the war from now." If respondents emphasized a strong and unwavering attachment to ethnicity, that would suggest that interest-based theory would be more useful than identity-based theory in understanding behavior in deeply divided, postconflict settings. Keep in mind that interest-based theory presumes an unproblematic and straightforward relationship to identity; the more fluid, capricious, complex constructions of identity seem to be, the more useful identity-based theory becomes. Interest-based theory also expects ordinary people to accept the contention that only ethnic group elites can properly define and protect the interests of their co-ethnics. These expectations assign little power to ordinary people in the multilevel network model.

Alternatively, identity-based theory would expect to find that individuals possess both a multiplicity of social identifications—including, but not limited to, ethnicity—with varying attachments to each of these social groups. This approach asserts that individuals play an active role in refining their self-understandings through everyday social interaction and experiences with actors in the multilevel network.

In answering questions about nationality categories, most respondents did select the ethnic-based categories that dominate census options. However, individuals often complained that the categories did not suit their own conceptions of belonging. One quarter (25 percent) were unable to limit themselves to one group, despite the census's insistence that citizens choose one identity. As we saw, Dragan's response to my request for specification of his census-defined nationality was "Serb" followed by a set of nested and increasingly inclusive identifications.

Another example is Petar, a former communist bureaucrat who stayed in Sarajevo and participates in a multiethnic professional association of World War II veterans. Before the war, Petar declared himself as a Serb and Yugoslav; after the war he calls himself a Bosnian and Yugoslav. His declarations favor political affiliation, which is consistent with socialist teachings. His unwillingness to discard "Yugoslav" suggests his nostalgia for the previous system, while his decision to drop Serb may be in part a defensive mechanism that downplays his ethnic ties to a group that Bošnjak nationalists hold responsible for the war. His strategy also supports Marilynn Brewer's (2001) expectation that strong connections to several social groups create pressure for individuals to recognize bonds to those groups rather than to embrace only one. Petar expressed his tie to Bosnians though his decision to stay among his multiethnic neighbors during and after the war. He expressed his tie to Yugoslavs by his activism in the World War II veteran's organization that honors the generation that built the Socialist Yugoslav state. His activism indicates that his choice of the Yugoslav label was purposeful. It is noteworthy that rural inhabitants were quicker to settle on ethnic or religious labels—a process encouraged by custom, lack of urbanization, and international organizations distributing aid.

Many Bošnjaks were not satisfied with ethnonational labels, which continues a tradition of frustration with official categories (Hadžijahić 1974; Bringa 1995). This may also be a legacy of the Socialist state changing the census categories for those of Muslim background over time. Middle-aged Ditka felt that the official categories have never matched her self-understanding and those of her family:

> In 1991, I couldn't declare as a Muslim and . . . I'm not Croat, and I'm not Czech, because that is what my husband is, even though his father is Czech and his mother is Slovene. My mom is Muslim, but in the 50s she declared as a Croat. On my birth certificate, it says Croat. My father was born into a Muslim family in Bihać, but declared himself a Serb. In 1991, I declared myself a Yugoslav.

The variety of collective labels that Ditka uses to describe herself and her family illustrates begrudging adaptation to official labels, not enthusiastic internalization of them. Ditka's story also conveys confusion about the official categories since it *was* possible in 1991 to declare as a Muslim. In short, the official categories will always be a rearguard effort to impose a severely simplified frame on a complex reality.

Not all persons of Muslim background embraced the push begun by elites of the nationalizing state during the war to bolster their ethnonational distinctiveness by declaring themselves to be Bošnjaks. These elites promoted the term "Bošnjak" to resist claims that persons of Muslim heritage in Bosnia are merely Croats or Serbs who practice Islam. Instead Muslim respondents more often stayed with Muslim as their nationality. Some, such as Munira, resented having to categorize themselves at all: "Before the war, I declared as a Yugoslav in the sense of a citizen; if I *must* identify myself, then I'm a Bošnjak." Similarly, Avdo, a Bošnjak who stayed in Banja Luka despite being expelled from his apartment, felt forced into choosing his ethnonational group because the extremists used violence to tear apart his prewar circle of colleagues of diverse backgrounds. Absent a pluralistic group, Avdo could only safely resort to his own, a consequence of the violence that was far from accidental.

A stroll through Baščaršija, an old part of Sarajevo, during Ramadan in 1998 provided an opportunity for Armin, a high school student, to clarify the label that best fit him and its meaning. After we heard celebratory gunshots, I asked if he was observing Ramadan. Armin laughed heartily and explained, "No, I'm Bosnian." Clearly he felt that calling himself "Bosnian" conveyed his secularism. The term did not have the same connotation for most minorities, however, who felt that Muslims had hijacked the term along with the state. One symbol of this was the message on the public phones arrayed along one side of a Sarajevo post office. Before spelling out the directions for making a call, the telephones with an LCD display scrolled a salutation for Ramadan. Those most likely to declare themselves as Bosnians were those who declared their prewar nationality as Muslim despite the potential of "Bosnian" to serve as a civic or political identification, similar to the term "American."

When Yugoslavia disintegrated, state authorities removed supraethnic categories like "Yugoslav" and elevated ethnonational categories in state-authorized and internationally accepted business in Bosnia. These steps compelled a segment of the population to reconsider its nationality. Though nearly half of my minority respondents declared their census-defined nationality differently before the war than they did after the war, individuals tried to choose categories with consistent meaning. For instance, many respondents who avoided ethnic labels in favor of political terms like "Yugoslav" before the war shunned ethnic labels after the war as well. The testimony and behavior of respondents like Petar, who continued to identify himself as a "Yugoslav" after the war, suggest that minorities chose non-ethnic classifications or used multiple classifications to express rejection of the idea that one ethnic category could describe their self-conception rather than as a defensive move to protect themselves from nationalists.[11]

Predictably, ethnically "mixed" persons expressed particular frustration with nationality categories, claiming that they could not fit themselves into the narrow boxes. As Novka, whose father is Muslim and mother is Serb, sighed, "These categories are not adequate for the way I feel." Bosnians tended to see the official ethnonational categories as artificial labels that failed to define their sense of self. Even those who declared their nationality in ethnic terms attached varying meanings to those labels. This sentiment becomes clearer in the following testimony individuals gave about their social ties.

Attachment to Social Groups

Do ethnonational communities form the basis of the in-groups to which individuals identify? To find out, I asked respondents to specify the groups with which they shared a sense of community, the groups in which they felt more comfortable. Interest-based theory would expect Bosnians to respond by identifying their ethnic group in a manner consistent with the messages of the nationalizing state and minority activists. But only two respondents who now live as minorities identified their in-group in culturally exclusive terms.[12] One was Ivo, a priest who specified "Catholic," but even he made a point of adding, "but I work often with others."

Much to my surprise, the most common response was "none." Most replied that they did not feel better with any one group. Mina elaborated on why she did not identify with any particular group by mentioning how her neighbor reached out to her even at a traumatic time. "When my neighbor's son, who is Muslim, was killed, she immediately called to tell me. She blamed it on Alija," meaning Alija Izetbegovic, Bosnian president and Bošnjak leader at the time. Mina's story conveyed her comfort with

---

11. This contradicts findings by Sekulić, Massey, and Hodson (1994, 95), who argue that, before the war, minorities chose "Yugoslav"—the predominant supraethnic category at the time—as a neutral and defensive posture. Further research is needed to determine minorities' motivations for choosing supraethnic labels.

12. As Bringa (1995) suggests, Bosnians from villages would respond differently to this question, probably placing a greater emphasis on ethnoreligious identity.

individuals who refrained from blaming an entire ethnic group, such as Serbs, for crimes committed during the war. The mix of educational backgrounds of these respondents, ranging from primary school to university, suggests that this response was not offered merely to meet the expectations of internationals assumed to favor reuniting and reintegrating Bosnia. Urban respondents simply refused to pick one group to provide solidarity and to represent their interests.

The next most popular category consisted of those who sought out likeminded individuals. These respondents indicated that they prefer to *choose* an in-group whose members share important values and act according to those values rather than accept the proposition that those who share their ethnicity must share their interests by definition. The likeminded trait mentioned most often was treating people as human beings rather than as members of some ethnic group. In describing to me the group to which she felt closest, Renata, an NGO activist who stayed throughout the war in Sarajevo, expressed discomfort in specifying a particular group and rejected classifying people according to ethnicity:

> I guess that I prefer to be with people who . . . look at other persons as humans, regardless of their political party or their religion. The war uncovered these types of people, . . . people [who] helped me during the war.

Though Renata's cultural heritage, which she identified as Croat and Catholic, was important to her, she did not believe it determined the group to which she felt the closest sense of community. Instead, she identified most with those who recognize the basic humanity that connects individuals. Renata's recognition that these individuals helped her survive the war indicates that she feels close to them both because she shares their beliefs and because she has had positive experiences with them. Renata's mention of specific encounters with persons of other backgrounds bolsters the credibility of her answer.

Here we see a common theme, that the war was a traumatic test that definitively revealed those who value the humanity in others regardless of ethnicity and those who judge people by their ethnicity; for Bosnians, the war was a seminal event that compelled reconsideration of their selfunderstandings and their social relations. Treating others as humans was a mantra voiced by those who rejected ethnonationalism—most often those living as minorities or at least in relatively diverse areas.

Minka, who endured both World War II and the most recent war in Sarajevo, echoed Renata's sentiments. She associated with a circle of people who "never looked at her and her husband in terms of nationality, but only as humans." Reflecting on her reasons for remaining in Sarajevo led her to reveal the meaning she attached to her Serb background:

> Once . . . someone asked, "Why do you say you are Serb, when you are from Bosnia?" I couldn't even say. My mother [said she was Serb,] and [so] I always did. I didn't think about it. My sister even attended a Catholic school and sang in [its] choir. . . . [Like me,] my other sister married a Croat. I never paid attention to religion. During the First Yugoslavia I went to the cathedral and to the synagogue to hear their choirs.

During a visit to pay respects to Bošnjak acquaintances during the Muslim holiday of Bajram, Minka also displayed her knowledge of Islamic prayers (in Arabic, no less) and customs. Her upbringing had downplayed religious differences and guided her behavior in diverse settings. Minka's mention of concrete experiences and her social behavior (discussed below) suggests that she puts these tolerant views into practice.

Rajko, a Serb who stayed in Sarajevo, where he worked as a policeman, told me he felt closest to "people who stayed" during the war. After pausing to reflect, he continued earnestly, "People don't look upon me, not that I know of, as a Serb." Rajko's sense of attachment to urbanites who endured the siege was reinforced by his belief that fellow long-term Sarajevans shared his upbringing and judged him based on his character and his actions of helping defend the city.

Regardless of ethnic background, most urbanites found it difficult, even unpleasant, to specify a single group with which they felt a special sense of community. "Well, if I must . . ." was a common sentiment, clearly conveying their resistance at being confined to one group. These responses stood in contrast to those from Bosnians living in areas where they were majorities, where about half of Croats (47 percent), for example, identified exclusive ethnic or religious groups as those to which they felt particularly close (USIA 1997, 193).[13]

The refusal of minorities in Novo Sarajevo and Bihać to identify mainly with their ethnic group does not conform to the interest-based model for divided societies, which assumes that ethnic attachments drive interests.

13. The USIA survey compelled respondents to identify only one group whose beliefs they felt were particularly close to their own. This rigidity means that it probably did not capture the diversity of belongings felt by the inhabitants of Croat-dominated and Serb-dominated areas of Bosnia. Only 15 percent of Serbs living as a majority expressed exclusive cultural identifications, a surprisingly low figure given other evidence on the relatively high ethnic distance expressed by Serbs living as a majority (USIA 1999). This suggests that a wide range of those living in Bosnia are dissatisfied with the ethnonational proposition that ethnicity determines interest.

Instead it suggests that the minorities who remained in Bošnjak-dominated urban areas continue to assert an identity that they themselves work to define. Of course, this identity requires some degree of acknowledgment by society, even if it is not necessarily the most powerful elites in the multilevel network. It also shows how ordinary people quietly contest the official categories and identities that are promoted by the nationalizing state and minority activists. Observation of minorities as they go about their everyday lives reveals how difficult it is for individuals to practice their self-understandings in broad social settings when doing so risks ostracism or other retribution. This becomes even more challenging in the political realm (chapter 5).

Multiple Social Cleavages

Data from nine separate nationwide surveys also contradict the expectations of interest-based theory. Instead, they confirm that ethnicity is only one of several significant social divisions in postwar Bosnian society. Bosnians see the greatest social distance between categories of class, between (ethnic-based) nationalities, and between refugees and persons who stayed in Bosnia during the war, according to research by the World Bank (Dani et al. 1999) (table 2.2). This survey supports the findings from my interviews that most Bosnians do not identify most closely with members of their own ethnicity or feel the most removed from people of other ethnicities. This and other nationwide surveys conducted after the war reveal a society where ethnicity in not the only basis for the in-group.

Nonetheless, the divide between people of different ethnic backgrounds is clear to any observer in Bosnia. Its depth is illustrated by the low levels of willingness to engage in intimate interethnic relationships and by the consistently different attitudes that members of each ethnic group tend to express. Few Bosnians of any background now express a willingness to marry someone of different ethnicity (see table 1.3).[14] But Croats are the least willing to enter into a mixed marriage, while Bošnjaks are the most willing (UNDP 2003a). Logically, support for less intimate mixing, which occurs in venues such as schools, neighborhoods, and the workplace, is higher (UNDP 2003a; European Values 2004; see chapter 5).

To explore whether regional demographic settings and migration decisions influence levels of ethnic tolerance, I analyzed data collected by the

14. Surveys conducted by the UN Development Programme depict the opinions of Bosnians who live largely in localities where they are among the majority. They do not identify those few respondents who live as minorities.

Table 2.2. Social distance between different social categories

Categories listed for social distance[a]	Serb (%)	Bošnjak (%)	Croat (%)	Average (%)
Rich vs. poor	58	43	12	38
Between different (ethnic-based) nationalities	57	12	29	32
Refugees from abroad vs. persons who stayed	38	29	15	27
Between members of different political parties	37	21	11	23
Rural vs. urban	12	21	5	13

Source: Dani et al., 1999, table 5.

$N = 3,120$ persons in a nationally representative sample covering all of Bosnia.

[a]Expressed in percentages of people reporting high social distance.

State Department (USIA 1998). I isolated Serbs and Croats who had always lived in areas dominated by their co-ethnics, those who used to live in areas where they were in the minority but relocated to majority areas, and those who stayed in areas where they are in the minority. Responses to three propositions about ethnic relations indicate that individuals now living as minorities are more tolerant than those who have always lived among co-ethnics and those who recently relocated to areas where they are now among co-ethnics (table 2.3).

One-third (33.3%) of Bosnian Croats who chose to remain a minority agreed with the proposition that they would not object to their child marrying someone of a different ethnicity, while only 11.8 percent of Croats who relocated from minority to majority areas concurred. The gap between opinions on whether Croats, Muslims, and Serbs can now live peacefully together again is a whopping 63.8 points, with 84.2 percent of Serbs currently living as minorities expressing support as compared to only 20.4 percent of Serbs who relocated.

These data on ethnic tolerance shatter assumptions of interest-based theory that ethnicity is enough to determine values or views on social relations. The relatively higher tolerance of those living as minorities[15] is

15. Whether living as minorities or a majority, Bošnjaks tend to possess similar views toward interethnic relations. About the same percentage of Bošnjak relocatees or displaced persons (78.6 percent) and minorities (76.6 percent) supported the proposition that "I be-

Table 2.3. Attitudes on ethnic relations, by ethnicity and postwar migration status

| | Bosnian Serbs | | | Bosnian Croats | | |
Proposition	Minorities who stayed[a] (%) (N = 38)	Minorities who relocated (%) (N = 93)	Stayed in the majority (%) (N = 505)	Minorities who stayed (%) (N = 48)	Minorities who relocated (%) (N = 51)	Stayed in the majority (%) (N = 817)
Croats, Muslims and Serbs can live peacefully together in the country	84.2	20.4	20.8	79.2	31.4	37.1
People can feel safe even if they aren't the majority nation in their country	39.5	11.9	11.8	41.7	15.6	21.0
Wouldn't mind if my child married someone of another ethnicity	52.6	8.6	8.1	33.3	11.8	7.4

Sources: U.S. Information Agency (USIA) 1999. Thanks to Dina Smeltz for providing extra data on minorities in her samples.
[a]Bosnian Serbs are now a minority in central Bosnia, Bosnian Croats are a minority in central Bosnia and the RS, and Bošnjaks are a minority in Herzegovina and the RS.

surprisingly consistent with research on ethnic tolerance in Yugoslavia conducted before the war (Massey, Hodson, and Sekulić 1999), when the state officially supported tolerance. Many of those living as minorities reject the idealized multiculturalism so typically promoted by transnational actors but view some degree of diversity as a normal fact of life, even in postwar Bosnia.

These views also suggest the influence of the rhetoric of many local minority activists who tend to view interethnic relations in Bosnia as a glass half full. Leaders of a multiethnic group of high school students in Mostar in 2004 explained why they worked with students "from both sides of the river" separating Bošnjaks from Croats. They characterized the youth in the city as only 10 percent "extremist" and 10 percent "not extremist" in their views about ethnicity. The remaining 80 percent were "more or less neutral" and needed to be persuaded to be open to difference through experiences of working together on concrete projects to improve the lives of all of the city's youth.

Bosnians portrayed their experiences with interethnic relationships as falling into a consistent pattern, perhaps to reinforce the correctness of their decisions to both me and themselves. A distinguishing factor among respondents who stayed or returned to areas where they are now in the minority was the better interpersonal relations they reported with peoples of diverse backgrounds. They were more likely to characterize relations with their neighbors on the eve of the war as unchanged or improved than were respondents who relocated to areas where they are now in the majority. Those who stayed or returned could point to manifold concrete experiences with people of other ethnic backgrounds before, during, and after the war as evidence for this pattern of good interethnic relations. They pulled out their photo albums to show me friends of other ethnicities with whom they had vacationed, maids of honor of other ethnicities, and so on. They also discussed occasions when neighbors, students, and coworkers of other backgrounds reached out to them at important times. For instance, Minka appreciated that her daughter's Bošnjak colleague had risked his life to run bread and milk from his family's bakery across the firing zone of central Sarajevo to Minka's ill husband.

Does one's social identity lead to ethnic tolerance, or does tolerance

lieve that Croats, Muslims, and Serbs can live peacefully together in the country." This anomaly can probably be explained by the prewar dispersion of Bošnjaks throughout Bosnia and the fact that Bošnjaks have no option other than Bosnia for a homeland (USIA 1999).

lead to that construction of social identity?[16] My research suggests that the influence runs in both directions. Such a process is similar to that envisioned by David Snow et al. (1986), where those who appeared more open to diversity before the war tended to view future social relations through that prism, acknowledging and probably privileging social relations that most closely fit their prior understandings and expectations. Given the policies of the nationalizing state and the national-level minority activists, it is difficult to believe that the minorities who wound up in Bošnjak areas would suddenly have more tolerant views after the war. No, they probably were fairly tolerant to begin with.

Pressure to produce socially desirable answers to surveys funded by transnational actors obviously cannot explain the widely divergent levels of ethnic tolerance, especially since the bulk of respondents were not shy about expressing intolerance. A more plausible alternative is that minorities are making the defensive transition to being among so few of "their own" or possibly that their greater contact with those ethnically different has increased their tolerance. Such an interpretation is consistent with that made by scholars (Massey, Hodson, and Sekulić 1999, 689) who found the same effect in the prewar period.[17] My observation of individuals, across natural social settings and over eight years, can help evaluate these contentions in a way that one-shot interviews cannot.

Articulating Self-Understandings in Everyday Life

The big question is: Do these lofty, even noble, self-understandings and attitudes about interethnic relations, expressed by so many individuals during interviews and surveys, hold up during actual social interaction in Bosnia? During participant observation, I did not ask about self-understandings because I wanted to see how individuals expressed and re-

16. Gibson and Gouws (2000; 2003) argue that openness to multiple social identifications or lack of a strong attachment to a particular cultural group facilitates the tolerance of difference. They acknowledge that tolerance instead may help determine openness to multiple social identifications. Alternatively, education may help determine tolerance. However, research on tolerance in prewar Yugoslavia (Hodson, Sekulić, and Massey 1994) and postwar Croatia (Massey, Hodson, and Sekulic 1999) found that education had no statistically significant impact on ethnic tolerance.

17. American blacks who live in more diverse situations express the highest levels of racial tolerance (Sigelman et al. 1996). Literature on racial tolerance among American whites asserts that the relationship between diversity and tolerance is contingent on factors such as competition over the same scarce jobs, levels of education, and demographic balance (Pettigrew 1998; Oliver and Mendleberg 2000).

fined their notions of self in natural settings during everyday social interactions and contact with actors in the multilevel network.[18] Beyond their interaction with family and close friends, minorities often refined their self-understandings by contrasting themselves to out-groups.

Let us be frank: In the broad daylight of the tense postwar public, presentation of self often diverged from privately held meanings. Looking only at those whom I both interviewed and observed, the self-understandings they practiced in real life tended to be less inclusive than those they expressed in one-on-one interviews. Given the public settings where members of the multilevel network in practice push ethnicity as the only accepted identity, this is logical. Nonetheless, even in the harsh reality of social life, individuals articulated self-understandings that failed to conform to the unidimensional categories promoted by any of the most powerful actors of the multilevel network.

Informal Groups

Small informal groups are an important venue in which individuals refine who they are and where they fit in society. In informal groups, individuals interact in a way that expresses either the commonalities they have with other individuals or groups or the distance they feel from them (Tajfel 1978).

Visiting is a Balkan tradition that provides a window into social interaction in small group settings that are often highly selective. When a member of an urban minority turns to this or that person for camaraderie, that is a powerful affirmation of affinity in a real context, away from the idealized setting of the interview room. My observations suggested that visiting focused on camaraderie usually involved people who shared the burden of minority status. In other words, minorities tended to seek each other out for the purpose of camaraderie. This contrasts with visiting oriented toward practical exchange, which more often brought minorities and Bošnjaks together in Bihać and Sarajevo, a process I discuss in chapter 4. Serbs often met over coffee and cigarettes in their homes to gossip, discuss family, decry discrimination from the nationalizing state, and lament the altered demographics of their cities.

18. The testimony presented in this section to illustrate this process is consistent with the tone of testimony gathered while in the field. I checked this by comparing my narrative against a random sample of text about social identity and distance from my field notes (available upon request). I used the qualitative data-analysis program, NUD*IST (Scolari 1997), to assist in interpreting the data I collected. It can call up systematically and within context all discourse on the topic of interest throughout my field notes and contained in answers to my interview questions.

In one visit that I observed, Ljubica stopped by to let Zlata know the news from her family in her putative homeland of Serbia, which was under NATO bombardment at the time. Over coffee, Ljubica vented about Sarajevo's deteriorating social atmosphere.

> LJUBICA: I never paid attention to people's names [which often indicate ethnicity]. But I visited the clinic I retired from and I looked at the staff list. I didn't know a *single* person. Serbs make up fewer than 5 percent of those employed here.
>
> ZLATA: They probably left [the city], like most educated people. Educated people don't see a future here.
>
> LJUBICA: I've lived in Sarajevo for 50 years, and I don't see anyone on the street I know. Imagine that! You can't find educated people here in Sarajevo anymore.

In this conversation, Ljubica and Zlata identified their out-groups. The first is the nationalizing state that prioritizes hiring Bošnjaks. The second are those who lack "education," which refers to both those with little schooling and those who engage in unenlightened social behavior like judging people by their ethnicity. Left unsaid is that this group, too, consists largely of Bošnjaks.

Urbanites of all backgrounds expressed clear distance from those displaced from rural areas into the city. During Minka's visit to pay her respects to a couple whose nephew had died, the conversation turned to current social relations in the neighborhood. Host Edhem, a Bošnjak who had stayed in a Serb-occupied suburb of Sarajevo, told Minka, "My wife and I don't associate with the displaced persons; they don't have our upbringing." Edhem reached out to Minka, a Serb, by blaming the decline in cosmopolitanism on the influx of displaced persons from the countryside, his out-group.[19] Even though those displaced in Sarajevo are largely Bošnjak, their rural upbringing was enough for Edhem to classify them as "others."

Looking at the opinions expressed during visits involving the majority group helps clarify whether the disdain for rural newcomers is a cover for ethnocentrism. Bošnjaks in both Sarajevo and Bihać frequently distinguished long-term city residents from co-ethnic newcomers from rural areas of Bosnia. During a visit from their Bošnjak neighbors, one of my hosts, Mirsada, blamed persons displaced from villages—fellow Bošnjaks—for disrupting the neighborhood utility service by failing to pay their bills.

19. Despite the time that long-term urban residents devoted to professing their cosmopolitanism, their collective denigration of villagers reveals their own intolerance.

Discussion about neighborly relations sparked Ahmet, a Bošnjak who stayed in Bihać, to provide another illustration of the type of upbringing that urbanites feared the rural newcomers lacked—mutual respect for difference:

> There are two kinds of people. The displaced persons are peasants who want you to live as they do, according to their traditions. . . . They say *merhaba* and observe religious holidays. They dress differently; [women] wear headscarves. They don't like urban lifestyles.

Other than exchange greetings, Ahmet stayed clear of his new neighbors because he did not identify with their practices. The social conversation of long-term urbanites indicates that class and urban–rural divisions are significant social cleavages that can cut across ethnicity to create an "in-group" of those who strive to emulate what they consider a modern ideal.[20]

Urbanites who stayed in their towns during the war also told stories that conveyed the significant distance they felt from those who fled. Zorica, who stayed in Sarajevo during the war, had trouble connecting with fellow "mixed" acquaintances who had fled the city at the beginning of the war for Republika Srpska. "They [those who fled Sarajevo] will *never* understand what we went through!" she exclaimed, as she agitatedly lighted another cigarette after a visit by these acquaintances.

Franjo, a Croat who stayed in Sarajevo, provided another illustration of the divide between those who stayed and those who fled. He told of a night out with a high school friend who had fled to Germany during the war but returned afterward. Franjo was disgusted by his friend's stories of constant partying in Germany. He commented, "I couldn't listen to it. . . . We didn't call each other again. And he is *Croat.*" Franjo's wartime experiences of defending the city and living without utilities, security, or a reliable supply of food were so different from those of his schoolmate that he had difficulty communicating with him. Disparate wartime experiences trumped shared ethnicity. The division between those of the same ethnicity who stayed and those who fled decreased over time, but it never disappeared. Those who stayed continue to believe that refugees' experiences not only were easier than theirs but also advantaged them in the competition over scarce resources.

20. A follow-up survey conducted by the World Bank (Dani 1999, 71) and my research revealed more intense distance between those originally from rural and urban settings than table 2.2 suggests. Distance between urban and rural inhabitants may have been underestimated in the World Bank survey if Bosnians conflated class and settlement categories, which often overlap in practice.

Formal Groups

Participation in formal voluntary groups such as NGOs involves a greater degree of choice than does informal neighborhood visits. Individuals can choose whether to participate in NGOs and, if so, which ones. They also must expend more effort to involve themselves in voluntary groups than in walking next door for coffee. Voluntary groups are larger than those formed during visiting, thus creating more possibilities for disagreement and for complaining about out-groups.

Ljubo, a journalist who returned to a suburb of the capital in 1998, participated in the Serb cultural organization Prosveta in Sarajevo. During a roundtable discussion on reconciliation, to which Prosveta had invited Croat intellectuals and other members of the city's cultural elite, most of them minorities, Ljubo described his out-group as anyone who accepted essentialist identities. He included in this group transnational donors who categorized him as a Serb and assumed that ethnicity determined his interests. The interest in reconciliation on display during the roundtable served to separate the group from ethnocentric Bošnjak elites, ill-informed transnational actors, and secessionist minority activists who ran a parallel Prosveta organization in the Republika Srpska.

In Bihać, a group that brought together young people to work for democratic dialogue served as a gathering place for like-minded youth to hang out and to engage in grassroots work in their local community. A planning meeting for a seminar on education inadvertently provided the opportunity to express a little animosity toward one of the most prevalent out-groups in the Bihać pocket—those Bošnjaks who supported rebel leader Abdić's movement for autonomy. During the meeting, Hamdo, a Bošnjak who was crippled while fighting in the war against the Serbs and the autonomists, objected to inviting unemployed teachers who had supported Abdić and made plausible claims of workplace discrimination based on their political activism. For the many Bošnjaks who stayed and fought to protect Bihać, the idea of reconciliation with Abdić supporters was as unthinkable as reconciliation with their Serb neighbors who had fled. Expressing a common sentiment among Bošnjaks in Bihać, Hamdo asserted that "Abdić is not really human." Activist Ditka pleaded for the participants to live up to the organization's mission, explaining that "as an NGO, we must invite everyone" concerned about the topic of the seminar, "including those who conducted war against us." Though the NGO successfully cosponsored the seminar with Abdić supporters participating, the disabled veteran decided not to attend. In Bihać, this NGO was rare in even attempting to organize an inclusive in-group committed to dialogue.

The experience of my host Jovan in a Sarajevo chess club illustrated how, under some conditions, even mixed voluntary groups can promote exclusive in-groups. Jovan, a Serb who had fled Sarajevo for Serbia at the beginning of the war and now returns regularly to visit his wife Ana, who had chosen to stay, played chess at every available opportunity. One evening Jovan returned from a downtown chess club and said that one player, frustrated by Jovan's victories, derided him for having served as an officer in the Yugoslav army. Several factors explain why this chess group was unfriendly toward Serbs like Jovan. These include Jovan's temporary status in Sarajevo, the relatively low levels of education of members of hobby associations (Hooghe 2003), and the fact that a little chess playing cannot overcome years of resentment toward Serbs with military experience.

Everyday Life

Beyond the confines of their closest neighbors' homes and voluntary organizations, minorities often confronted a more hostile environment in their everyday lives. Names often caused minorities trouble in public. Jelena, who returned to Sarajevo after the war, broke into tears in 1999 while describing the reactions of Sarajevans to her name: "My name is Serb, and I am proud to be a Serb. But I must prove to people that I am not a četnik[21] [a Serb extremist who fought during World War II]!"

Mina, a retired teacher of "mixed" background, found that some of her Muslim neighbors treated her differently depending on the social context. Mina endured the war in Sarajevo with those she considered "her people" and generally felt that there was a sense of mutual respect among her neighbors, particularly the long-term residents. But there were exceptions. Some of the Muslim men greeted her only if there was nobody else around. If they happened to be with friends when they saw her in the bustling courtyard of the apartment complex, they would not greet her. Mina did not seem upset by this disrespectful behavior because "they had never been my friends" or otherwise part of her in-group. Instead, she found camaraderie among a group of former colleagues who happened to be "mixed" like her. Minorities found it difficult to convince the Bošnjaks they encountered in everyday public settings to refrain from assuming that their interests arose out of their ethnic background, in other words relegating them to an out-group.

21. Četnik forces were the official resistance force of the Serb-dominated Yugoslav government in exile. They committed atrocities during WWII (Stokes 1993, 222). During the 1990s and 2000s, many Bošnjaks and Croats used the term "četnik" to label those they considered to be Serb extremists.

An exchange between minorities and staff at a gym offers another illustration of the possibilities for the frequent humiliation that minorities face in everyday life. Looking to shed a little extra weight she had put on over the holidays, my host Ana joined me one evening at the gym. She asked for information about membership, and the gym's receptionist responded coolly. After the receptionist asked Ana for her name, she furrowed her brow upon hearing the answer, asking in a suspicious manner, "Are you from Sarajevo?" "Yes," responded Ana. The question implied that Ana's Christian background—signaled by her name—probably meant that she did not belong to the city's predominantly Bošnjak community. On the walk home, Ana moaned about the woman's small-mindedness. While the receptionist did not deny Ana membership or call her names, her behavior certainly seemed intended to make Ana uncomfortable and to relegate her to the Bošnjak-majority city's out-group.

Despite often uneasy interethnic interactions in their hometowns, minorities frequently experienced even more strained relations with their co-ethnics living in areas where they were in the majority. Such troubled experiences reinforced these minorities' beliefs that ethnic background did not determine their interests. For instance, Mira, a journalist of Serb background who stayed in Sarajevo, told me of her jolting visit to Lukavica, a Serb-dominated municipality near Sarajevo to which many Serbs from downtown Sarajevo had fled. Mira was there to report on the suburb's reactions to the 1999 NATO bombing of Kosovo:

> As I approached [Serbs in the market], it was immediately clear that I was an outsider. People asked if I was from "that side" [the Federation]. They called me a traitor. I asked some about their homes in Sarajevo. One said that in order to visit his prewar home he needed an escort from the NATO peacekeepers. To this, I responded, "Why?! There is freedom of movement!"

Though Mira lived only twenty minutes away from Lukavica, she felt that her experiences living in Sarajevo were light years away from those of her co-ethnics living in this Republika Srpska suburb. That her co-ethnics living in an area where they are in the majority labeled her a traitor for remaining in Bošnjak-dominated Sarajevo cemented Mira's estrangement from them.

Contact with the Nationalizing State

All Bosnians dreaded interacting with self-interested public officials who are a part of daily life. But minorities were doubly anxious about dealing with officials of a nationalizing state perceived to focus on solidifying control of the majority group and on making minorities' lives miserable. Those seeking the return of occupied property often felt that municipal officials were out to obstruct their claims long enough so that the applicants would give up on returning. I could see that Tamara, now a refugee with her husband in Serbia, felt this way as I accompanied her on what turned out to be fruitless visits to different local institutions dealing with property in Sarajevo.[22] Tears formed in her eyes after one encounter with housing officials. Vuk, a displaced person, also felt this way, as his claim for the return of his socially owned apartment in Bihać had been mired for nearly a year in the *papirologia* (the local bureaucracy's Byzantine maze of paperwork). One problem was that the nationalists stacked local bureaucracies with those opposed to the return of minorities. When he asked a municipal housing authority about his claim, Vuk repeated his legal rights and appealed for empathy:

> VUK: But the squatter in my apartment is not a refugee [a status that entitled them to special rights for temporary occupancy during the war].
> CLERK: I myself am a refugee, from Bosanski Novi [in Republika Srpska].
> VUK: Well then, as a refugee, you understand my position!
> CLERK: Except that the municipality official in Bosanski Novi hasn't even agreed to *accept* my application for return.

Vuk's appeal to a common in-group, minorities who had suffered displacement, fell on the deaf ears of a resentful official. While the displaced housing official's property claim had been blocked by Republika Srpska municipality officials, she knew that Vuk's appeal to Federation municipality officials would eventually result in the return of his apartment. She may also have questioned whether Vuk was sincerely interested in returning.

Reactions to Bosnia's Independence Day illustrated minorities' conflicted views about the Bosnian state. Observance of Independence Day spurred conflict in Ana's state institute, which was staffed roughly according to ethnic quotas mandated by the Dayton constitution and controlled by political appointees. As a form of protest against the Bosnian state, the deputy director at work—a Croat and a member of the national-level HDZ elite—ordered that Croat employees ignore the holiday and report to work. But one of Ana's colleagues, a Croat, did not go to work, so the next day the deputy director pointedly asked her about her absence. She replied that it was a state holiday, not a religious one. The grip

---

22. After years of effort, Tamara finally reclaimed her socially owned apartment in 2001.

of the nationalizing state and minority activists over employment, particularly in the bureaucracy, enabled them to obstruct reintegration.

Interaction with Transnational Actors

Faced with the discriminatory environment cultivated by the nationalizing state and national-level minority activists, ordinary people often appealed to transnational humanitarians. As an attempt to undo ethnic cleansing, transnational humanitarians created incentives for individuals to emphasize their interrelated statuses as ordinary folk, minorities, and victims deserving of generous international support.

I observed these processes during my visits with international voluntary organizations that were there to assist with housing reconstruction for returnees. During one visit with an international humanitarian and her Bošnjak translator, Edim, to a Serb hamlet outside of Bihać, Serb returnee Kosta made coffee for us on the fire pit next to his partly reconstructed home, which lacked water and electricity. He asked the humanitarian workers to help him replace some of the farming equipment he had abandoned when he fled. Kosta talked about hating displacement and resenting the measly pension he was getting. He asserted that during the war, "we were defending Knin," a Serb-dominated town in neighboring Croatia. Kosta's self-description as a victim who suffered while defending Serbs angered Edim, who refused to translate Kosta's story for his British colleague, leaving me to do so. Edim urged me to reject Kosta's assertion:

> Kosta was for a greater Serbia. We didn't want this war. We voted for Bosnia and not for a Muslim Bosnia. . . . Serbia and Croatia wanted to divide Bosnia and Herzegovina. Then they started messing with people here. . . . We didn't have weapons. They had lists [of people to eliminate]. . . . We didn't.

Edim viewed Kosta as an aggressor, indicating the gulf between Bošnjaks who stayed and Serbs who returned after the war, particularly men who fought for opposing armies.

As a foreigner, I often provided an opportunity for Bosnians to present their self-understandings. An invitation to lunch with college student Danica's family in 1999 spurred a lengthy discussion about self-understandings that diverged along generational lines. Danica and her brother spent the war in Poland and Croatia, respectively, while their parents stayed in Sarajevo. Their father, who grew up in Bosnia, asserted a non-ethnic self-understanding, but his children defined themselves ethnically. The family sparred over various issues: the relationship between the

Bosnian and Croatian languages (Danica and her brother seeing them as significantly different, their father seeing them as the same); Croatia's then president, Franjo Tudjman (Danica and her brother viewing him positively, their father negatively); and the relationship of the Croat-dominated southwestern region of Herzegovina to Bosnia (Danica and her brother viewing it as Croat, their father viewing it as belonging to the state of Bosnia-Herzegovina). In a story about her father's birthplace in northwestern Bosnia, Danica explicitly identified her father as Croat. He rejected this label, calling himself "a Bosnian, as are all people who live in Bosnia." Shaking her head in frustration, Danica summarized her family for my benefit: "This is a typically mixed family: Here you have a Bosnian, my dad; a Pole, my mother; and two Croats, myself and my brother." If there is a lesson here, it may be about young Sarajevans who return at the end of the war and face pressure from all sides—the nationalizing state in Sarajevo, putative homelands, and minority activists—to collapse their self-understanding to ethnicity. Under those conditions, young people may have reached for cultural identifications, such as Croat, as a prism to help interpret events.

The impact of experiences on self-understandings during formative years can differentiate persons even within the same generation. Only two years separate Seka and her sister, Violeta, children of a "mixed" marriage of a Serb and Croat, but they spent their most impressionable years in different social environments, which played a role in their distinct self-understandings. When their grandparents whisked them out of Sarajevo to Vojvodina at the beginning of the war, Violeta was old enough to have attended primary school in Sarajevo—Seka was not. On return, Violeta seemed undaunted about reentering public school despite its domination by Bošnjaks. Violeta's grandmother described her as "not religious," and Violeta even dated a Bošnjak for six years. But attending public school in Sarajevo was more difficult for Seka, who felt excluded by the Bošnjaks in her secondary school. Their grandmother noted that Seka "feels Croat, Catholic. She recognizes to which community it is most practical to belong. And this is better than to none." Emphasizing her Croat and Catholic self-conception helped Seka get accepted at Sarajevo's highly respected Catholic school.

Stubbornly Clinging to Self-Conceptions

Youth like Danica, Violeta, and Seka have refined their prewar understandings of self through their everyday interactions with members of the multilevel network who trumpet ethnicity as the only valid identification. Each tends to believe that her cultural background has varying implications for interethnic relations. The views and behavior of urban middle-class minorities strongly suggest that they possess a variety of self-understandings. The term "self-understandings" rather than "social identities" seems appropriate because urban minorities tended to *struggle* with official nationality categories and efforts to specify a social group with which they identified. These self-understandings fail to conform to the conceptions pushed by any single member of the multilevel network. As a result, most of these minorities feel they do not fully belong anywhere in the postconflict Balkans. How, if at all, these self-understandings influence decisions about where to make a home is the subject of the next chapter. Its answer will help determine what kind of Bosnia will be rebuilt.

3

The Dilemma of Migration

Mina [a retired teacher of Serb and Croat background]: I stayed in Sarajevo because I feel that here is my place, these are my people, and this is my life and country. I *chose* to stay here.

Milan [a pediatrician of Serb background]: Return doesn't mean just the return of one's house, but the return of one's town. . . . It is not the streets that make a town, but the people. . . . I'll return to Sarajevo when its prewar population is restored.

In chapter 2, we saw how individuals living in areas dominated by another ethnic group try to forge self-understandings that often do not fit the ethnically based identities promoted by the nationalizing state and national-level minority activists. But what goes into the decision about whether to relocate, where to rebuild their lives? The migration decisions that Bosnia's minorities have made—to move within Bosnia, to stay put, or to move next door to their putative homeland—reveal a great deal about forces shaping reconstruction in Bosnia.[1] On the one hand, ordinary people with prewar homes in areas where they are now in the minority are confronted by daunting opposition to the very idea of their living as minorities mounted by putative homelands, the nationalizing state, national-level minority activists, and a good portion of local minority activists. These forces exert pressure to relocate to an area where they would be in the majority.[2] On the other hand, transnational actors seeking to reverse ethnic cleansing offer minorities incentives to accept living in their

1. Here, I am interested in the choices that individuals make between living in their original homes where they are in the minority versus living in places where they are in the majority. For example, the most feasible choices for a Bosnian Croat from Sarajevo would be to stay in the city, where he is in the minority, or to relocate to a predominantly Croat area of Bosnia, such as Herzegovina, or to his putative homeland of Croatia.

2. Unless otherwise specified, I use the term *relocate* to indicate movement to an area of Bosnia or the former Yugoslavia where a person would be among the majority.

prewar homes as minorities. For those displaced by the war, this means embracing the unprecedented right to return to their homes of origin.

Theories and policies about migration rest on assumptions about how locals think, feel, and behave. This literature often relies on policy descriptions and socioeconomic data to make arguments about the forces underlying migration decisions. With the notable exceptions of political geographers Bob Kaiser and Elena Nikiforova (2006), Jon Fox (2003), and Alexander Diener (2005), few scholars have rolled up their sleeves and investigated the resonance of migration policies among ordinary people on the ground. This chapter focuses directly on the common people and the stories they tell about deciding where to try to reconstruct their lives. In addition to those who have been displaced and those who have returned, I look at an understudied group: those minorities who endured the war in their homes and have decided not to move, to rebuild their lives in the same place (Malkki 1995b). If, as is commonly believed, people make choices about migration based on hopes for a better life, what constitutes a better life? Who decides? How do they choose?

These are not merely decisions about where to spend the next several years or so. Like most citizens of developing states, Bosnians are less mobile and far more rooted in communities than Americans are. Furthermore, Balkan peoples view the sociability of their local communities as a central aspect of their customs and lives (Bringa 1995; Gordy 1999). Attachment to local communities runs even deeper in rural areas, where many people have long family ties and own homes they have built largely on their own or with the help of neighbors.[3] So Bosnians' decisions about where to rebuild their lives cut to the heart of the matter, both for the residents themselves and for activists trying to remake Bosnia.

At bottom, this is a battle for the hearts and minds of minorities in the region, a struggle particularly acute between transnational actors and national-level minority activists. A look at how ordinary people make sense of the policies intended to influence their choices about migration identifies who is winning that battle, and why. We can begin to see what postwar policies contribute to regional stability by eliminating large populations of disgruntled minorities and displaced persons ripe for manipulation by extremists.

---

3. The connection to urban areas is usually weaker because World War II and Tito's modernization efforts have resulted in many relative newcomers living in urban areas (Ramet 1996). Until 1996, most property in urban areas was socially owned. Nonetheless, some urbanites—even minorities—have generations-long ties to urban areas.

The Identity-Based Approach to Migration

Identity-based theory challenges interest-based theory in its conception of the decisionmaking process behind migration. While interest-based theory assumes that ordinary people accept the communal labels, values, and interests promoted by group activists and then use them in their decisions about migration, identity-based theory *investigates* these contentions. The identity-based approach leaves open the possibility that not all individuals embrace the idea, pushed by nationalists, that interests and values are inextricably linked to ethnicity. It questions the premises of interest-based theory that ordinary people mechanistically calculate the costs and benefits associated with decisions according to stable values determined by ethnic group elites (Taylor 1988; Shingles 1992). Identity-based theory instead anticipates that people attach variable meanings to social categories and incentives (Walsh 2004; McAdam 1982).

The identity-based approach conceives of decisions about migration as guided first by an individual's self-concept (Hugo 1981), rather than necessarily by profit and a desire to be among co-ethnics. A person's sense of self helps him filter the incentives offered by the competing members of the network to relocate or not. Recall from chapter 2 how interviewees such as Goran with strong ties to several groups (in his case Croat and Bisčani) tried to balance those groups in formulating their self-understandings. Giving up strong ties to a location is not a simple matter, as interest-based theory sometimes makes it out to be. All things being equal, a person whose self-concept arises out of a dense network of ties to multiple groups capable of providing psychological and practical support is better equipped to get by in an area where she is in the minority than someone who prioritizes ethnicity. The testimony of Mina and Milan illustrates this dynamic. Depending partly on a person's notion of self, values, and social ties, a displaced person can view a private house as an economic asset to sell to support relocation or as a home to reclaim and permanently return to. Reconstruction assistance dangled by transnational actors is likely to lure a displaced person into returning *permanently* to her prewar home only if she can find a job and is attached to those in her prewar locality.

The personal stories that Bosnians tell about migration are important. An individual's *perception* of her motivations and the process of making sense of incentives have significant consequences for ethnic diversity. The decisionmaking processes of the individuals I encountered in the field did not conform to the expectations of interest-based theory. They also turned out to be more complicated than identity-based theory predicted. When respondents discussed their decisions about migration, they did not necessarily specify their sense of self as the predominant motivator. Instead, they often dwelled on concerns about family, property, and jobs. Nonetheless, reflecting on their decisions about where to rebuild their lives compelled them to consider whether the path that practical interests pushed them toward was compatible with their sense of who they are.

Seeking to Uncover Stories about Migration

In interviews, I asked minorities to discuss their reasons for staying in, returning to, or relocating from their homes. The topic of migration is a politically charged one in the postconflict period since those who fled were often charged with betrayal, if not worse. As a result, participant observation in many ways provided better opportunities to hear the stories that Bosnians told about where to rebuild their lives and how their social experiences influenced their decisions. Bosnians shared these stories while sweeping the rubble that was once their homes, celebrating their return to reconstructed homes, meeting with real estate brokers to sell their homes, or waiting for the umpteenth time in the municipality housing office to try to reclaim their property. Though my focus is on those who stayed in or returned to prewar homes, I also talked with Bosnian Serbs who left Sarajevo and Bihać to relocate to Serb-majority Republika Srpska.[4] Following returnees to villages allowed me to understand how migrating to urban areas differed from migrating to rural areas.

People from Sarajevo and Bihać explained their migration choices with complex stories about evaluating incentives offered by those I describe as actors in the multilevel network.[5] Minorities who stayed in or returned to their prewar homes offered more multifaceted reasons for their decisions than did Bošnjaks, who were living where network actors wanted— among the majority in Sarajevo and Bihać.[6]

Before delving into the narratives about migration, it is important to investigate the possibility that minorities felt that they lacked the conditions necessary for making a choice. Interest-based theory could argue that those who remained as minorities or those who returned did so merely because they were compelled to do so, out of lack of resources to start a life elsewhere. Testimony revealed that most minorities felt that

4. Comparative methodology (Geddes 1990) requires attention to both those who returned and those who relocated in order to isolate the factors motivating minorities.

5. Again, I used qualitative database software to systematically call up discourse, in this case on migration, in my field notes and then use the program to aid in analysis.

6. Unless otherwise noted, all interviews were conducted in 1999.

they *had* been able to make some kind of choice, although most viewed it as a constrained one. Minorities I talked with in their fifties, the latter stage of their working years, who stayed in their homes during the war often felt that they had the most limited choices. They believed that they lacked real options because they had often invested in property, jobs, and communities and were hesitant to risk those investments to move and "start over again from scratch." A 2001 survey of returnees—most minorities—strongly suggests that individuals after the war felt they had exercised a degree of choice in deciding to return to homes of origin. In that survey, just 13 percent of respondents who returned to their prewar homes reported being "pushed" into returning by the immediate prospect of expulsion from temporary shelter (Sweeney 2001). It was the *Bošnjaks* I interviewed who were the most likely to mention this feeling of being stuck. Unlike Serbs and Croats, Bošnjaks knew that they had no other homeland to consider.

Participant observation provided the best opportunity for me to understand the options my hosts felt they had about migration, their views on the constraints they faced, and their reasons for living in Sarajevo or Bihać. In chapter 1 we saw that the dynamics of return to urban areas have differed from the dynamics of return to rural areas because the former almost always requires the eviction of temporary occupants from the majority group. Return to urban areas has tended to be more individualized, with leaders from formal neighborhood organizations (*mjesne zajednice*) playing a smaller role than in return to tighter-knit rural areas. Those who fled Sarajevo did so at different times and ended up displaced in different areas, often outside of Bosnia. The exodus of the vast majority of Serbs from the comparatively small town of Bihać just prior to its encirclement was more organized, and its inhabitants mostly resettled in clusters around Prijedor and Banja Luka, the major Serb-dominated towns near Bihać. In contrast to the political support that the SDA-dominated nationalizing state generally provided to minorities seeking to return to Croat- and Serb-dominated parts of Bosnia, Serb and Croat national-level activists worked vigorously in favor of *relocation*. This meant that Serbs and Croats seeking to return had to overcome the opposition of many coethnic *and* Bošnjak activists. As a result, Serbs and Croats who desired to return to prewar homes usually had to appeal to transnational actors or local minority activists, who were often supportive but weak.

While return to Sarajevo and Bihać was contentious, it did not risk igniting the level of violence possible in towns controlled by those suspected of and eventually indicted for committing war crimes, such as Bugojno, Prijedor, Srebrenica, Stolac, or Zvornik. Early efforts to return to such towns were met by violent personal attacks, booby traps, arson, and drive-by shootings; local police were often implicated in this violence. In contrast, officials from international humanitarian organizations and local minority groups concurred in 1999 that no such violence targeted minority returnees to either Sarajevo or Bihać.[7] However, a minority making a claim to property that jeopardized the shelter of displaced families who had not been offered alternative housing by city authorities risked reprisal.[8] Furthermore, up until 2002, the predominantly Bošnjak police periodically abducted male returnees to the outlying suburbs of Sarajevo on merely the suspicion of committing war crimes (Democratic Initiative of Sarajevo Serbs 2002). Local Serbs advocating return successfully appealed to international officials to free them quickly. But it understandably took only a few scattered abductions to discourage Serbs from returning. Returns to Bihać, where real estate was far less valuable than in Sarajevo and where Bošnjak demographic dominance was never threatened, did not generate any security incidents in 1999. Though minorities' sense of safety in Sarajevo and Bihać increased over time, so did the competition over scarce jobs, leaving the vast majority of minorities unemployed and making returns that occurred later in the postwar reconstruction period even harder to sustain.[9]

Stories Hosts Told about Migration

The role of practical concerns about work and property was much more evident in observation than it was in interviews.[10] But Bosnians wove emotional ties into their decisionmaking as well, as my hosts demonstrate. For instance, Ana, born and raised in Bosnia, indicated in 1998 that

7. UNHCR officials and Serb activists in Sarajevo conveyed that personal security concerns should not prevent minority return to Sarajevo in most cases (Interviews, January 1999). Officials with UNHCR, the International Police Task Force (IPTF), and the leading Serb NGO in Bihać reported no incidents that jeopardized the security for minority returnees in 1999.

8. Property legislation imposed by transnational actors after the war obligated local authorities to provide alternative housing to displaced persons evicted from property that had been only temporarily assigned to them. Urban housing authorities often lacked the political will and sometimes the capability, however, to meet this obligation.

9. Interview with Federation Ombudsmen officials, Bihać, July 1999.

10. Those whom I observed were probably more likely to include "down and dirty" issues because observation over months helped me develop deeper relationships with them than with those interviewees with whom I was not able to spend time outside the interview setting. Participant observation also allowed Bosnians enmeshed in varying situations in everyday life to generate a diversity of reactions that one-shot interviews or surveys could not.

practical concerns had led her to stay in Sarajevo for the medium term. But the isolation eventually led her to plan to leave:

> I stayed because of my property and my job . . . [but] I have no one here. My friends and family have gone elsewhere. I am waiting to see what it will be like. Most likely, I will sell the apartment and spend a little time in Serbia [with my husband], a little with my son [in Republika Srpska], and a little with my daughter [abroad]. Sarajevo was such a cultured city, but now it's full of peasants. There are Muslims who don't like the nationalist leadership. But unfortunately most do.

Ana's narrative of migration reveals that the lure of economic incentives is not enough to overcome the alienation she experienced in a city dominated by Muslims who do not share the cosmopolitan orientation she appreciates. Having stayed and worked as a clerk in a Federation institution throughout the war in Sarajevo, Ana had maintained a small network of neighbors and colleagues who helped her survive the postwar trauma (see chapter 4). When I first met Ana in 1997, she emphasized that she was the only member of her family who had been able to stay in her home. Over time, her family had taken advantage of more aggressive efforts by the international community to implement property rights. In 2002, her parents were among the first to return home to their Herzegovinian village, where they ran a successful agricultural pharmacy that they started with international seed money. Such efforts did not influence her son, Lazar, however, who by 2004 had joined her daughter in emigrating to the West to pursue economic opportunities and an environment free of discrimination prevalent in the Balkans. Throughout it all, Ana continued to work in Sarajevo with a plan to leave the city after retiring.

Lazar, in his twenties, had lived in Cyprus, Serbia, and Republika Srpska since fleeing Sarajevo with his father during the war. He was even more pessimistic than his mother about Bosnia and his ability to find a place in it. Explaining in 1999 why he hoped to emigrate to Canada, Lazar felt that he could not live a normal life in Bosnia. He bemoaned the lack of job opportunities for minorities:

> If you're from a Muslim area, and you've been away . . . and you reapply for your former job, now they employ only Muslims. It is the same in other regions of Bosnia. . . . State companies have . . . an ethnic key [quota]: a certain percentage Muslim, another percentage Serb, etc. . . . I don't want to be worried about the names of the people with whom I associate. It is primitive. Almost all of those who didn't think this way have already left Bosnia.

Identifying as a young cosmopolitan and lacking his mom's prewar work experience and property, Lazar saw the exodus of like-minded citizens as devastating his possibilities for a future in Bosnia. In 2002, he realized his dream of immigrating to Canada, where he began to study computer science at a two-year college.

A mix of practical and emotional concerns also influenced my host Zlata's arduous decision to return to Sarajevo only temporarily. A widow who returned in 1996 to Sarajevo after spending the war in Serbia caring for her then-ill husband and young granddaughters, Zlata welcomed me into her home in 1999. Though born in Serbia, she had spent the bulk of her adult life in Bosnia with her husband, a Serb born in Bosnia who had served in the Yugoslav army. Because she had returned within days of the reintegration of Serb-held suburbs into Sarajevo in early 1996, Zlata was "lucky" enough to be able to reenter her apartment before squatters could claim it. She was not early enough, however, to prevent vandals from stripping everything from her apartment, right down to its plumbing and her dentures. Zlata told me several months into my stay that she had returned to settle her ownership of the apartment before selling it. She planned someday to return to her hometown in Serbia's Vojvodina province to be where her late husband was buried. When the international-led property rights process provided her with the paperwork confirming her ownership of the apartment, she sold it and moved out of Sarajevo in 2001, partly because, in her words,

> Here [in Sarajevo], I'm visited only by my friend from my hometown and by my daughter's family. . . . I know that my [new Muslim] neighbors don't want to have contact with me. [Pointing to her apartment's pock-marked walls] Look! . . . Those holes in the wall are from snipers from the Muslim side. No, I don't want to stay.

As with Ana, Zlata felt alienated from a postwar Sarajevo dominated by Muslims displaced from the countryside to the point that it encouraged her to relocate from her home of thirty years. Zlata's preference to relocate to Serbia became her only option when Bosnian authorities rejected her application to resume receiving social services from Sarajevo rather than from the area of her displacement—Serbia. This illustrates the role of political manipulation of social services in thwarting returns. Visits to Zlata after she relocated to the village of her birth in Vojvodina, in 2002, 2004, and 2006 found her engaged in subsistence farming and socializing with her family. She was satisfied that she had left an uncomfortable community in Sarajevo. Her decision was motivated by her attachment to her hometown and to her late husband, her alienation from the newcomers to Sarajevo, obstruction on the part of Bosnian authorities, and lingering insecurity about life in Sarajevo.

In 2004, I lived with Zlata's daughter Sandra, her Croat husband Stipe, and their two teenaged daughters Violeta and Seka, all of them born in Bosnia. Like many middle-class citizens of Sarajevo, Sandra and Stipe had tried to emigrate, twice in their case. First, they had applied to emigrate to the United States but were rejected. Then, after continuing his work for an engineering firm in Sarajevo during the war until 1994, Stipe left his besieged hometown to live with wealthy relatives in Zagreb and to find a job. After a month with no success and no offer of additional help from his relatives in Zagreb, Sandra advised him to return to Sarajevo, where he took over his apartment again and resumed his job as a budget officer that he had held for twenty-three years. Stipe was fond of telling war stories, including one about how he bartered with his colleagues—mainly Muslims—to get what his family needed to survive. Sandra, who fled to join her mother and daughters in Vojvodina after weathering a year of war in Sarajevo, returned with her daughters immediately once the fighting stopped. She felt that finding a job with an international organization in Sarajevo as a clerk was critical in her family's survival. When efforts to emigrate failed, they used their resourcefulness and prewar connections to secure jobs and cope with postwar Sarajevo.

The insecurity they felt was largely financial. Sandra's contracts, with an international organization, were only short-term—months at a time. In 2006, she felt compelled to quit after the international organization moved its office to a location requiring a nearly four-hour commute every day and reduced her hours to part-time. Stipe began to receive his salary in full and on time only after 2000. Both of them worried that Violeta and Seka, now attending Sarajevo University, would not be able to find jobs in Bosnia due to their lack of connections to the nationalizing state, which were eminently more important for employment than was merit.

Because Kristina, who rented me a room in mid-1999, did not have children, she did not have to factor such concerns into her decision about migration, as Sandra, Stipe, and other hosts did. Though her background was Slovenian, she had spent her entire life in Bosnia and did not consider Slovenia to be her homeland. She felt that it was natural to stay in Bihać, where she had spent her professional career. Her late husband—a Serb—left a Serb suburb of Sarajevo in 1992 for Bošnjak-majority Bihać for safety. He left because of threats directed at him after he publicly criticized Serb nationalists. He was a victim of in-group policing enforced by national-level Serb activists, who consider co-ethnic dissenters as much of an enemy as those who are ethnically different. When he died during the war, Kristina took solace in the knowledge that people of all ethnicities came to pay respects and to help with the burial. She also took these gestures of help as concrete signs of the basic humanity of Bisčani, which encouraged her to stay. Kristina never expressed feelings of insecurity, even though she received verbal abuse over the phone during the war. Her dismissal of that threat as an exception accorded with the philosophy that seemed to guide her though difficult postwar times: "When I lost my husband and mother within six months, I decided to emphasize that which is still good in life." In practice she was trying to ignore the things that disturbed her, including the behavior of Bošnjak newcomers from villages to Bihać.

As a returnee struggling to regain her property rights, Ilinka had a more difficult time than Kristina in looking past the hostility she confronted. Ilinka—an ethnic Macedonian who had lived and worked as a nurse at the city hospital for thirty years in Sarajevo, including most of the war—finally fled with her ill husband to his hometown in Montenegro just before the war ended. She took me in during the summer of 2002. Ilinka said that she returned there after the war because she wanted to live in her own apartment, which had been originally allocated to her by her employer, the hospital. She felt that her Sarajevo apartment was her home and turned down the possibility of living in an uninhabited apartment in Montenegro that her daughter owned. Since 1996, Ilinka had been battling with the Federation's legal system to regain her legal right to the apartment, which the hospital had reallocated to another employee after she and her husband fled at the end of the war. She took over the apartment again in 2001 even though her right to it had not yet been settled. During my stay, she came home one day understandably exasperated from yet another inconclusive battle in court about her apartment. She appealed to me to use the connections she assumed I had as an American to gain her an audience with staff in the Office of the High Representative (OHR). When I suggested that she talk to local officials working for the Dayton-mandated Commission on Real Property Claims, she dismissed this suggestion with a rant to the effect that local institutions cannot help her because they lack power. This was a typical example of minorities rebuffing local institutions and officials and instead relying on networks to reach the most powerful people possible—the transnational officials running OHR, in this case—even though they did not deal with individual cases of property disputes. The court finally awarded her the apartment in 2003; when I visited in 2004, she was sharing it with her daughter, who had moved back to Bosnia full time. Ilinka's pension and income from her daughter's work as a contractor for international organizations helped them survive in postwar Sarajevo.

The migration decisions of my Bošnjak hosts were less complicated than those of my minority hosts. Mirsada and Alija stayed throughout the war in Bihać because of their attachment to their homeland and their desire to thwart what they viewed as the Serb nationalist project to force Bošnjaks to leave Bihać in order to capture it. When I asked Mirsada if they considered leaving for Liechtenstein, where her brother had long lived, she replied fatalistically:

> We planned to leave when we saw the Serbs fly out of Bihać from the Yugoslav army airport. But I simply couldn't leave. I thought that if I left, I would never come back. I decided if I die here, then it is meant to be.

They had no other homeland and were committed to rebuilding their lives in Bosnia. Alija, who served in the Bosnian army on the front lines defending Bihać, has been enraged at transnational actors "for failing to stop the Serb aggression against Bosnia" ever since I first met him in 1996. Mirsada and Alija, who had lost their private shop during the war, earned money after the war by renting out the space to an international organization. By 2002, even they were expressing concern about future opportunities for their teenaged daughter and sought to find a way for her to study in the United States. Their concern was echoed by other Bošnjaks over time as they became less and less hopeful that the reconstruction of Bosnia's economy, society, and political institutions would ever provide the conditions needed to resume "normal" lives.

The stories of my hosts illustrate that the practical concerns about jobs, property, and the general economic environment are critical factors when minorities decide where to live. As the international community improved security conditions and moved more aggressively to ensure the implementation of property rights at the end of 1999, economic factors played an increasingly important role in migration decisions (Poggi et al. 2002, 116). All things being equal, it makes sense that individuals would seek to live in an area where they were, or could become, employed, the place holding out the best promise for future prosperity. Though Bošnjak-majority areas have a better economy than Serb-majority areas—partly due to the concentration of international organizations there—and should in theory attract Serbs displaced from Republika Srpska and Serbia, workplace discrimination, or the fear of it, may undercut the supposed benefits for Serbs of living in Bošnjak areas.[11] This is especially the

11. Given that Croat-majority areas offer a higher standard of living than Bošnjak areas, it is not surprising that a higher percentage of Bosnian Croats than Serbs relocated from chiefly Bosnian areas. According to the Federation Ombudsmen in Bihać, "The employment situation is so bad, generally, that it's difficult to determine [discrimination]. Unlike other places, there was no mass firing of minorities in Bihać at the beginning of the

case for Serbs who do not speak English, a skill most often necessary for jobs with international organizations that provided both high salaries and nondiscriminatory environments.

Although economic factors were important considerations, for most hosts they were only one of several factors that influenced their decisions about migration. Of my six hosts, only Ilinka relied solely on economic considerations to decide where to live. This finding is consistent with the responses of those I interviewed (discussed below).

Most of my hosts also considered their connections to people and to the town where they lived before the war in deciding whether to rebuild their lives there. Stipe lacked deep emotional ties to the community in which he was raised, but he had the connections to endure the war in Sarajevo and to support the later return of his family. He felt let down by his relatives in Zagreb and by the general reception he received in his putative homeland of Croatia. Stipe's experiences and decisions do not fit the expectation of interest-based theory: that he would want to relocate to Croatia. This theory contends that he would have calculated the costs of returning to a Bošnjak-dominated area—especially during the war—as greater than returning to his co-ethnics in Croatia, who were expected to eventually offer him work and a home.

Stories Interviewees Told about Migration

Those I interviewed often combined utilitarian factors and emotional attachments. Irena, of "mixed" background, mentioned ties to her parents and to her hometown, Bihać, together with the confidence that her skills would enable her to get a job with an international organization, as factors motivating her to return. Asked if she was worried about facing a discriminatory local economy after her international employer closed its offices in Bosnia, Irena expressed surprising confidence that her job experience would ensure that she would find employment with a Bosnian firm. Even though Davor emphasized remaining in Sarajevo because of his shoe repair business, he revealed during an interview that his confidence in his business was rooted in the belief that he could convince his customers of the quality of his craftsmanship regardless of his—or their—ethnicity.

Nela's willingness to give up a job in Serbia to return to Sarajevo in 1998 also fails to fit the economic emphasis of the interest-based theory.

---

war. . . . But you can be sure if a Bošnjak and a Serb with the same qualifications are applying for the same job that the Bošnjak will get it" (Interview, July 1999, Bihać).

Though her background is Serb, Nela's sense of self and her lived experiences in Sarajevo before the war helped her filter new information she received as a refugee in her putative homeland. Nela's narrative about migration opened with her belief that she was "closer to people" in Sarajevo than in Serbia. Seeing herself first and foremost as a Bosnian, she ruled out job and housing incentives offered by her putative homeland and minority activists in Republika Srpska:

> I could have gotten some kind of apartment in Serbia, and I already had a job. But I didn't want to. I'm a *Bosnian*. . . . As I was leaving Sarajevo during the war, I realized that virtually all of my friends were Muslim. . . . I can't live in a place that is ethnically pure. I don't think that way. I raised my son to think as a human. I could also obtain a job in Republika Srpska, but I can't see that as a possibility.

Nela's attachment to a mixed community and to humanism enabled her to use a multiethnic network of prewar colleagues to help secure her reemployment in Sarajevo. In the introduction, we heard about Nela's frustrating experiences with the nationalizing Bosnian state authorities, transnational actors, and minority activists and about how these experiences reinforced her reliance on informal ties to diverse colleagues for returning to Sarajevo and for coping after the war.

Because it took four years before transnational actors compelled local authorities to evict the temporary occupant of her apartment and because she received no aid, Nela's return could not have been motivated by the carrots dangled by Dayton's implementers. Ordinary people like Nela nudged international officials into implementing aggressively nondiscriminatory property legislation by tenaciously hounding transnational actors about restoring property rights.

Gordon, a Serb who stayed in Bošnjak-dominated Zenica throughout the war and continued teaching there afterward, told a story about social ties that was similar to Nela's story. The help that he and his wife—a Muslim—received from colleagues, acquaintances, and friends during the war convinced them to remain in their home in Zenica despite the rebuff they received from humanitarian organizations with religious connections and the local government, which disapproved of their mixed marriage. Predrag, another teacher of Serb background, asserted that "good experiences with Serbs and Muslims" in his prewar workplace and his activism in non-nationalist politics influenced his return to the town of Bosanski Petrovac. Having a multiethnic network can increase a person's sense of belonging to a mixed community; it also makes one feel safer. Slobodan, a Serb who returned to a hamlet near Bihać in 1998, asserted that even though he knew that there were "crazies around," he had not felt unsafe because of his professional reputation as a sawmill worker. "People know me," Slobodan said assuredly, that is, people knew he treated people fairly regardless of their ethnic background. In these four cases, it was the informal connections and the reputation established through repeated behavior—not the formal state institutions such as the courts, housing authorities, police, or international organizations—that instilled a sense of personal security in those living as minorities.[12] Furthermore, there is a long tradition in Bosnia of the role of reputation in bringing about justice.[13]

Minorities who lack the psychological and concrete connections to their hometowns that Nela, Gordon, Predrag, and Slobodan possessed could not conceive of coping as minorities and were committed to relocating to areas where they would be in the majority. Take Mladin, a Serb who decided to relocate from Bihać to Banja Luka, where he worked as a high school gym teacher. At a Banja Luka café where Serbs met with a Bošnjak real-estate broker to sell their homes in Bošnjak-majority areas, Mladin portrayed his decision as natural given his feelings of alienation in his hometown:

> I can't live with Muslims. Even in World War II, we [Serbs] were victims. . . . I never felt like a minority before April 1992 [the start of the war]. . . . I left Bihać because (1) civilized people left Bihać, [including] 20,000 Muslims, 15,000 Serbs, and five of my friends; (2) of my job; and (3) of security [concerns].

Like Ana, Mladin laments the exodus of "civilized" people from his hometown. But unlike Ana, Mladin is clear about his unwillingness to live with Muslims, connecting his decision to a historical narrative of Serb victimization. Mladin viewed return as an artificial project that the international community had forced on the peoples of Bosnia. He is as convinced of the illogic of returning to a mixed community as Nela is of its

---

12. Because I lack data on these individuals' prewar support networks, I must rely on self-reporting, which is susceptible to reinterpretation. As a result, minorities who stayed during the war or returned just afterward may exaggerate the positive qualities of the interethnic relationships they had before or during the war.

13. Journalist Chuck Sudetic (1998, 58) writes about a Muslim from Eastern Bosnia who fought for the Germans in World War II and who professed that confidence in his reputation helped convince him to return to his village after the war: "'Tito announced that all could return to their land, that the people could decide who was guilty and who was not,' Avdija said. 'I hadn't harmed anyone or killed anyone. I never committed any crime. So I came back.'"

soundness. He also believed that it was impossible for the international community to protect returnees: "It only takes one crazy person to kill me." Returnee Slobodan agrees about the existence of "crazies" and the inability of state or international organizations to protect returnees, but not about the implications of these facts. Slobodan felt that his local reputation and connections could help him address this problem, while Mladin could not see how he could overcome such insecurity.

Milan, a Serb who relocated from a Sarajevo suburb to eastern Bosnia, echoed Mladin's reasons for moving, including an unwillingness to share a neighborhood with Muslims and a fear of radical demographic change. As we saw in his epigraph to this chapter, Milan no longer felt connected to Sarajevo: "its population has completely changed. Tens of thousands were expelled from Sarajevo . . . and now it is Islamicized." Milan repeated charges made by Serb nationalists that Bošnjaks intend to create an Islamic state. When I asked about his views on living once again with his neighbors, he responded, "We can live side by side—but not together." Milan also worried about employment discrimination in the Federation, even though he thought that his school chum directing the clinic where he had worked would be willing to help him reclaim his old job. That one connection was not nearly enough, in his mind, to overcome the risks of what he would have to give up should he return.

Marko, a Serb who relocated from Bihać to Banja Luka, also feared trading what little he earned on the black market in Republika Srpska for the risk of never finding a job in Bihać because of the tight job market or possible employment discrimination. Marko believed that his former colleagues would help him start a new business "that would employ returnees as well as people generally." But he believed that the ruling nationalists would obstruct it. As a result, he had reclaimed his apartment in Bihać, but he visited there only on weekends. He spent the bulk of his time living with his family at his mother's place in Banja Luka while his daughters attended university there. Marko was straddling the fence, leaving his options for return and relocation open. Urbanites belonging to the majority group and those urban minorities who had stayed throughout the war often resented this opportunistic behavior of straddling.

While Marko's unwillingness to commit to return was based largely on judgments of financial insecurity, both Zoran and Natasha linked their hesitancy to return to their prewar homes to their personal experiences of interethnic hostility. Zoran's experience with his long-term neighbor, a Muslim, in Bihać just prior to the war cemented his decision to remain in a community where he is part of the majority group:

I had lived in my house for thirty years. There were families in two houses in my neighborhood to whom I was particularly close. The owner of one house came to my house with a gun and told me to leave or he would kill me. I was raised with, and played with, my evictor.

This betrayal by someone Zoran thought he had known well deeply soured his view of the possibility of close mixing. The results of Zoran's experience with intimate violence is consistent with survey research conducted in Croatia that found that people who experienced personal tragedies, such as the killing of a family member or forcible eviction, are more fearful of those ethnically different and are less tolerant of diversity (Kunovich and Hodson 1999, 655). Like other men of draft age who were displaced, Zoran's participation in the army—in his case, that of the Republika Srpska—increased his hesitancy about the reception he might receive should he return to Bihać.

After relocating to Bratunac, Natasha, a Serb, was startled by the hostility she experienced from a family who moved into her old neighborhood near Sarajevo just after the war. She was attempting to rebuild her family's prewar home in one of Sarajevo's suburbs, but the animosity convinced her to give up in 1999. Only after the situation in her prewar neighborhood had calmed down in 2004 did Natasha and her family feel comfortable enough to return.

Building or Rebuilding Home

Whether staying or returning, minorities who emphasized their emotional attachments often linked a particular place and the people associated with that place. This combination of connections to place and its people was the most common conception of *home*, not a mere physical structure. These places included their town of residence, their birthplace, the town where they and their children grew up, or, more rarely, the entire country of Bosnia-Herzegovina. In the first epigraph of this chapter, Mina explained that she stayed in Sarajevo because of her feeling that she belonged to the city, its people, and the way of life there. In response to my question about whether she considered leaving, she shook her head and said, "This is my home; I'm not a nationalist." Given that Mina felt the closest to the people and the town of Sarajevo, it was logical that she would stay in the capital. A desire to be among family and close friends was likewise a reason that Nikola, a Serb who spent the war at his weekend house in the Republika Srpska, gave for returning to Bihać in 1996 and resuming his job in the municipal bureaucracy.

Minka explained in a matter-of-fact way that she stayed in Sarajevo because she and her family had lived there for a long time; there was no reason for them to leave. She mentioned that they had a large weekend house on Bosnia's Adriatic coast, adding that their lack of connection to people there played a role in their decision to stay in Sarajevo: "In Neum, we did not associate with the locals—they were privileged." She ended the story of her migration decision by emphasizing the ties of her family to Bosnia: "We are Bosnians."

The decision of minorities to remain in or return to their prewar homes seemed to be strengthened by their alienation from co-ethnics living in areas where they are in the majority. As we saw in chapter 2, Mira's co-ethnics in a Serb-dominated suburb who distrusted her for living in Muslim-dominated Sarajevo reinforced her decision to remain in Sarajevo. This is not to say that she was wholly satisfied with the atmosphere in Sarajevo; she readily criticized SDA's leaders for their nationalist policies. This criticism of her political leaders demonstrates that she is not blindly mimicking the rhetoric of the nationalizing state as either an internalization of its ideology or as a defensive strategy to present to an American. Despite her dislike of SDA, she continued to feel more at home in Sarajevo than she did anywhere in the Republika Srpska, where she spent her childhood. Another Serb respondent explained that he stayed in Bošnjak-majority Goražde because it was "his town." He refrained from visiting neighboring Serb-majority Kopaci because Serbs saw him as "some kind of traitor" (Lippman 1999–2000). Katica, a clerk who identifies herself as Yugoslav, decided to return to Sarajevo after working in Serbia during the war in part because of her lack of identification with the values of Serbs in Belgrade:

> I would not have stayed in Belgrade. People were insensitive when I was working there. In the summer of 1992 [during the Bosnian war], the hottest topic of conversation was which Greek island one should visit for summer vacation.

That citizens of Belgrade could so easily disassociate themselves from the mass human suffering occurring next door reinforced Katica's decision to return to her boyfriend in Sarajevo. Feelings of alienation in putative homelands have influenced migration decisions in other post-Socialist states. Research among Hungarians from Romania (Fox 2003) found that they were often verbally abused by co-ethnics while working in their putative homeland—Hungary—even though the government in Hungary provides incentives for Romania's Hungarians to work there. Such reactions reinforce the decision to remain living as a minority in Romania.

Serbs and Croats living in Sarajevo and Bihać with whom I talked often felt more attached to (or at least less alienated from) local places in Bosnia than to the exclusive areas dominated by their co-ethnics that were advocated by Serb and Croat activists. In addition, many minorities living in Sarajevo and Bihać did not see a benefit to relocating, partly because their attachment to the places where they had lived at the onset of war involved ties to the people living in those places. Simply put, they did not feel that their connections to their co-ethnics were necessarily stronger than their preexisting connections to groups with specific social bases or values. The importance of a sense of belonging for migration is supported by a 2001 survey of 500 returnees, virtually all minorities. When asked to explain their reason for returning, a majority of respondents—53 percent (265)—said that they were motivated by their desire to return to their home and to their neighbors with shared experiences (Sweeney 2001, 2).[14] Twenty-two percent (110) of respondents also said simply that they had returned because of their homes. Bosnians construct their notion of "home" as the place where they feel they belong the most. They may not always feel completely comfortable there, but they have a hard time feeling more "at home" anywhere else.

Contrary to the programs of the most powerful actors in the multilevel network, Bosnians prioritize "home" over "homeland." These narratives and experiences challenge the idea of an immutable connection between ethnic identity and a "historic homeland." In the stories they told me about their migration decisions, Serbs and Croats now living in Sarajevo and Bihać were much more likely to bring up the ties they had to specific local people and places than to mention connections to Bosnia-Herzegovina as their "homeland," a goal of transnational actors.

These findings on the concept of home and on the attachment to home are supported by the innovative field research of social scientists working among minorities in other divided societies. Diener's (2005) research on Kazakhs from Mongolia found that these minorities often expressed "intense feelings of place attachment for regions" *outside* their nominal homeland of Kazakhstan. Anecdotal evidence about Serbs who returned to Croatia similarly suggests that concepts of home influenced decisions to return (Hundley 2000). And Izhak Schnell found that feelings about deep roots in an area in Israel and lack of belonging to areas of the occupied territories significantly influenced the decision of Palestinian citizens of Israel to stay in Israel (1994, 92–94). These cases persuasively argue that ideas about home affect minorities' decisions about migration.

Though the options available to Bosnians and the incentives they can

---

14. Respondents were allowed up to three responses (Sweeney 2001, 2).

exploit are also important in migration decisions, they are not static factors; Bosnians *interpret* them to see if they are consistent with their sense of who they are and where they belong. Bosnians' narratives about migration highlight their sense of self as important. But sociological research (Snow et al. 1986) suggests that once one decision becomes more feasible than another, Bosnians probably adjust their migration stories to at least approximate those narratives held up by their immediate community as "correct." Mira's dissatisfaction with the reception by her co-ethnics in Republika Srpska, for example, was probably amplified by the sustained rhetoric of relative tolerance she heard among the professionals in her Sarajevo circle. This process of readjustment, however, cannot account for the decisions that some minorities made after the war to either return from areas where they were displaced during the war or to relocate to be among the majority: These decisions reject the "correct" choice touted by the immediate community at the time. Furthermore, minorities who stayed in or returned to Sarajevo did not mimic the rhetoric of multiculturalism that savvy Bošnjak political leaders or transnational actors regurgitated. Instead, they discussed the tough situations they were compelled to navigate nearly every day.

Investigating an Alternative Argument

To plumb the interest-based argument's contention that socioeconomic factors suffice to explain decisions about migration, I turn now to a quantitative approach. I conducted a statistical analysis of a large survey of refugees returning from Western Europe to Bosnia that was administered by the International Organization for Migration (IOM 1999).[15] IOM offices in Bosnia developed and distributed this survey to all former refugees whom it had assisted in returning from Europe, where they had been staying under a status of temporary protection while war raged in their country of origin. Upon the signing of the Dayton Peace Agreement in November 1995, most European host countries maintained that Bosnian refugees were legally obligated to return to Bosnia (Koser and Black 1999).

15. Between 1998 and mid-1999, the IOM's regional offices in Bosnia surveyed more than 27,500 returnees upon their arrival in Bosnia as they provided refugees with one-time financial assistance on behalf of the German Federal Ministry of the Interior and the government of the German Federal States. Virtually all of the IOM respondents returned from Germany, which hosted the largest number of Bosnian refugees, some 345,000. Special thanks to Fran Sullivan for authorizing the analysis of these comprehensive data on Bosnian returnees.

Multivariate regression makes it possible to assess the individual effect of each factor on return. In addition, the large sample helps analyze factors and their relationships beyond the ones I was able to uncover from the stories of the smaller group I observed and interviewed. The survey is limited to refugees who temporarily resided in Europe before returning to Bosnia in 1998 or 1999.[16] Because it was distributed only fifteen days after a refugee's return to Bosnia, the survey reflects the first migration choices of those who returned from abroad. Thus, limitations on the data set rule out medium- to long-term migration decisions from the analysis.[17]

I constructed a model to predict the likelihood that a refugee leaving Western Europe who had lived as a minority in prewar Bosnia would return to his original home or relocate elsewhere in Bosnia. Socioeconomic and demographic factors in the migration model for individuals include age, employment status, ethnicity, income, gender, education, and property ownership, all of which the interest-based model anticipates play a role in migration. The model took into account experiences such as losing a family member during the war. It examined attitudes about returning to Bosnia. My model also explored the local dynamics of the violence and the environment for return.[18] It incorporated municipal-level factors that could affect migration, including the following indicators of the municipality's political environment for minorities: the percentage of municipal assembly seats occupied by non-nationalists,[19] the percentage of minorities cleansed from a municipality during the war, and the municipal housing office's record of compliance with property legislation. Other municipal-level demographic factors included population density and percentage of Croats. Finally, I took into account the entity in which the prewar home is now located (the Federation of Bosnia and Herzegovina [the Federation] or the Republika Srpska). Unfortunately, the survey did not contain questions about self-identification or social identity. Nonetheless, the migration

16. Because of the survey's sampling, the findings gleaned from its analysis cannot be extended to the migration of those displaced *within* Bosnia or within former Yugoslavia.

17. In 1998 and 1999, concerted political obstruction and sometimes the destroyed housing stock meant that it was highly unlikely that a returnee from Western Europe would quickly be able to repossess his prewar property. Obstruction to minority returns weakened only after Dayton's transnational implements placed concerted pressure on intransigent local authorities beginning in late 1999.

18. I used a multilevel mixed-effects maximum likelihood model that expects the data to be grouped around municipalities.

19. The strongest non-nationalist parties in 1997 were the Social Democratic Party (SDP) and the Party of Independent Social Democrats (SNSD), though many other tiny non-nationalist parties also participated.

Table 3.1. Predicting the return of a minority who spent the war in Western Europe to his prewar home in Bosnia

Independent variables	b	s.e.
Individual-level variables		
Age	**.027**	.010
Education	.003	.008
Serb background	**.336**	.061
Unemployed	−.010	.036
Pensioner	−.032	.078
Worked abroad	−.002	.019
Income	−.006	.005
Property owner	−.009	.011
Gender	−.020	.020
Desire to return to Bosnia	**.042**	.017
Experience of a family tragedy	**−.089**	.023
Local and regional-level variables		
Percentage of non-nationalists in local legislature	.136	.138
Percentage of municipality's minorities cleansed	−.124	.124
Compliance of municipality with property legislation	.207	.207
Municipality's population density	.000	.000
Percentage of municipality that is Croat	−..017	.058
Entity of prewar home	**.607**	.148
Constant	.896	.148

Source: International Organization for Migration (IOM) 1999. I appreciate the IOM's permission to make use of the data they collected on refugees returning to Bosnia–Herzegovina for this book.

Note: The survey asks whether individuals returned to their prewar municipalities, rather than to their specific prewar homes. See appendix E for coding of variables. Many minority respondents were automatically dropped because they did not provide essential information. This is one sign of the problems involved in conducting a survey in Bosnia.

$N = 1410$

Log Likelihood: −327.601

Bold results are significant at $p < 0.05$.

Probability $> \chi^2$: 0.000

model can systematically evaluate the role of socioeconomic factors that interviewees may have been hesitant to discuss and structural factors that may have lurked behind some of the migration decisions.

My migration model found that several demographic factors (an individual's age group and ethnicity), attitude toward return to Bosnia, personal experience of loss (suffering a family tragedy), and the entity where a minority's prewar home is located systematically affected the probability that a minority would return to his original home rather than relocate (table 3.1). These statistically significant factors are bolded in table 3.1. A minority was more likely to return home if he was older, was not a Serb, had expressed a desire to return to Bosnia, had escaped a close personal tragedy, and had a home in the Federation. What are missing from these statistically significant factors are the socioeconomic variables that the interest-based theory anticipates drives migration.

Demographic Factors

The model helps clarify the role of age, which also emerged as a factor in my interviews. The older a returnee from Western Europe was, the more likely she was to return to her home in a minority area of Bosnia. This finding cannot be explained by the conventional wisdom on migration that it is easier for older people to return, because they can get their pensions no matter where they live. This is because the vast majority of the respondents were not yet pensioners (97 percent were younger than 59 years old). So increasing age, even ignoring that the eldest are pensioners, independently increases the probability that a minority returned home. This finding dovetails with results from a recent survey of 500 returnees to the Federation that found that only 3 percent (15) of respondents had returned in order to receive their pensions (Sweeney 2001, 2). Older minorities seem more heavily influenced by their emotional and concrete attachments to their homes, neighbors, and places they consider to embody their roots than young people (UNHCR 1998b; Dani et al. 1999). I found that younger minorities were more preoccupied with their financial prospects than their elders were—and more willing to move to try to do something about it. Twenty-something Jovan assured me, "Return is generational-based. Old people want to be with their own; young people want economic opportunities." This was partly reflected in the high percentage of split families, in which older members stayed or returned while young adults relocated. My interviews indicate that older generations possess psychological and practical resources that allow them to cope better than youth with the discriminatory environment they confront as minorities.

Refugees of Serb background were the least likely to return to their prewar homes in areas where they would be a minority. Why? First, Serbs have been made to feel less welcome than Croats in the Federation. Serbs face the greatest obstacles in returning to Bošnjak-majority areas because of their legal status as minorities until 2000 and the social intolerance of the majority, partly a product of the legacy of atrocities committed by Serb extremists.[20] Second and related, Serbs are less interested in living in ar-

---

20. This interpretation is a reminder that the model cannot account for several structural factors that could influence a minority's ability to return home. These factors include levels of damage to minorities' property and living alternatives available to minorities.

eas where they would be in the minority (Dani et al. 1999).[21] The cited surveys also consistently show less support for a multiethnic Bosnian state among Bosnian Serbs and Bosnian Croats in comparison with Bošnjaks, who realize a viable Bosnia requires that they live among others (see chapter 5).

Desire to Return to Bosnia

My statistical analysis demonstrates the power of one subjective factor on migration. Those refugees who expressed a *desire* to return to Bosnia were more likely to return to homes in areas where they are in the minority. Overall, few refugees returning from abroad who had lived in areas controlled by another ethnic group before the war were happy about returning to Bosnia. Less than a third of minorities in IOM's survey expressed a desire to return to Bosnia. Those minorities who wanted to return despite the formidable obstacles presented by postwar conditions likely bring significant psychological resources to their arduous effort to return to their original homes. Since the economic prospects in Bosnia are poor, those minorities who expressed a desire to return probably did so out of a sense of belonging to the country and their homes.

Entity of Home

A refugee who was displaced from a home in the Federation was more likely to return to that home—at least initially—than a minority who was displaced from a home in the Republika Srpska. One quarter of those respondents who lived in areas of the Federation where they were in the minority before the war (1,876 persons) had not returned to their original homes by 1999 after entering Bosnia (IOM 1999). For those respondents who lived as minorities in areas of the Republika Srpska before the war (1,851 persons), that percentage skyrocketed to 90 percent. Several dynamics explain why minority return has been easier to the Federation than to the Republika Srpska. First, non-nationalists were more successful in the 1997 local elections in the Federation than in the Republika Srpska. Non-nationalists captured an average of 28 percent of votes for the local legislatures in the Federation as opposed to 14 percent in the Republika Srpska. In a similar pattern, while an average of 75 percent of minorities were cleansed from municipalities in the Federation, an average of 95 percent of minorities were cleansed from municipalities

21. A survey by the U.S. Information Agency (1998, 51) provides more specific information. It found that 77 percent of Bošnjaks, 47 percent of Bosnian Croats, and 24 percent of Bosnian Serbs who were displaced were planning to return to prewar homes.

in the Republika Srpska. Furthermore, the rate of compliance with internationally designed property legislation on the part of municipal housing authorities was significantly higher in the Federation in 1997 and 1998 (just prior to the IOM survey) than in the Republika Srpska. All this evidence emphasizes the importance of entity dynamics for minority return. In 1998 and 1999, the authorities in the Republika Srpska were steadfastly opposed to minority return and urged their residents to adopt the same stance. Those minorities who had homes in the Republika Srpska were more likely to relocate than to return, even if they wanted to return.

The powerful forces that differentiate the dynamics for minorities in the two entities overwhelm the possible influence of local political factors. Municipalities governed by a higher percentage of non-national political authorities saw more minorities return home as well. But that correlation is not statistically significant at the municipality level—only across entities. The poor performance of non-nationalists in the 1997 local elections meant that there were too few non-nationalist politicians to address one of the most contentious aspects of the Dayton Peace Agreement: allowing minorities who desire to return to do so.

Tragic Experiences

A visit to a village near Prijedor to which minorities had just begun to return in the spring of 1999 illustrates the difficulty of minority return to the Republika Srpska in this period. The wartime experience of the village influenced prospects for return. As was typical for the region, troops from the Yugoslav army had surrounded the village and shelled it at the beginning of the war. Then Serb extremists, some of whom were later convicted by the International Criminal Tribunal for the former Yugoslavia of crimes against humanity, systematically killed most Bošnjak men and expelled the rest of the villagers to prison camps or to Croatia in the spring of 1992 (Oberschall 2000). Efforts by the villagers to return in previous years had been met with such concerted violence that return did not occur until the international peacekeeping force used tanks to escort returnees and then deployed permanently there. Though state officials in Sarajevo and local minority activists emphasized the political motivations for pushing return—preventing the formation of an ethnically pure Republika Srpska—ordinary families who returned emphasized the emotional ties to their own homes and land as driving their return. For example, hostess Jasmina told me she had returned because "someone else's home is nothing to live in," echoing a sentiment I often heard from rural returnees.[22] Jasmina's former neighbor, Silvana, a pediatrician, chose instead to relocate to Sanski Most, the closest Bošnjak-dominated town. In explaining why she relocated, Silvana replied that it had been too much to watch armed men force her husband out of his home at gunpoint in 1992, the last time she saw him alive.

This traumatic story illustrates the power of intense experiences on migration. And the statistics confirm this influence. According to the model, Bosnians who survived the war without suffering the death of a close family member were more likely than those, like Silvana, who did suffer such a loss, to return to an area where they would be in the minority. In the IOM sample, 16 percent of minorities from the Republika Srpska and 10 percent of minorities from the Federation reported the death of a close relative. The impact on minorities' behavior of suffering a family tragedy in Bosnia tracks with the narratives of the relocatees with whom I talked. Violeta's Bošnjak boyfriend, Haris, was not interested in returning to his hometown of Foča because his father had disappeared there while in the hands of Serb soldiers. Instead, he and his mother sold their apartment there to relocate to Sarajevo. Experience of family tragedy, combined with continued nationalist rule, increased insecurity and intolerance of others and severed key connections that could have assisted with return and reintegration.

In sum, several demographic factors, subjective views, and personal experiences helped explain why some minorities returned home and others did not. Statistical analysis of the returnee survey, however, found that *none* of the factors anticipated by the interest-based argument for migration decisionmaking affect decisions to a significant degree. Income, employment status, profession, and ownership of property exerted insignificant influence on the behavior of survey respondents.

Perceptions of Common People Matter

Analysis of interview, participant observation, and survey data calls into question the assumptions of interest-based theorists that discrete cost-benefit analysis drives postwar migration in Bosnia. Minorities consider their emotional ties to communities when they decide where to rebuild their lives. They seek to reconstruct their lives in a community that

22. Vera told me that "good people" cannot be comfortable in someone else's home. "We say, 'God, give me a rag rug rather than someone else's hand-woven carpet'" (*Daj mi Bože moje ponjave radije nego tudji čilim*).

they feel comfortable calling "home." This is not to downplay the formidable tools that political leaders use to direct migration in the wake of war or the resource constraints that Bosnians confront. Though they may have initially "wound up" in a community through circumstances beyond their control, minorities endeavored to remain there only if they felt some kind of attachment to it, which they evaluated and reevaluated through social interaction. It was their self-concepts, not their ethnicity per se, that helped them make sense of conditions in deciding where to try to rebuild their lives. To weather the discriminatory environment in which they live, minorities rely on emotional and practical ties to people in their local community. Their struggle to cultivate and maintain these helpful ties is the subject of chapter 4.

4

Sites for Building Bridges

Vera [a Catholic who stayed throughout the war in Sarajevo]:
If I or other minorities stayed among ourselves, we wouldn't
be able to survive. Really, only Muslims can help me survive.

The decision of minorities to remain in their homes, whether they waited out the war there or returned after it, is only the first step in an arduous process of reintegration. A key goal of the transnational actors' reconstruction project for Bosnia and other areas of the Balkans is for minorities to rebuild their lives in their homes of origin. Few have studied how ordinary people react to the new institutions designed by transnational actors to assist reintegration. While transnational actors can provide the seeds to encourage reintegration, they can do little else. The policies favored by elites of the nationalizing state, national-level minority activists, and the putative homelands assist in practice only those minorities who relocate to majority areas (see chapter 1). Such policies demonstrate that the Bosnian state is unwilling to spearhead a process of reintegration of minorities any time soon. This puts the onus on minorities who want to reintegrate to find their own ways to do so.

A grassroots process of integration is likely to focus on economic and social dimensions. Specifically, minorities need to develop sustainable livelihoods and find ways to live among—or alongside, at least—members of the majority group (UNHCR 2003a). Vera's acknowledgment above that she needs help from Muslims is a reminder that for urban minorities in Bosnia, each dimension of the integration process requires positive interethnic relationships. In an atmosphere where many Bosnians have been radicalized by war and exclusivist politicians dominate the multilevel network, under what conditions can minorities in Bosnia build cooperative ties to the dominant ethnic group?[1]

---

1. Some ideas expressed in this chapter appear in Pickering 2006.

Social Networks and Social Capital

Integrating into a postwar community is difficult for all Bosnians. But the process is especially challenging for those minorities in Bosnia who hope to integrate into a diverse community. These minorities lack strong allies in the multilevel network who can assist them.

Given the findings about migration decisions described in chapter 3, it seems reasonable to conclude that individuals will seek to integrate into communities that they view as consistent with their self-understandings. Those individuals who feel strongly attached to their ethnic group will seek security and social assistance from among their co-ethnics. This type of strong in-group affiliation decreases their interest in building the kind of interethnic cooperation that could help them reintegrate into a diverse society. In comparison, those individuals who do not feel as strongly attached to their ethnic groups are less likely to feel that the set of people who can provide help is limited to co-ethnics. Such people may feel attached to multiple social groups or to one non-ethnic one, giving them a bigger stake in forging interethnic cooperation that can assist their integration. This interest in building positive cross-ethnic relationships is reinforced by the practicality of everyday life in the nominally diverse communities in which they live. Social and work lives place minorities in situations where they must interact with members of the majority group. The literature on social capital and social networks identifies alternative pathways that those who seek integration into heterogeneous communities can use to build cross-ethnic cooperation in everyday life.

Social capital is "the ability of actors to secure benefits by virtue of membership in social networks or other social structures" (Portes 1998, 6). The "bridging" (culturally inclusive) and "bonding" (exclusive) dimensions of social capital help explain the integration process. Most individuals need *strong* ties that bond them together with similar people and provide them with social support (Colletta and Cullen 2000; Hurlbert, Haines, and Beggs 2000). This is particularly true after traumatic events such as war. To integrate (Putnam 2000, 22–3) and advance (Granovetter 1973; Burt 1997), however, individuals also need *weak* ties that cross the salient social cleavage—in this case ethnicity. The problem with close friends is that they share too much of the same social connections with you, so there is little new they can offer you. Minorities seeking to integrate need concrete aid from people of other ethnicities, which arises from social networks that forge interethnic cooperation. At the level of the state, bridging social capital is also necessary to support democracy in diverse societies (Dowley and Silver 2002).

But where and how can minorities build culturally inclusive coopera-tion that would help both them and postwar Bosnian society as a whole? Studying individual interactions and networking can help us understand this process because social capital arises out of resources rooted in social networks (Lin 2001, 3). Social network theory suggests the necessary characteristics that institutions must have to enable people to forge ties that bridge ethnic divisions. First, institutions must be culturally diverse. Diversity is partly determined by the ability of individuals to select into different institutions (Mondak and Mutz 2001, 16). The more leeway in-dividuals have to select into institutions, the more likely they are to choose homogeneous and exclusive ones. On the other hand, the fewer opportunities that persons have to choose involvement in institutions, the more likely they are to find themselves in heterogeneous and inclusive ones. Second, institutions need to promote weak ties that are acquain-tance-based rather than friendship-based. Individuals seek out those similar to them—culturally, socioeconomically, and ideologically—for strong, intimate relationships (Laumann 1973; Finifter 1974; Huckfeldt 1983). So strong ties actually do not promote diversity. Third, institutions must possess a norm that at the very least allows for interethnic cooper-ation. Finally, venues need to promote repeated, mutually dependent in-teraction among persons from different backgrounds. This helps builds trust, even if the initial encounter is mistrustful and the relationship remains acquaintance-based (Seligman 1997). Even where no effective authorities promote cooperation, it can emerge if individuals rely on rec-iprocity (Axelrod 1981, 69). Ditka put it simply: "If your hand is open, you can both offer and receive; if your hand is closed, you can do neither."

Personal networks rooted in everyday life offer the best possibilities for interethnic cooperation because they are furthest away from the political realm, where issues are generally viewed in zero-sum terms. Postwar surveys found that Bosnians are much more likely to turn to personal net-works of *informal* institutions (family, friendship, colleague, and neigh-borhood networks) for support than to formal institutions (national and local government, the judiciary, the police, and the army), which they in-stinctively distrust (Cushman 1998; Djipa et al. 1999; Sweeney 2001, 2). Of these informal institutions, neighborhoods, voluntary organizations, and workplaces allow individuals to develop the weak ties needed to bridge divides.[2]

2. While these venues may overlap (e.g., some voluntary organizations are also work-places), social networks that minorities form are initially rooted in a specific venue where they emphasize a particular role (e.g., paid-activist/employee, volunteer, or beneficiary). My

Sites for Generating Bridges

In the setting of postwar Bosnia, all of the institutions hypothesized by social network theory to generate ties across ethnic lines have suffered politicization that limits their ability to cultivate interethnic cooperation.

Neighborhoods

Before the war, however, urban neighborhoods in the Balkans were primary sites for promoting cross-ethnic ties. Urbanites in socialist Bosnia could not typically choose their place of residence, which was often allocated by employers. As a result, ethnically diverse city neighborhoods emerged that, to varying degrees, survived the war. Combined with the poverty of Socialist Yugoslavia, these neighborhoods forced individuals of different backgrounds to work together to solve practical problems. Slavenka Drakulić (1993a, 183) depicted an important coping strategy for socialist citizens: "Because there is no such thing as a self-sufficient communist household, you depend fatally on your neighbor for all kinds of favors, from borrowing coffee, . . . or cursing politics . . . to getting your child enrolled in a better school." The Balkan tradition of the neighborhood (*komšiluk*) promotes cooperation (see chapters 1 and 2). A middle-aged Serb, Ljubo, believed this meant that "you should be able to turn to your closest neighbor for help, before you turn to your own brother." *Komšiluk* played a more prominent role in rural areas than urban ones, where Bosnians had more opportunities for social interaction beyond the neighborhood and where the pace of city life left little time for socializing. Bringa (1995, 66) found that the widely practiced ritual of neighborhood coffee visiting in heterogeneous rural areas of Bosnia promoted practical exchange, interethnic communication, and multiple collective identifications. Yet the neutral institutional structure of good neighborliness, which is based partly on *communal* belongings, such as ethnicity or religion, rather than on individualism, can easily be perverted for nefarious ends. As discussed in chapter 1, national-level minority activists during the war sought to destroy the inclusive, cooperative capacity of the neighborhood by demonizing those ethnically different, disrupting mechanisms for mutual respect, fomenting fear, and encouraging intimate violence, particularly in rural areas (Bougarel 1996). After the war, the competing projects pursued by actors in the multilevel network to remake

---

focus on domestic, not international, voluntary organizations and ordinary people rather than elites—who are most often employed by nongovernmental organizations as activists, somewhat decreases the extent of overlap of these social venues.

Bosnia included plans to remake the neighborhood. The nationalizing state and national-level minority activists have used administrative tactics to manipulate property laws and social services to try to create and solidify homogenous neighborhoods. Transnational actors favoring Dayton's multiethnic goals have endeavored to counter this project by rewriting property laws, encouraging their enforcement, assisting return, and funding formal neighborhood organizations (*mjesne zajednice*).[3]

Voluntary Organizations

Voluntary organizations are another institution capable of generating the kind of social capital that can bridge unlike groups. Voluntary groups can serve a political function by helping citizens hold authorities accountable (Tocqueville 1994). Less studied is how voluntary organizations help ordinary people forge ties that cut across ethnic lines (Bell 1975). Ashutosh Varshney's (2001, 7) multicity study found that heterogeneous civic associations in India increased communication and created shared interests among persons of different backgrounds, thus promoting interethnic peace. This suggests possibilities for citizens seeking to integrate into postwar Bosnia. But unlike Indian civic organizations, whose traditions stretch back to the 1930s, Bosnian civic organizations lack deep roots. Socialist Yugoslavia did create opportunities for local participation, for example, in voluntary civic associations (*udruzenje gradjana*) that focused on sports or culture and were linked to the Communist Party only in a loose way (Poggi et al. 2002, 80). Yugoslavia's one-party state, however, constrained other opportunities for participation until the early 1990s (Šupek 1975; Županov 1975; Križan 1989). The tendency for individuals to join organizations with members from their own social group and the salience of ethnicity in general meant that as socialism fell, many of the new organizations formed in its wake were monoethnic. Some of these monoethnic organizations were connected to nationalist parties and contributed to the conflict, overpowering local multiethnic groups opposed to partition (Oberschall 2000, 994–95). During the war, new nongovernmental organizations (NGOs) grew out of international projects providing services to victims of the violence (Sali-Terzić 2001, 139). Promoting inclusive NGOs and ones focused on increasing political accountability, the rule of law, and civic engagement is a strategy the West has embraced to support cross-ethnic cooperation and democratization

---

3. Despite receiving international assistance, these formal neighborhood organizations established in socialist Yugoslavia remain weak (Poggi et al. 2002, 69–76) and thus provide little capacity for supporting bridging ties.

after war. Understanding the views and behavior of minorities in Bosnia helps us figure out how well this will work there.

Workplaces

Workplaces also suffer from concerted nationalist pressure, but several characteristics make them better suited than neighborhoods and voluntary organizations for building bridges in postwar Bosnia. Workplaces generally promote weak ties and create opportunities for repeated, horizontal interaction between employees with similar authority focused on tasks that promote interdependent relationships (Minard 1952; Mondak and Mutz 2001; Romann and Weingrod 1991, 144–45). Robert Putnam (2000, 87), overlooking the possibilities of inclusive and interdependent work relationships between racially diverse employees, worries that most U.S. workers consider their colleagues to be "merely" acquaintances. But it is exactly the weakness of those ties that make them so ideal for building diverse links. Workplaces do not explicitly promote interethnic cooperation; this status allows them to serve that end under the radar, which makes them all the more effective. Before 1990, it was difficult for individuals to select their workplaces in Bosnia. Just before the war, citizens overwhelmingly viewed interethnic relations in the workplace as good—even when they evaluated them as bad in more general contexts (Baćević et al. 1991, 144–49). Nonetheless, the failure of Socialist Yugoslavia to sustain economic growth (Comisso 1979; Woodward 1995b), facilitate cooperation among republics (Ramet 1992), or maintain avenues for social mobility (Denitch 1973) produced frustrations that politicians manipulated. After the 1990 elections, the nationalizing state and minority activists continued the Balkan tradition of patronage (Woodward 1999). In Sarajevo, several minorities I met who had enjoyed high-status jobs before 1991 became victims of discriminatory hiring and firing. This included Jovanka, a professor at Sarajevo University who had been fired during the war because she was a Serb and an outspoken social democrat. Ultimately, urban minorities desperate for work could hardly avoid interacting with Bošnjaks after the war.

Uncovering Concrete Ties

Asking and observing how ordinary people in everyday social contexts interpret and react to elite policies helped us understand the different decisions that minorities made about migration. Similarly, the perspectives and actions of minorities can help us identify the conditions under which even these marred institutions help minorities develop interethnic cooperative ties. In applying the social network approach to interethnic relations, I combined interviewing and observation to focus on concrete ties. I observed the interethnic interactions of my six host families in Sarajevo and Bihać as they went about their everyday lives in real-life settings such as neighborhoods, workplaces, cafés, markets, and farms. I gauged the strength of a tie by looking at the amount of time, the emotion, the degree of confiding, and the supply of services (such as material aid, socializing, or interaction) that characterized the tie (Granovetter 1973, 1316; Marsden 1990, 442). I also noted the ethnic and social background of those involved in the tie.

My initial focus on Sarajevo and Bihać—which differ in terms of demographics, socioeconomics, politics, and history—allows me to investigate whether a similar pattern for cultivating bridges persists despite these sites' differing demographic, socioeconomic, political, and historical dynamics. The two sites also differ significantly in the general availability of voluntary organizations. I also explore sites that minorities find suitable for developing bridging ties in Republika Srpska.

Wading Upstream

Bosnians interested in forming bridging ties struggled with the consequences of the exclusive nationbuilding programs that putative homelands, the nationalizing state, and national-level minority activists pushed during and after the war. For urban minorities in the Federation, these consequences included raw wartime memories, propaganda, impoverishment, an influx of rural Bošnjaks, and an exodus of intellectuals. Systematic observation of how Bosnians viewed the effectiveness of neighborhoods, voluntary organizations, and workplaces in building interethnic cooperation suggested that mixed (i.e., multiethnic) workplaces were a superior venue for minorities to use reciprocity to build bridging networks. This is because the comparatively limited selectivity of the workplaces promotes relative diversity. Mixed workplaces also allow colleagues to focus on tasks and remuneration while they repeatedly interact with their coworkers, who are often of different cultural backgrounds (figure 4.1). While nationalist control of many workplaces drastically reduced the number of mixed workplaces, most minorities in Sarajevo and Bihać had to work somewhere if they wanted to get by. And the vast majority did not have the luxury of working only among those who shared their ethnicity. The next most useful venue for building bridging networks is the mixed civic association, a voluntary organization with a broader-based membership than advocacy NGOs have. The fact that

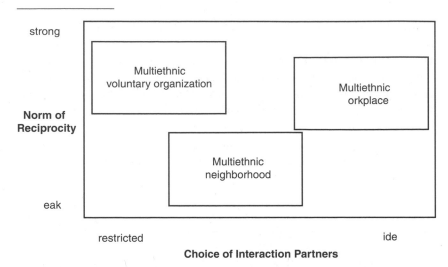

Figure 4.1. Dimensions of venues that may facilitate interethnic interaction.

Bosnians have wide leeway in choosing to participate or not in civic associations means that few Bosnians choose to participate in these voluntary organizations and, even if they do, most of these groups are dominated by a single ethnicity. Nonetheless, those rare occasions when mixed associations do arise provide individuals with norms and opportunities for the repeated and mutually dependent interaction that reinforces bridges.

In my discussions with minorities, they reported a significantly higher percentage of positive interethnic interactions in the workplace than they did in the neighborhood.[4] Analysis by a qualitative database program indicated that 83 percent of interviewees' interethnic interactions in the workplace were neutral or positive, and that 95 percent of interactions were between individuals who are minorities and individuals of the majority group.[5] In contrast, only 64 percent of interethnic interactions in the

    4. Statistical tests on these data gathered through participant observation and interviews confirm that these differences are statistically significant. *F*-tests show that the differences are significant at the 0.001 level.
    5. To analyze these data, I divided testimony from interviews and observation into paragraph-sized text units. I spent the most time observing or listening to Bosnians talk about interacting with neighbors (953 text units), followed by colleagues (937), and local NGO members (699). Of these interactions, the number of interethnic encounters observed or mentioned was 159 with neighbors, 111 with colleagues, and 80 with NGO members. I calculated the percentages of interethnic interactions characterized as good, neutral, or poor with each social group by dividing that number of a particular quality of interethnic interactions by the total number of interethnic interactions.

neighborhood were neutral or positive, and only 60 percent of interaction occurred between members of minorities and the majority. While interethnic interactions in mixed local voluntary organizations were overwhelmingly neutral or positive (95.5 percent), interactions were largely among activists, and again, only 61 percent of interaction occurred between members of minorities and the majority. Furthermore, fewer ordinary (i.e., nonactivist) minorities belonged to voluntary organizations (one-third) than worked, this despite high levels of unemployment. A look at Bosnians' behavior in neighborhoods, voluntary organizations, and workplaces reveals the conditions under which the venues are successful in cultivating cross-ethnic ties.[6]

Tense Neighborhoods

Minorities had difficulty building inclusive ties in their neighborhoods largely because of a combination of the relatively strong ties expected according to tradition and the calculated demographic changes that occurred around the war. Ethnic engineering threw together small numbers of urban minorities and their long-term Bošnjak neighbors with many newly transplanted Bošnjaks. Many of these transplants, either displaced from rural areas or politically connected to the ruling nationalists, were shuffled into the property of minorities who had fled during the war, even if only temporarily. Such temporary residency measures often took years to undo. This massive upheaval created tensions between native urbanites and the newcomers, as we saw in chapter 2. The prospects of having to socialize with or seek help from people with such different upbringings and political outlooks further turned long-term urbanites against the cultural expectations of relatively close relations with neighbors. These dynamics tended to discourage the forming of weak ties focused on mutual help with new neighbors. Those who had spent considerable time living in towns—regardless of ethnicity—most often characterized their relations with their new neighbors displaced from villages as "superficial," often confined to the exchange of greetings.

After this common response, however, minority and majority interviewees characterized the situation differently. Native urban residents who were Bošnjaks conveyed that while they did not feel close to displaced Bošnjaks, they did not distrust them as much as they did Serb neighbors who returned after the war. So long-term urbanites who were

---

6. The tenor of the data I use below is consistent with the data I collected overall, as indicated by randomly selected text from my field notes. Randomly selected text on interethnic relations from my field notes is available on request.

Bošnjaks tended to describe their relations with Bošnjak displaced persons as "good." Mirsada, for example, occasionally helped two Bošnjak families who had recently settled in her neighborhood after fleeing from nearby villages despite her frustration with the presumed unwillingness of some displaced Bošnjaks to pay their utility bills. At the same time, she refused to communicate with a former colleague, a Serb who fled before the war and had just returned to her prewar home in Bihać. Mirsada considered this Serb's initial flight from her hometown as betrayal. In contrast, long-term urbanites who were Serb, Croat, or ethnically mixed, characterized their relations with these new neighbors as "distant" or "strained." In fact, *no* minority respondents believed that they had "good" relations with their new neighbors.

The improved implementation of property rights allowed more Bosnians to return to their prewar homes after 2000 and somewhat eased the contention over scarce apartments. Ivan, a thirty-something Croat who stayed in Sarajevo throughout the war, felt that the social situation had improved between 1996 and 2002 because quite a few persons who had been displaced from rural areas had returned to their prewar homes, opening Sarajevo up for long-term urbanites. For most long-term urbanites, however, their neighborhoods remained chiefly Bošnjak, which was a source of tension. The behavior of informants in their neighborhoods clarifies the neighborhood's role in integration.

The views of my hosts Mirsada and Alija illustrate the situation that many minorities confronted in neighborhoods. Mirsada and Alija led the most ethnically exclusive lives of my host families. As members of the majority group, they have fewer incentives for engaging in interethnic cooperation than minorities do. Even so, Mirsada not only ignored Serbs, she also felt that their silent exodus from Bihać just before the war was a betrayal that freed her from any obligation to engage in reciprocity. She ruled out friendship with Serbs, believing that refusal to accept their reintegration into the neighborhood would discourage Serbs from returning. Norms of interethnic betrayal and reciprocal punishment permeated their neighborhood.

Vera demonstrates a common reaction of minorities to such an inhospitable atmosphere. She distrusted new Bošnjak neighbors from the countryside who arrived during the war. Like Mirsada and Alija, I have known her since 1996. For almost the entire time I knew her, she felt so vulnerable in public that she confided, "If I value my head, I can't voice my opinion." When UN police officers conducting routine work came to check up on her in 1998, Vera "kept quiet" about pressure she was feeling because she was sure that the translator accompanying them would tell officials with the nationalizing Bosnian state about her complaints. She feared that she would suffer some form of reprisal if she reported her problems. Nonetheless, Vera realized that she needed to interact with some neighbors, so she did so strategically, through the practice of selective reciprocity. This emphasizes an individual's careful choice of partners for cooperation. Vera reached out to one Bošnjak neighbor to establish enough rapport for a relationship of mutual help. She took care of her neighbor's children when they were locked out of their apartment, an act that allowed Vera to ask her neighbor to take care of her apartment when she later went on vacation. As with the players in Robert Axelrod's (1981) prisoner's dilemma game, Vera's efforts to form cooperative ties with an acquaintance were not motivated by friendship but rather by the knowledge that her stake in future interaction was large enough that it was in her interest to cooperate with at least selected Bošnjaks. "I help them and they help me. I'm forced to do this; I have no other choice." In this manner, Vera successfully developed a weak tie to her neighbor that revolved around practical help as opposed to intimacy indicated by confiding.

Host Zlata found the environment in her urban neighborhood so stifling that she confined her ties to members of her ethnically mixed family and a few non-Bošnjak neighbors who embraced reciprocity or the notion she described as "pay back in kind" (*milo za drago*). Because her Croat neighbor had fixed her toilet, Zlata would help him with something he needed, such as mending or cooking. Zlata repeatedly expressed disappointment with the unwillingness of her new Bošnjak neighbors to engage in reciprocity in a way that respected difference, as urbanites did instinctively. After returning from the store one morning, she shouted, "My neighbor just greeted me with '*Merhaba!*' ["hello" in Turkish]. . . . This is no kind of neighborhood. . . . I will use a greeting that communicates with people regardless of their nationality!" Her neighbors' use of exclusive language symbolized their aversion to forming even the weak ties that might bridge divides of culture and upbringing. Zlata's status as a former refugee who had *returned* and her neighbors' status as formerly displaced persons who had *relocated* emphasized competing group interests and further soured the possibilities for cooperation. While Zlata always intended to move to Serbia to be closer to her late husband buried there, her decision to leave Sarajevo was hastened by the lack of cross-ethnic ties developed there when she returned after the war (chapter 3).

In confronting a similarly difficult environment in his neighborhood, Dragan refused to abandon his efforts to build bridges with his neighbors. To reclaim his family home in the Sarajevo suburb of Ilidža in 1999, Dragan had to confront the squatter who had taken it over. The squatter had

physically attacked him the year before when Dragan had finally persuaded local housing authorities to authorize his eviction. When Dragan
realized that neither the local authorities nor voluntary organizations
were going to be any help in his quest for reintegration, his first reaction
was fear. His second reaction, however, was to turn to a strategy of reciprocity with neighbors:

> I came to believe that there must be other people who think like me. I de-
> cided that if I show others that I'm sincere, that I don't hate them, then
> they will respond in the same way.

His approach was less selective than Vera's, as it included reaching out to
people who posed threats to him. The first overture he made to the former squatter was refraining from pressing charges over the assault. He
believed that limiting his ties to the small group of people who were similar to him would not help him integrate into his local community that
had been transformed by war. Dragan was proud that he and the squatter, who now lived next door to each other, had reached a level of begrudging coexistence where they regularly exchanged greetings. His
approach to increasing his sense of security was to engage with the people around him by appealing to values he believed they shared: civility
and sincerity. This is similar to the approach that Torsten Kollind (2005)
found among Bošnjak returnees to the Herzegovinian village of Stolac,
who reached out to Croats by emphasizing inclusive notions of "decent
people." By 2002, Dragan's efforts to coexist with his new neighbors was
faring better than his efforts to find a stable salary and build social ties of
varying levels of intimacy. Though he still hoped he could rebuild a normal life in Ilidža, Dragan and his family felt worn down by social exclusion, job discrimination, and crime (which disproportionately affected
minorities).

Hosts Stipe and Sandra had never been close to their neighbors. Stipe
socialized with neighbors more than his wife, especially over drinks at
neighborhood pubs. Sandra played down the importance of neighborhood visiting; she was more likely to visit with family and friends from
her prewar job or from her university study than with any of her neighbors. One reason became apparent after I dropped a shirt off the clothes-
line into the courtyard of their apartment building in 2004. This blunder
required asking a downstairs neighbor for access to the courtyard to re-
trieve it. Sandra disliked having to ask because the neighbor had been unfriendly during the war. One time, while their children, Violeta and Seka,
were playing in the building's courtyard during a lull in the shelling, this
anxious neighbor yelled at them, "I hope the Serbs bomb you!" The chil-

dren shrugged off the incident by attributing the outburst to the neighbor's general anxiety problem, citing her tirades at other neighbors who made noise. But Sandra took the comment as a more malevolent sign of the neighbor's intolerance.

Host Mara faced an unusual situation in her small apartment complex in Sarajevo—most of her neighbors were minorities, like her. She regularly participated in coffee visits with her neighbors, who were predominantly Serb. When I lived with her in 2002, Mara was anticipating a new next-door neighbor, a Bošnjak. Even though the family had not yet moved in and she had not yet met them, Mara paid their phone bill, which had been wedged in the hinge of the neighbor's apartment door. "I would hate for them to waste money to get the phone reconnected; I hope that somebody would do the same for me." She not only felt that making such a gesture was appropriate, she also hoped that it would elicit a generous act in return, especially since a next-door neighbor was someone with whom she should be on good terms.

In Bihać, Kristina had good relations with the Bošnjak couple who had been her next-door neighbors for years. The neighbors borrowed household items from each other, on occasion letting themselves into empty apartments with spare keys. They also exchanged weekly coffee visits. But when she needed practical assistance requiring more effort, Kristina turned first to her mixed family members and to her colleagues at the Federation institute from which she had recently retired.

Distant Voluntary Organizations

Tense neighborhood environments such as those in postwar Bosnia could encourage individuals interested in cultivating bridging networks to turn to inclusive voluntary organizations, whose norms are more hospitable to mixing. All the more so, since transnational actors devoted resources to cultivating them. But I found that ordinary people looked at NGOs differently than civic activists. While activists relish the opportunity to use voluntary organizations to build bridging networks with fellow NGO leaders, ordinary people in Bosnia avoid participating in voluntary organizations because they feel that these groups do not meet their needs. Only when they encompass more than a small group of activists and are responsive to ordinary people in local communities can voluntary organizations help build grassroots-based bridging social capital in Bosnia.

International donors have focused on building NGOs that *advocate* for liberal democratic ideals. Due to their structure, these advocacy groups foster horizontal connections and repeated interaction among tiny groups of activists, not ordinary people. Networks of activists compose the "mid-level" segment of a peace constituency critical to rebuilding postconflict societies (Lederach 1997, 94–97; Gagnon 2002, 216–17). To be an effective bulwark against war, however, this middle segment needs support from below. Advocacy groups do not generate such support because the ties they promote between activists and ordinary people, while largely positive, are often hierarchical. A World Bank study found that a large majority of Bosnians who were members of NGOs expected "the one-way delivery of various public services and benefits" (Poggi et al. 2002, 80–81). Unlike civic associations (neighborhood or professional associations, cooperatives, youth groups, sports clubs), advocacy groups do not provide ordinary people with opportunities for repeated, inter-dependent interaction that can generate "mutual reciprocity . . . and the broadening of social identities" (Putnam 2000, 76).

According to interviews I conducted and local surveys, minorities who feel their rights have been violated sometimes turn to local advocacy groups for help (Srpsko Grandjansko Vijece 1998; Helsinki Committee for Human Rights 2001). Advocacy groups are also successful in encouraging ordinary people to use the legal system to settle disputes. But interviewees were rarely satisfied with advocacy groups and often did not stick with them. A common complaint of my contacts was that advocacy groups were impotent in the face of opposition from authorities, as the experience of Serb returnee Tamara, who was trying to repossess her apartment, illustrates. Despite appealing to three local voluntary organizations offering assistance with property rights, Tamara was not able to enter her home until two years later. During my stay in Bosnia, I saw this grueling scenario repeated over and over again in towns across the country.

Bosnians who remained aloof from local groups frequently told me that voluntary organizations were not interested in *their* everyday needs.[7] These opinions did not vary by locality. Widespread skepticism of the intentions of voluntary organizations and their activists stemmed partly from international funding. Bosnians believe that local voluntary organizations pay more attention to the demands of international donors than to the needs of Bosnians. Many minority interviewees viewed NGO workers in Bosnia as opportunists driven by high salaries and perks unavailable from the local economy. Dragan fumed in 2002 that international donors funded organizations he considered corrupt instead of

---

7. While activists and other elites distinguish two types of voluntary organizations— mass organizations, or citizens associations, and NGOs (*nevladine organizacije*) (Poggi et al. 2002, 80)—many ordinary people I spoke with lump voluntary organizations together.

directly supporting aspiring entrepreneurs like himself. Multiple studies (Chandler 2000; Poggi et al. 2002) confirm broad public cynicism about local NGOs. A 2002 study by USAID concluded that many NGOs in southeastern Europe "still have tenuous links with their communities" because of their orientation toward international donors (Stuart 2003, 10).

Scholars have warned that international assistance to NGOs can wreak havoc on local social relations by creating new "haves"—local NGO activists who enjoy high salaries, travel, and other privileges—and "have nots"—all other Bosnians (Sampson 1996; Wedel 2001; Ghodsee 2003). Donor policies can even harm the spontaneous development of bridging social capital by imposing goals. For example, donors have sometimes compelled women's organizations that pride themselves on not focusing on ethnicity to work toward "ethnic reconciliation" (Helms 2003). Assistance that targets only one group—for instance, minorities—in effect pits groups against each other (Demichelis 1998). A recurring complaint of Bošnjaks I interviewed was that international aid that prioritized minority returnees over those who had stayed and suffered through the war was unjust. A World Bank report urges international actors to take a holistic approach to reconstruction by both encouraging groups that developed bridging ties (e.g., multiethnic youth groups) *and* incorporating existing groups that produce bonding ties (e.g., cultural organizations) (Poggi et al. 2002, 2).

Those civic organizations that have seen some success in building ties across ethnic lines include groups that are responsive to local needs and supportive of interests that are not ethnically defined. A teenager of mixed background who returned to Bihać boasted of helping form a youth group that organized meetings for five hundred youth from areas throughout Bosnia. The first meeting was successful, she asserted, because "kids want to meet people from different places and they can talk about [shared] concerns." In Mostar, three teenagers of different backgrounds spoke of their youth group, which produced interethnic cooperation as a by-product of working together on concrete tasks in the local community.

Further, research has found that an essential component for women's voluntary organizations to be successful in transitional societies is their willingness to take up issues of immediate interest to their constituents (Cockburn 1998; Carothers 1999, 217). For instance, a women's organization with mixed membership helped reintegrate Sladjana, a Serb returnee, by teaching her skills and connecting her to like-minded people.

> Aside from my family, at the beginning of my return, [a women's organization] was the number one thing that helped me feel included in life.

There were computer exercises and workshops to meet people with the same problems, people who think the same, people who can help others find work. . . . It's very important to meet people and not to fear them.

Sladjana appreciated this organization because it met some of her pressing needs for concrete skills and connections to others in Sarajevo's tumultuous postwar community.

In support of Varshney's (2001) research, an ethnically mixed network of small business associations formed in central Bosnia produced concrete benefits for its participants by bringing about necessary changes in the law and increasing profits. A transnational activist implementing the project indirectly confirmed the virtue of weak ties: "People participate to improve their businesses, not to find a spouse." Because ethnic cleansing intensified the traditional homogeneity of Bosnian villages, the best way to forge multiethnic ties through voluntary groups in rural areas was by developing a network of homogeneous smaller groups. The best recipe would result in broad, multiethnic organizations that build on indigenous ideas and traditions (Gagnon 2002, 227) and reach out to their communities with "practical services that have immediate, tangible effects on people's lives" (Richter 2002, 56).

Possibilities in the Workplace

There are several reasons that networks initially formed in mixed workplaces were more useful than those formed in mixed voluntary organizations. First, Bosnians need work, and when they are at work, they are focused on fulfilling responsibilities. And since there was no explicit pressure to form ties in the workplace, people felt free to establish ties of varying intimacy with colleagues. Most minorities I interviewed had no choice but to work in predominantly Bošnjak workplaces. Of the institutions I examined through observation and interviews, mixed workplaces had the lowest ethnic selectivity and the most individualist norms (see figure 4.1).

The mixed workplaces that best promoted cooperative interethnic behavior encouraged repeated interaction among colleagues of different backgrounds on a horizontal basis. This reinforces findings by Nan Lin (2001) that engaging in reciprocity is most feasible when strangers are in similar functional positions. The workplace is necessary, at least initially, to develop ideals of professionalism, which can then facilitate interethnic cooperation at work and even among colleagues in other social venues. Those respondents who found workplaces useful for interethnic cooperation were most often involved in white-collar jobs in the public sector, even though quite a few of them had only a high school education. Several interviewees worked in the private sector, including a cobbler and a journalist.

For Zorica, who had limited contact with her Bošnjak neighbors, the workplace was helpful in developing cross-ethnic identifications and cooperative relationships. She found selected Bošnjak coworkers and students at the public school where she taught who downplayed ethnic markers and emphasized shared beliefs in self-criticism and inclusivity. She met some of her colleagues after work, for coffee and cigarettes at cafés or in homes. She felt that their views and behavior contrasted with the nationalist ideology of most parents of students and of the school's administration. The connections that Zorica formed at work, ranging from weak (with her students) to moderate strength (with selected colleagues), were important to her since most of her close friends had left Bosnia. Like Zorica, Ivan felt that his workplace, a newspaper, allowed him to get acquainted with like-minded people who felt that cultural backgrounds were not terribly important.

My host Ana also depended more on Bošnjaks from her multiethnic workplace than on people from her neighborhood, where experience with betrayal and discriminatory housing allocation prevented her from drawing on resources that could otherwise have arisen from local interethnic ties. This was the case even though she disagreed with the ethnic quotas in the Federation institution where she worked.[8] Ana formed relationships with her colleagues of varying strength across ethnic lines. To earn extra income, she sold black-market textiles to her colleagues. Visits to Ana's workplace revealed that she also frequently drank coffee and socialized with colleagues of different backgrounds during and after work. On religious holidays, she exchanged cakes and celebrated with them. Though she did not describe her Bošnjak colleague Anisa as a friend, Ana occasionally saw movies with Anisa and confided in her about her children. These coworkers established inclusive identifications based on professionalism and mothering. To express solidarity with her colleagues, Ana displayed in her office a 1994 newspaper photo of her and Anisa peering out from the window of their mortar-pocked office during the war. This photo suggests the powerful unifying experience of working together during war. Ana's connections at work provide psychological support and help her to solve practical problems. The mutual confiding, time spent together outside the office, and even the photo indicate that Ana and Anisa have ties of considerable meaning.

8. The influence of quotas on interethnic cooperation deserves further research.

A common theme expressed by my interviewees was the belief that their professional skills, which could only be demonstrated in the workplace, enhanced their reputation at work and often in the community as well. Maja, a nurse of Croat background, asserted that emphasizing professionalism and avoiding politics was the key to maintaining good interethnic relationships at the Sarajevo hospital where she worked. This included "getting along fine" with a Muslim colleague whose son had died in a Croatian prison camp. Cobbler Davor boasted that his customers included the city's mayor as well as Muslims from neighborhoods thick with other cobblers. His business success both broadened his self-understanding and contributed to his respect in the community. Serb returnee Blagoje, a sawmill operator, believed that his reputation from his prewar work in Bihać enabled his current positive relationships with Bošnjaks: "Because of my trade, people know me." Nela appreciated that fellow teachers (mainly Bošnjaks) thought so highly of her that they successfully lobbied for her reemployment. As Mark Granovetter (1973) found, these stories show that cross-ethnic connections with acquaintances helped minorities improve their financial situations and to reintegrate into the community.

Many Bosnians thought that the most valuable function that international NGOs, intergovernmental organizations, and, to a lesser extent, internationally supported local NGOs was providing jobs, not services, for locals. This was because a stable salary was their primary concern. In addition to offering good salaries, many international NGO workplaces allowed Bosnians to develop bridging ties around professionalism and shared experiences. Consider, for example, Nikola and Selma, displaced persons of "mixed" and Bošnjak backgrounds respectively, who worked together at an international humanitarian organization. During a break in one of my several trips with them to visit returnees, Selma volunteered, "Nikola and I are united by the fact that we are not in our original homes." Moreover, they had both sought to reclaim and return to these prewar apartments. Selma tried to help Nikola get his apartment back. International organizations, whether they are intergovernmental ones, such as the UN or the Organization for Security and Cooperation in Europe (OSCE), or nongovernmental ones, such as the International Rescue Committee, offer temporary havens and financial rewards that insulate those inclined toward individualism from the more chauvinistic Bosnian society. Donors, however, are impatient and often quickly shift their attention and resources from one global crisis to the next, reducing the number of these sites for building bridges. By 2005, many donors had radically reduced their aid to Bosnians and international efforts to implement Dayton. As a result, most international organizations do not offer sustainable alternative employment. Internationally supported local NGOs are even more precarious.

While people of working age who were employed had the best opportunities for developing bridging ties, even retirees kept some former colleagues in their personal networks. For instance, retiree Minka maintained a large bridging network of acquaintances, which she cultivated mainly from her own and her family's work and everyday economic activities. Her broad background as a socialist bureaucrat, a native Sarajevan, and the wife of a Croat made it easier to forge connections. The first time Minka invited me over for coffee in 1998, she and her husband had just returned from a visit to her hairstylist's home. She explained, "During the war, she brought us food. We were acquaintances before the war, but we didn't visit each other's homes. . . . [Today] we brought her a few gifts." Minka believed that the war "showed who was human and who was not." On reflection, she mentioned that Muslims helped her family survive the war. In addition to the aid offered by her hairstylist, her seamstress loaned her money, her daughter's colleague sent bread, and her dry cleaner delivered milk and cheese. As a comparison, her family received no help from her sister-in-law in Serbia and little help from most of her neighbors. In the winter of 1999, at the end of Ramadan, I accompanied Minka on a visit to her dry cleaner's; on other occasions, I went with her on visits to five other groups of acquaintances. These visits sometimes involved specific requests for help. For example, she asked her seamstress's husband if he could get an elusive part for her toilet. A common theme of the conversations during these visits were the exchange of similar experiences of surviving the terror of war and the wrenching postwar conditions. Other common topics were the observance of important rites of passage and traditions. In 2004, Minka took pride in relating how her family—especially her grandson, who had just completed his military service, and her daughter, a teacher in Sarajevo—had navigated around discriminatory authorities.

Ana's retired husband Jovan sometimes hosted former colleagues of Bošnjak background, hospitality that was reciprocated. Even though he had fled to Serbia during the war, two of Jovan's guests included colleagues who had fought for the Bosnian army during the war. These divergent wartime experiences did not fundamentally change the positive relationships Jovan had established with his colleagues at work before the war. For example, Adil, a former colleague, used his connections in the Bosnian army to help Ana and Jovan's family during and after the war in ways that their friends could not, since none of Jovan's friends had fought with the Bosnian army. During one conversation, Jovan and his colleague discussed parenting concerns and disapproved of the role of Islam in Bosnian politics—common values that bridged cultural divides. The omission of certain sensitive topics—such as which ethnic group had suffered the most during the war or what kind of Bosnian state should be built—implied an empathic understanding on the part of these colleagues.

What the social ties of these Bosnians have in common is that they were *initially* formed in a workplace or economic setting. In the workplace, the primary (though not only) role of Bosnians was as coworkers. They were able to appeal to professionalism, common values, and interests that were usually not ethnically specific as a way of establishing ties of varying strength. Minorities took advantage of the relative freedom of the workplace to form a wide variety of ties to forge weak to moderate connections that met their desired level of interethnic cooperation—from material aid to confiding. In *none* of these workplaces were relations between superiors and minorities in mid- to rank-and-file positions very positive. Ana knew that her boss was an SDA activist and his deputy an HDZ activist. As a result, she was guarded around them. For ordinary minorities, what mattered most was dependable salaries, bosses who were not hostile, and sustained horizontal relations with colleagues.

Simple inattention on the part of managers could sometimes harm the workplace's atmosphere for interethnic cooperation. Sandra mentioned that a Bošnjak colleague with whom she had very weak ties lashed out at her one afternoon. Workers in her office had turned on a TV set to watch a soccer game between teams from (Bošnjak-dominated) Sarajevo and (Croat-dominated) Široki Brijeg. After the TV coverage showed Široki Brijeg fans shouting epithets at Bošnjaks, Sandra's embittered Bošnjak colleague directed his frustration with the nationalist soccer hooligans onto the first minority he encountered—who happened to be Sandra. He turned to her and "suggested" that she change the name of her oldest daughter, since it was the female version of the name of a convicted Serb war criminal. The ability of a trigger such as sports competitions to damage the work environment demonstrates the fragility of venues for interethnic cooperation, as well as the power of sports to divide rather than unite (Orwell 1968).

People without regular work were doubly disadvantaged because they lacked both a salary and an obvious venue for these sorts of social ties. One evening in 2002, Dragana, a neighbor who had recently returned from Belgrade, stopped by the home of my hosts Sandra and Stipe. The guest envied what she perceived as the successful integration of Sandra and her family, wistfully commenting, "You are a successful case of return: You and your husband work, your children study [at Sarajevo University]; you were accepted." Dragana then contrasted this "happy story" with her own inability to find steady work and the dispersal of her immediate family. As isolated as she was, Dragana's strategy for making ends meet was a bridging one that involved subletting a room in her apartment to a medical student of Bošnjak background. Sandra later confided that she worried that the social isolation of Dragana, whose main activity was to "sit and stare at her apartment's walls," was contributing to her depression. Psychologists conducting research on Bosnians in the postwar setting have found that steady work produces psychological benefits for victims far beyond those expected by Western experts (Bell 2005). Full-time work has even improved the mental health of Bosnians suffering from post-traumatic stress.

Full-time employment eluded many young minorities, like Dragan, who were too young to have worked before the war and thus had no ties to resurrect afterward to help them find a job. By 2002, Dragan was exhausted by his continuous struggle to find steady work. He had not been able to get a loan to start a small business, so he had been working off and on as a truck driver. Unlike his girlfriend, Dragan lacked the English skills that might have helped him land a coveted, albeit short-term, job with an international organization. So he reluctantly considered going to Germany to work as a guest worker. Without steady employment, it would be hard for him to provide a solid financial foundation and cultivate the bridging ties necessary for reintegration.

Forging Bridges beyond Bihać and Sarajevo

Returnees to ethnically homogeneous hamlets had far fewer opportunities than urbanites to engage in interethnic cooperation with colleagues. Nevertheless, everyday economic activities (such as shopping in town stores or markets) and work served as the primary venues for interethnic interaction for these rural returnees. Work for minority returnees to hamlets in the Federation sometimes required cooperation with predominantly Bošnjak businesses in nearby towns. One Serb who had recently returned to a Serb hamlet found a job as a lumberjack in a nearby town that is predominantly Bošnjak. He was proud that a colleague—a Bošnjak—had already visited him. Dušan, a Serb who returned to a hamlet near Bihać, found employment as manager of a trout farm owned by Bošnjaks based in Bihać. These cases indicate the potential of workplaces in small towns to help reintegrate returnees even to nearby rural areas dominated by another ethnic group. In the prevalent pattern in the postwar countryside, most returnees to this Serb hamlet, however, either commuted to jobs in areas where their ethnic group predominated or remained in their hamlets to farm on their own.

Do these conditions for developing and using bridging ties for integration into Bošnjak-dominated areas after war differ for minorities living in the Republika Srpska? There are reasons to believe they do.

National-level minority activists (largely based in Banja Luka, the largest town in the Republika Srpska) who have taken on the role of nationalizing parastate elites in the Republika Srpska have more explicitly expressed antipathy toward, and implemented policies hostile to, minorities than the Bošnjak-dominated nationalizing state. The legacy of higher levels of ethnic cleansing in the Republika Srpska contributes to minorities' feelings of vulnerability there, both in the large towns and the smaller villages. The few who have returned to the Republika Srpska tend to be clustered in isolated hamlets or neighborhoods, which also heightens insecurity among minority returnees to the Republika Srpska (see table 1.2). One focus group study of Bošnjaks in the Republika Srpska in 2001 found that most of them felt threatened (IDEA 2001, 14).

Observation and interview testimony of minorities in the Republika Srpska reveal how they cope with postwar society. Spending time with minorities in the town of Banja Luka and in a village near Prijedor revealed differences between the experiences of minorities in areas of the Federation and the Republika Srpska, as well as between urban and rural areas of the Republika Srpska. In 1999 in Banja Luka, I talked with minorities who had been evicted from their homes but had remained displaced within Banja Luka throughout the war. Transnational humanitarians called these people "floaters" because they had been floating from one temporary shelter to another for years. One floater had lived with his family in a neighbor's garage for eight months before moving into one room provided by the Bošnjak humanitarian organization Merhamet. Others lived in garden sheds or even in their own cellars while squatters occupied their homes. Only a few had been able to reclaim their homes by 2000.

Transnational humanitarians working with floaters described many of them as people lacking the resources and connections to leave Banja Luka.[9] Most were not evicted from their homes until 1995. At that time, a portion of Croatian Serbs driven from their homes by Croatia's offensive to recapture Serb-held regions adjacent to Bosnia ended up in Banja Luka and evicted many of the remaining minorities. Resource-strapped Banja

9. Interview with Pax Christi officials, Banja Luka, October 1999.

Luka then confronted the burden of caring for refugees, a social group not present in Sarajevo or Bihać.

Merhamet's soup kitchen illustrates the role that local voluntary groups can play for supporting minorities in the Republika Srpska. It provided a place where displaced minorities found both practical and social support. It was mostly Bošnjaks who made up the community at the soup kitchen, although some Croats also spent time there. One Croat who did so described it as a place where "people are treated as human beings." It served as a safe haven for minorities who found it difficult to function within Banja Luka's larger community, which in 1998 was 94 percent Serb (UNHCR 1997), more homogeneous than Novo Sarajevo or even Bihać.[10] One floater described his strategy for coping in mixed social settings: "I shut up." The minorities in the Federation who felt the most vulnerable did the same thing.

There were limits to Merhamet's capacity to assist integration. Merhamet was a local organization to which Bošnjaks retreated for social and psychological support, largely from members of their own background. It lacked Serbs and did not help minorities to develop bridging ties. This matches findings in other postconflict settings that the more hostile the atmosphere for interethnic relations, the more heavily minorities seek psychological support through the exclusive ties of bonding rather than the inclusive ties of bridging (Colleta and Cullen 2000). In general, the extremely difficult economic conditions for people of all backgrounds in the Republika Srpska meant that they spent less time engaging in social interaction than people in the Federation (Poggi et al. 2002).

In those rare instances when minorities in the Republika Srpska interacted with Serbs, they used bridging mechanisms similar to those I observed in Bihać and Sarajevo. For example, I observed soup kitchen employees—Bošnjaks—reach out to an electrician—a Serb—who had been hired to patch up the faulty wiring. This exchange occurred in the context of *work* tasks. Initially they invited the electrician to drink coffee with them, a shared cultural tradition, during his break. While sipping her coffee, employee Jadranka complained about the unwillingness of the rural squatters in her home to take care of her fruit trees. The electrician returned the overture: "What is the hometown of the refugees?" Jadranka replied "Knin," a town known to grow the same fruit trees as in Banja

---

10. My discussions with minorities in Banja Luka focused on floaters who would be more vulnerable than those minorities who remained in their homes there throughout the war. Those minorities who managed to remain in their homes during the war represent a miniscule portion of the already tiny local Bošnjak population.

Luka. The electrician shook his head in agreement with her about the inexcusable behavior of the refugees. "They *must* know how to take care of fruit trees then." He further volunteered that he was a displaced person who was hoping to return to his prewar home. The electrician and the soup kitchen employees connected through their common experience as displaced urbanites who sought to return home.

As this setting illustrates, minorities in Banja Luka made distinctions among Serbs. They distinguished between domiciles (natives) in Banja Luka, displaced Serbs from rural areas of Bosnia, and refugees from Croatia. They also recognized that long-term Serb domiciles of Banja Luka faced pressure from extremists within their own Serb community during the war, though this acknowledgment did not extend to forgiveness. After their eviction in 1995 by Croatian Serbs, Fadila and her husband felt that they had little choice but to buy a bus ticket to a refugee camp in Croatia. They returned in 1997 and lived in a friend's shed while they petitioned for the return of their illegally occupied private home. Fadila was furious at the Croatian Serb refugees for what they did but refrained from heaping blame on domicile Serbs. "No domestic Serbs touched us, though no one dared protect us either." Darija, also evicted in 1995 by refugees, volunteered that she believed the claim of her long-term Serb neighbor that she "didn't dare do anything to help us during the war." Acknowledging that domicile Serbs in Banja Luka faced pressure from extremists within their own ethnic group helps her cope with her family's return to the neighborhood. Neither Darija nor the floaters who remained displaced mentioned receiving practical help from Serb neighbors. This indicates a more strained neighborhood environment than in Sarajevo or Bihać, where even minorities who felt the most vulnerable, such as Vera, selectively engaged neighbors from the majority group.

Another way that minorities in the Republika Srpska coexisted with Serbs was by refraining from discussing topics sure to provoke controversy. Anders Stefansson (2004) found that Bošnjak returnees to Banja Luka tried to connect with selected Serbs in their neighborhood by focusing on shared concerns, such as the trauma of displacement and poverty, while intentionally avoiding politically sensitive topics. Neighborhoods in Banja Luka were tenser for minorities than neighborhoods in Sarajevo or Bihać.

Seeking out Serbs deemed appropriate and decent was a strategy minorities used not just for coexistence but also for finding work. The only way that floater Vesna, a single mother fired from the city's largest department store in 1993, was able to make money was by cleaning the homes of Serbs. Vesna cultivated this work out of a network of former employers whom she felt had treated her fairly. She learned the hard way that accepting work from employers beyond her network meant risking confrontation with those who would refuse to pay her for her informal work. Former floater Darija, whose family had just reentered their home after the refugee family occupying it moved into internationally funded alternative housing for refugees in Banja Luka, was in better shape. Her husband was a repairman who managed to find work here and there, and her sons had found a social circle at school. Simply put, none of these Bošnjaks would have been able to survive in Banja Luka without building bridging networks with Serbs, who were essential in helping them find work.

As difficult as it was for minorities to cultivate bridging ties in Banja Luka, it was a gargantuan task in the village near Prijedor mentioned in chapter 3. All Bošnjaks had been cleansed from this village in 1992. The first families began to return in 1999, under the protection of peacekeepers. The Bošnjak returnees avoided domestic Serbs, whom they identified as participating in their expulsion and suspected had killed many of the village's Bošnjak men. In contrast to the situation in Banja Luka, returnees seemed more willing to engage with Serb refugees from Croatia because they had settled in the village only after its cleansing and thus could not have participated in the evictions.

Consistent with my findings in urban areas, it was through work that the rare majority–minority interaction occurred in the village. My Bošnjak host paid one refugee to help him build a shed. I also observed Bošnjak returnees interact with Serb construction workers who were paid by transnational humanitarians to rebuild returnee homes. These interethnic interactions, however, were brief.

Furthermore, the main work in the village for the returnees was in their own garden plots. This, together with the remittances from their adult children in Germany, helped my Bošnjak hosts cope. They even avoided shopping at the corner store run by a domicile Serb and instead found a way into Sanski Most, the nearest town across the interentity boundary line. With so many of their male family members having disappeared during the war, the returnees also sought practical help by developing a barter network to exchange services. Largely due to the legacy of the village's intimate interethnic violence, however, these practical networks were not inclusive, as was often the case in Sarajevo and Bihać, but narrowly restricted to Bošnjaks. The economically depressed condition of the village, like most villages in the Republika Srpska, only exacerbated interethnic tensions.

At the time I visited the village in 1999, only a handful of Bošnjak families had returned. By 2004, some ten thousand Bošnjaks had returned (Judah 2004). But these returnees led lives separate from their Serb neighbors. Returnee children attended a separate school in the village that taught the Bošnjak curriculum, suggesting that younger generations would also lead parallel lives. Simply put, positive interethnic relations in the village were practically nonexistent. Nonetheless, in those rare cases were interethnic cooperation emerged, it tended to be in the workplace and among individuals who forged weak ties partly based on some shared experience or sentiment.

Large surveys with nationally representative samples corroborate my findings on the possibilities for cooperation in the workplace. A survey conducted by the World Bank in 1999 indicated that it was in the venue of the workplace that Bosnians, regardless of ethnicity, expressed the greatest support for interethnic cooperation (Dani et al. 1999, para. 69). The majority of Bošnjaks and roughly half of the Serbs and Croats expressed willingness to share the workplace with members of other ethnic groups. Indeed, respondents expected to work in ethnically mixed environments. A survey by the UN (UNDP 2003a, 48–50) indicated that 63 to 85 percent of Bosnians were willing to work with a colleague of another ethnicity, compared to 50 to 59 percent of Bosnians in favor of interethnic cooperation in schools or in the neighborhood.[11] A 2002 survey by the World Bank (Poggi et al. 2002, 9) found that while citizens in Bosnia reported interethnic socializing had declined since the start of the war, that decline was smaller in socializing with colleagues (35 percent) than with neighbors (47 percent). According to another survey, even Serbs, Croats, and Bošnjaks living in areas where they are in the majority expressed more support for cross-ethnic economic cooperation than they did for ethnic self-sufficiency (U.S. Information Agency 1997, chaps. 5–6).

High unemployment rates and nationalist control of most Bosnian workplaces significantly limit the current ability of workplaces to reintegrate minorities on a large scale. An increase in unemployment heightens competition for the few available jobs and provides opportunities for elites in deeply divided societies to blame economic problems on those ethnically different and claim rare jobs for "their own" (Olzak 1992; Woodward 1995a, 56). Several studies found a positive relationship between intense ethnic competition for scarce resources at the local level and the outbreak of violence in Bosnia (Hodson, Sekulič, and Massey 1994; Slack

11. These ranges reflect the varying levels of willingness of Bosnians of different ethnic backgrounds to engage in interethnic cooperation.

and Doyan 2001).[12] For minorities, the environment for jobs was less competitive during and just after the war than it was later. High unemployment further sours relations between ethnic elites who have fewer spoils to divide and between the employed and the unemployed. In my experience, however, it does not exacerbate interethnic relations between those already employed unless job security was tenuous. Nationalist control of many workplaces drastically reduces the employment opportunities for ordinary people who do not support nationalists. Several outspoken non-nationalist informants were fired during the war. As V. P. Gagnon (2002, 208) suggests, the creation of sources of stable employment and resources beyond the control of political parties would significantly contribute to the building of social capital supportive of democratization. Dušan, the trout farm manager, said he agreed with his Bošnjak colleague that the future for themselves and for their children "depended on creating work and building tolerance."

Fertile Venues for Bridging Ties

Faced with a mix of modern and communitarian traditions, ordinary people in Bosnia will seek positive interethnic relationships that vary in strength and frequency. Flouting the policies of the nationalizing state and national-level minority activists, ordinary minorities in several Bošnjak-dominated towns and even in Banja Luka recognize the need to develop multiethnic networks and to seek out selected members of the majority for practicing reciprocity. Social network theory helps us understand why these urban minorities found workplace settings more amenable for reaching out to ordinary people belonging to the majority than their neighborhoods or voluntary organizations. Mixed workplaces may provide opportunities for repeated interethnic interaction among colleagues of equal status, allow for norms of professionalism, and enable people to form relations of varied and appropriate intimacy with colleagues of another background. These characteristics and the financial stability provided by salaries make the mixed workplace the most fertile environment for promoting interethnic cooperation.

Social network theory emphasizes the need for voluntary organizations to allow repeated, horizontal interaction among ordinary people of

12. These studies that uncover a positive correlation between ethnic competition over scarce resources and high levels of intolerance during the war were conducted at the level of the municipality. As a result of this level of analysis, it cannot be inferred from these studies that the same dynamic exists at the individual or neighborhood level.

different ethnicities. This interaction is supported best by responsive, broad-based civic associations, not the narrow advocacy groups that have been favored by transnational donors. The particular venues that are most suitable for building bridging social capital will be influenced by the dynamics of individual localities. Observation of minorities in the Republika Srpska demonstrates that even with the rarity of mixed workplaces in the region, those minorities who managed to find them were often able to forge bridging ties there. In chapter 5 we look at why common people find it even more grueling to reach beyond ethnicity in the political arena than in everyday life.

5

The Plague of Politics

Jovanka [a middle-aged Serb from Sarajevo]: In Bosnia, even breathing is political.

If minorities are to build the bridging social capital necessary for reintegration, they need partners from the majority group who are willing to play down ethnic divisions. How have attitudes among the majority group about interethnic relations changed since the end of the war? And what might make it difficult to reduce intolerance and realize the inclusive statebuilding project of transnational actors? As Jovanka says above, in an ethnically mixed space in Bosnia, everything is political, everything is controversial. Of particular interest in this chapter is how Bosnian citizens who live as minorities conceive of politics and participate in formal political institutions even though they reduce their opportunities for representation.

Cross-National Patterns of Interethnic Relations

How do the views on interethnic relations of individuals belonging to the majority group in each of Bosnia's entities vary across the three ethnically dominant areas of Bosnia? How have they changed since the end of the war? There are distinct patterns in how people respond to these situations, and they have important implications for the reconstruction process.

The Bošnjaks are the dominant group in the Federation, and the Serbs control the Republika Srpska. Each group, in the areas they dominate, affects attitudes about interethnic relations and the ability of minorities to form cross-ethnic ties. During the bulk of my fieldwork in 1999, Bosnian Serbs in the Republika Srpska expressed less willingness to engage in interethnic contact than Bošnjaks living in the areas of the Federation where

Table 5.1. Increase in belief that Bosnian Serbs, Croats, and Bošnjaks will be able to live peacefully together

	Percentage who believed that Bosnian Serbs, Croats, and Muslims will be able to live peacefully together in 1995 (%)	*Percentage who believed that Bosnian Serbs, Croats, and Muslims will be able to live peacefully together in 2001 (%)*
Serbs	13	31
Croats	31	62
Bošnjaks	65	94

Sources: Sweeney 1999; Demeri 2001.

Note: The question wording was slightly different in 1995 and 2001. In 1995, respondents were asked whether they "believe the Croats, Muslims, and Serbs can live peacefully together in the country" (Sweeney 1999). In 2001, respondents were asked if they "believe in time, Bosnian Serbs, Croats, and Muslims will be able to live peacefully together again." Between 1 percent and 9 percent of the respondents chose "don't know."

they are in the majority (see table 1.3). Throughout the postwar period, these differences between Serbs and Bošnajks in the areas they dominate have endured. This probably reflects Serbs' greater pessimism about interethnic cooperation and their preference for separation, ideas reinforced by political rhetoric in favor of separation in the Republika Srpska and the mistrust of transnational actors. Yet over time, ordinary Bosnians have generally increased their willingness to coexist with those of other ethnic backgrounds (table 5.1).

Since the end of the war, more Bosnians of all backgrounds believe that Bosnian Serbs, Croats, and Bošnjaks will be able to coexist at the least intimate level; that is, simply live in the same country with other ethnic groups (UNDP 2003a). Most individuals express a willingness to share the same country with different ethnic groups, ranging from 63 percent (respondents in predominantly Serb areas willing to share the country with Bošnjaks) to 87 percent (respondents in predominantly Bošnjak areas willing to share the country with Croats) (UNDP 2003a). Support among Serbs for sharing the state with those who are ethnically different, however, is still lower than among Croats or Bošnjaks. One reason for optimism is the spike during the 2000s in support for minority returns, one of the most contentious aspects of Dayton. Between 1995 and 2004, citizens of all backgrounds and all areas of residence decisively increased their support for the return of refugees of another ethnicity to their towns (figure 5.1). This improvement is abundantly clear, even though different

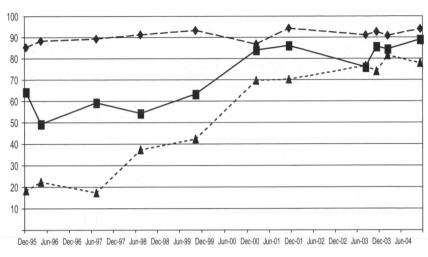

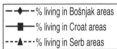

- - ◆ - - % living in Bošnjak areas
——■—— % living in Croat areas
- - - ▲ - - - % living in Serb areas

Figure 5.1. Increasing support for minority return to one's own village or town. Sources for 1995–99 data: U.S. Information Agency (USIA) 1998; Demeri 2001. Sources for 2001–5 data: UN Development Programme (UNDP) 2001–5.

data sources and sampling techniques make comparison difficult.[1] All three groups, whether they started out expressing tolerance or intolerance, jumped dramatically; the smallest increase was a whopping 18 points.

The most dramatic change occurred among inhabitants of the area that expressed the most opposition to minority return throughout the postwar period—the Republika Srpska. Between December 1995 and December

1. The source of data from 1995 to 1999 is the U.S. Information Agency (USIA), which was eventually folded into the U.S. Department of State. These sources report the views of Bošnjaks, Serbs, and Croats in areas where they live among the majority. These surveys asked, "How do you feel about refugees from another nationality group returning to your city/town/village?" "Support" includes those who responded that they strongly or somewhat supported return. The source of data from 2000 through December 2004 is the UN Development Programme (UNDP), which reports views by ethnically predominant areas and does not specify ethnic background. UNDP's sample of 650 in each ethnically predominant area contains 150 minorities. These surveys report those who responded "I mostly or strongly agree that people coming from the minority population who lived in this municipality before the war should return to their homes."

1999, Bosnian Serbs from Serb-dominated areas significantly increased their support for minority return, from 18 percent to 42 percent (USIA 1998; Demeri 2001). From February 2001 to February 2005, inhabitants of Serb-dominated areas—both Serbs and minorities—increased their support from 69 percent to 81 percent (UNDP 2000–2005).[2] While those living in predominantly Croat areas have also increased their support for minority return over the last ten years, the data reveal sensitivity to domestic political developments. For example, they indicate a dismal view of minority return that closely tracks the extremist shift in HDZ politics in 2001. Then, party activists advocated that Croats quit the Federation army and establish an entity for Croats within Bosnia. After that political crisis, support for minority return in Croat areas picked back up.

The startling increase in public support for minority return suggests surprisingly broad acceptance of the idea of return. What is less clear is whether Bosnians have internalized the idea of return or merely resigned themselves to minority return after seeing the concerted efforts of transnational actors to promote it.[3] The former is expressed by returnees, who often repeated to me the mantra, *"svak na svoj"*—"each in one's own home." On the other hand, it is possible that people express acceptance of minority return because they think that few minorities will be able to return permanently or that they are old and so will not threaten the dominance of the majority group in the area. My discussions with Bosnians suggest that reality lies somewhere between these two poles, tending toward the begrudging acceptance end. Distance from the war and an improved security situation has contributed to the acceptance of return. At the same time, Bosnians recognize that the extent of sustainable return will not threaten them. Regardless of the factors driving changes in attitudes toward minority return, the resulting modest increase in diversity will present greater opportunities for repeated interethnic contact.

At the more intimate level of the neighborhood, views on willingness to live next door to someone of another background have generally increased, a pattern consistent with support for minority return. Between 1997 and 2001, Bosnians decreased their objection to sharing the same

2. Even if we assume that all 150 minorities of the 650 respondents in each ethnically predominant area support minority return and subtract them from the sample, then the lowest percentage of Serbs from the Republika Srpska supportive of minority return ranges from 46.4 percent in February 2001 to 76 percent in 2005.

3. The acceptance of minorities living in close proximity is supported by the high percentage of minorities who have reported that they have not suffered verbal harassment or physical attacks in the past year (from 86.6 percent in Serb-dominated territory to 94.6 percent in Bošnjak-dominated territory) (UNDP 2001–2003). However, minorities may underreport security incidents because of their potential vulnerability (UNHCR 2005).

Table 5.2. Decrease in intolerance

	Percentage who mentioned that they would not live next to a neighbor of another religion in 1997 (%) (N = 1189)	Percentage who mentioned that they would not live next to a neighbor of another religion in 2001 (%) (N = 694)
In Bosnia as a whole	28	11
By entity		
In the Federation	18	7
In the Republika Srpska	46	22
By ethnicity		
Bošnjaks	19	8
Serbs	47	23
Croats	16	6

Source: European Values Study Group and World Values Survey Association 2004.

neighborhood with someone of another background (European Values 2004). As with views on sharing the country and supporting minority returns, attitudes about neighbors vary quite systematically according to ethnic background and region, with Serbs and those in the Republika Srpska being the least willing to live next to someone of a different religion (table 5.2).[4] On top of that, data collected recently by the UN Development Programme indicate that in Bošnjak-dominated areas, the relatively high tolerance of neighbors of Serb background decreased between 2000 and 2003, from 81.4 to 74.4 percent. This pattern may reflect tensions that increased partly as a result of a spike in the number of minority returns to predominantly Bošnjak areas between 2000 and 2002 (UNDP 2002).[5] Many natives of Bihać and Sarajevo expressed resentment that refugees returning from temporary havens beyond the Balkans appeared to secure international assistance with such ease.[6]

Since the end of the war, Bosnians have generally remained averse to

4. The World Values Survey does not ask about willingness to live next to someone of a different ethnicity. Religion, which often overlaps with ethnicity, is the next closest salient social division that it asks about. *F*-tests show statistically significant differences at the 0.001 level among the views of respondents of different ethnicity, as well as among inhabitants of different entities.

5. In 2002, the estimated number of minority returnees was 49,050 to the Bošnjak-Croat Federation (most to predominantly Bošnjak areas) and 34,740 to the Republika Srpska (UNDP 2002, 50). Furthermore, more returnees were Serb than Croat.

6. West European countries such as Germany, which took on a heavy burden of temporary protection for refugees from the former Yugoslavia, used assistance to prod refugees into returning permanently to Bosnia.

intimate interethnic relations, as indicated by their attitudes about interethnic marriage. These levels range from a low of 3.2 percent (respondents in predominantly Croat areas willing to have a family member marry a Serb in 2000) to a high of 38.5 percent (respondents in predominantly Bošnjak areas willing to have a family member marry a Croat in 2003) (UNDP 2003a). Given the thunder of nationalist rhetoric and the suffering everyone experienced during the war, the low levels of support for intimate interethnic mixing make sense.

Another way of putting it is that Bosnians have accepted coexistence but have rejected multiculturalism. They will tolerate difference, but they do not embrace it. This increased tolerance since the end of the war does contribute to peacebuilding. But the small size of that increase and the persistently low levels of ethnic tolerance among Serbs give advocates of inclusive statebuilding a good reason to worry. At the same time, these views and even modest levels of minority return indicate that the more exclusive statebuilding projects of the nationalizing state and parastate elites have not been an unqualified success.

Factors Contributing to Intolerance

If we want to understand the obstacles to transnational actors' peacebuilding efforts, we have to think clearly about the factors that reinforce intolerance. A national sample survey of Bosnians was conducted in 2001 (European Values 2004), giving analysts a splendid opportunity to understand about the structures that underlie both tolerance and intolerance. I created a model to explain religious intolerance among the predominant group in each entity, as indicated by Bosnians expressing unwillingness to live next to someone of a different religion (table 5.3). My statistical model investigates the influence of three sets of factors theorized to affect intolerance. The first is participation in civic groups that build social capital, as indicated in the model by participation in nonreligious NGOs and religious organizations. The second is approval of past and current statebuilding projects; these attitudes are indicated by views about the communist system and adherence to an overarching supraethnic Bosnian identity consistent with transnational actors' current goals, respectively. The third is general socioeconomic and demographic factors found in other settings to affect intolerance of difference (Oliver and Mendelberg 2000).

Statistical analysis confirms the divergent demographic and political dynamics at work in the entities. That is to say, residents of the two entities are approaching this problem quite differently. No one factor signifi-

Table 5.3. Explaining religious intolerance among majority groups in Bosnia's entities

Independent variables	Bošnjaks in the Federation (N = 400)		Serbs in the Republika Srpska (N = 161)	
	Coefficient	s.e.	Coefficient	s.e.
Attitudes and behavior				
Member NGO (not religious)[a]	−.552	(.416)	.196	(.442)
Religious attendance	−.060	(.093)	.440*	(.191)
Positive view of communist system	−.097	(.073)	−.107	(.066)
Supraethnic civic identification	.634	(.397)	−.192	(.413)
Demographics				
Age cohort	.320*	(.137)	.096	(.139)
Urban resident	.013	(.085)	−.243*	(.087)
Education	.096	(.110)	−.122	(.132)
Income	−.201	(.150)	−.117	(.155)
Unemployed	.715	(.446)	−.099	(.561)
Gender	.222	(.386)	.342	(.409)
Constant	-3.445	(1.616)	2.410	(2.494)

Source: European Values 2004.
Note: For coding of variables, see Appendix F.
* = significant at the 0.05 level.
Log likelihood (Federation) −104.429; Log likelihood (Bosnia's RS) −79.710
Probability > χ^2 0.05 (Bosnia's Federation); Probability > χ^2 0.05 (RS)
Pseudo R^2: 0.083 (Federation); Pseudo R^2: 0.117 (RS)
Percentage of responses on social distance correctly predicted: 91.5 percent in the Federation; 78 percent in the Republika Srpska.

cantly affected intolerance among both Bošnajks in the Federation and Serbs in Republika Srpska.[7]

Among Bošnjaks in the Federation, only age significantly influences intolerance. Older Bošnjaks expressed more intolerance than younger Bošnjaks in the Federation. To illustrate, the probability that an individual between 18 and 24 years old would express intolerance was 3 percent, while the probability that an individual 65 years old or older would express intolerance was 20 percent.[8] This is surprising, given the literature on political socialization (Jennings and Niemi 1981) positing that younger people would be more likely to internalize intolerance during the war. Yet

7. I used logistic regression to analyze these data. In this technique, the effect of a variable depends on where in the logistic curve we are evaluating the effect. This is because the effect depends on the values of all other independent (or explanatory) variables. In interpreting the effect of the statistically significant factors on intolerance, I selected a value for the significant independent variable of interest and kept other variables at their means.

8. I calculated the effect of age cohort at the value specified while fixing the values of all other independent variables at their means.

none of the 74 respondents in the 18 to 24 age group, Bošnjaks who would have been in their formative years during the most recent war, objected to living next to someone of a different religion. If anything, Bošnjak youth have internalized the folly of intolerance, it seems.[9] Many young people I talked with expressed anger toward self-interested, older politicians who led them into a war that one of them described as a "black hole" that swallowed up their lives and ruined their futures. They were denied much of what their parents could take for granted, including free higher education, expectations of a decent job, and vacations in the mountains or beaches throughout the region. Anecdotal evidence suggests young adults were probably more likely than older cohorts to have taken advantage of information technology and other resources provided by international assistance to connect to new people and knowledge.

One reason that young Serbs in the Republika Srpska did not express more tolerance than their elder co-ethnics may be the expectation of low benefits from transnational actors in comparison with young Bošnajks in the Federation. After the war, transnational actors punishing Republika Srpska parastate elites for not supporting the implementation of Dayton probably helps explain this difference. Interviews and assistance data suggest that young Serbs in the Republika Srpska were less likely to have positively interacted with or received aid from transnational actors than young Bošnajks in the Federation.

For Serbs in the Republika Srpska, one social practice and one demographic variable influence intolerance. Greater exposure to the divisive rhetoric that dominates the religious hierarchy and is a key component of nationalist ideology (Cohen 1997; Sekulić, Massey, and Hodson 2006) contributes to the intolerance of Serbs in the Republika Srpska. The probability that a Serb who rarely attends church expresses intolerance is 13 percent, whereas the probability that a Serb who attends church once a week expresses intolerance is 36 percent.

Serbs living in an urban environment in the Republika Srpska are less intolerant than Serbs living in rural areas. Contrast the probability that an individual who lives in a town of 10,000 to 20,000 will express intolerance—22 percent—with the probability that an individual who lives in a village with less than 2000 inhabitants will express intolerance—37 percent. Urbanites tend more often to mix with those of different ethnicities than people from rural areas do. In what can become a ""virtuous circle,"

---

9. A less sanguine interpretation of this relationship is that youth are more politically savvy and thus keen to downplay stereotypes and generate answers that they believe are socially desirable. The attitudes of youth on tolerance deserve further investigation.

such contact can work to break down stereotypes and slowly build trust (Pettigrew 1998; Kunovich and Hodson 2002), which leads to increased willingness to make contacts, and so on. What is surprising is that this process appears to prevail even in a situation of intense competition over scarce resources like jobs and housing. That minorities tend to be concentrated in particular neighborhoods within towns in the Republika Srpska and still make up only a tiny percentage of the urban population in the Republika Srpska probably temper competition. But urban areas in the Republika Srpska still allow for at least limited interethnic interaction, a possibility largely missing in villages.

One reason that urban environments do not appear to similarly decrease intolerance among Bošnjaks in the Federation is that many rural Bošnjaks from the Republika Srpska felt obliged to relocate to cities in the Federation. While an increasing number of Bošnjaks who were displaced have returned to their home villages, others have decided to stay permanently in urban areas, accelerating a natural process of urbanization of the country. Many of these "new urbanites," however, had spent the bulk of their formative years in rural settings, thus absorbing more ethnocentric views.[10] Also, these new urbanities are more likely to have directly suffered violence than the Bošnjaks who spent the war in more urban areas. The most contentious relations have often been between minority returnees and displaced Bošnjaks; these groups often compete directly for scarce jobs and housing. In the postwar context, urban areas of the Federation are not conducive to reducing intolerance among Bošnjaks.

Some factors conventionally thought to reduce intolerance did not affect Bošnjak and Serb views. Consistent with chapter 4's qualitative analysis, which found that NGOs rarely help minorities produce bridging social capital, statistical analysis found that membership in NGOs does not decrease intolerance among those in the majority. My interviews and observation suggest the ethnically homogeneous nature and shallow roots of many NGOs in Bosnia help explain the inability of civic participation to reduce intolerance.

Civic identification, considering oneself first and foremost a citizen of Bosnia also has no impact. This is not surprising given that supraethnic identification as a Bosnian has mainly taken hold only among Bošnjaks, which undermines the civic work the label can do. The Dayton constitu-

10. Urban areas in the Republika Srpska, such as Banja Luka, also experienced an influx of persons displaced from rural areas. However, many of the displaced are refugees from Croatia's Krajina. These refugees do not have citizenship in Bosnia and thus were probably excluded from the survey sample.

tion reinforces ethnicity as the basis for political participation and representation while providing no incentives for a civic identity. I found that many Bosnian Serbs and Croats resisted calling themselves Bosnians and instead conflated the labels of Bosnian (a civic identity) and Bošnjak (an ethnic identity). These findings point to the widespread perception that Bosnia is a nationalizing state of Bošnjaks and not a true civic state. Education also fails to decrease intolerance, as happens in most other societies. This is consistent with research on education and tolerance in Bosnia and the former Yugoslav region since the 1980s, when nationalists gained a firm grip over the educational system (Hodson, Sekulić, and Massey 1994; Donia 2000).

Neither did socioeconomic factors significantly influence intolerance. While respondents with lower incomes or no employment appear to be more likely to express intolerance, these differences are not statistically significant. Participation in the informal economy, particularly in the Republika Srpska, may help explain this anomaly. The vast majority of Bosnians are poor and have insecure employment prospects, which means that income cannot account for the *variation* in levels of intolerance.

This quantitative analysis helps identify factors that reinforce tolerance and that inclusive statebuilders should address. The influence of age on intolerance among Bošnjaks in the Federation suggests that transnational actors develop programs tailored to suite the specific practical and psychological needs of different generations. The power of religious institutions and urban-rural dynamics among Serbs in the Republika Srpska point to the need for transnational policies designed to encourage religious officials to moderate their teachings and to address the concerns of villagers.

Tiptoeing around the Political Battlefield

Social views about tolerance have political implications for the competing peacebuilding projects. Bosnians express divergent views about what kind of interethnic relations are preferred—or even possible—which affects the prospects for sustainable return and reintegration. Bosnians' attitudes begin to diverge even more sharply as topics move from the social realm to more explicitly political ones. We see this in views about what kind of Bosnia can peacefully accommodate all of its peoples. Bošnjaks continue to desire a united Bosnia with equal rights for all (UNDP 2003a). Between 2000 and 2004, however, there was no increase in support for the idea of Bosnia-Herzegovina as a state of equal citizens and peoples among Serbs and Croats, who continue to believe that a united Bosnia would in practice lead to Bošnjak domination and not equal rights (UNDP 2004b). More Bosnian Croats—31 percent—viewed greater autonomy as their paramount interest, while only 25 percent preferred Bosnia-Herzegovina as a state of equal citizens and peoples. For their part, more Bosnian Serbs (29 percent) viewed independence as their paramount interest than Bosnia-Herzegovina as a state of equal citizens and peoples (13 percent).[11]

But how preoccupied are voters in Bosnia with solving these divergent visions for Bosnia? Not so much, according to public opinion data. Since the end of the war, ordinary Bosnians have been most concerned with utilitarian issues. When given the choice between economic concerns or defense of ethnic interests, Bosnians of all backgrounds have over time increased their already strong belief that the government should primarily be solving economic problems.[12] This is consistent with Bosnians' conceptions of democracy; after equality before the law, the next most important tasks for government are meeting basic economic needs of the people and achieving economic prosperity (IDEA 2002, 22). Bosnians are also more willing to engage in protests if they involve economic issues rather than political issues (UNDP 2004b). Bosnians furthermore agreed that the obstacles to economic progress center on flawed privatization, corrupt politicians who are unwilling to advance concrete programs for economic growth, and lack of foreign investment (IDEA 2001).

In theory, increasing concern about the economy and agreement about the reasons for economic problems should create even better conditions for grassroots support of parties committed to addressing these concerns. Strong institutions, however, work against this. The ethnic party system, patronage, the war, and hierarchical political parties undermine pros-

11. In 2002, the top three state visions of each of Bosnia's three ethnonational groups were: (1) *for Bošnjaks*, 48 percent = Bosnia and Herzegovina (BiH) as a state of equal citizens and peoples, 21.7 percent = BiH as before the war, 17 percent = don't know; (2) *for Croats*, 30.7 percent = BiH as separate entities for each of three peoples, 24.5 percent = BiH as a state of equal citizens and peoples, 17.3 percent = don't know; and (3) *for Serbs*, 28.7 percent = independence for Republika Srpska, 26.9 percent = secession of RS to Yugoslavia, 16.1 percent = don't know (UNDP 2002, 51).

12. The importance assigned to economics, rather than ethnic interests, increased between 1998 and 2001. In 2001, those identifying "work to improve the economy and promote new jobs" as the highest priority for the government included 52 percent of Serbs (Bell 2001b), 47 percent of Croats (Bell 2001a), and 74 percent of Bošnjaks (Bell 2001c). Those believing in 2001 that the most important priority for the government should be "working to defend the rights of people of our own [ethnic-based] nationality" included 22 percent of Serbs (Bell 2001b) and 28 percent of Croats (Bell 2001a), though only 2 percent of Bošnjaks (Bell 2001c). This remained the second highest concern for Bosnian Serbs and Croats, the groups most dissatisfied with Dayton.

Table 5.4. Messages in 2002 election campaign in Bosnia

Campaign messages	As percentage of total campaign messages (%) (N = 244)
Ethnically framed issues	57
Anticorruption	12
Solving of economic problems	11
Stability and the rule of law	11
Movement toward the West	5
Change of leadership	4
Supraethnic solidarity	0

Source: A random sample of articles on the elections from local press in Bosnia in 2002.

pects for detaching grassroots concerns about the economy from nationalist parties. A party system dominated by ethnic parties exacerbates conflict by eliminating a moderate middle ground (Horowitz 1985, 291–98). Why is there no middle ground? Because by definition ethnic parties cannot win votes from other ethnic groups. This dynamic increases incentives to make radical appeals to mobilize the most votes within a party's ethnic constituency. In Bihać, the competition was so fierce for the Bošnjak vote during the first postwar elections in 1996 that SDA labeled Haris Siljadzić, leader of the Party For Bosnia and Herzegovina (SBiH)—the SDA's main competition—a "traitor" and had thugs injure him during a campaign visit. In such conditions, it is easy for elites to twist general disgruntlement with the economy into fear and anger toward enemies.

One elite strategy for framing grassroots concerns is campaign rhetoric. Content analysis of a random sample of local press coverage of the 2002 election campaign in Bosnia revealed that politicians did not respond to the electorate's concerns about the economy.[13] Instead, party elites propagated divisive, ethnically framed messages about protecting ethnic group interests, ethnic identity, and the threat posed by other ethnic groups and disloyal co-ethnics inside and outside the state (table 5.4).

Most campaign messages featured ethnic outbidding, a process in

13. I analyzed a random selection of 350 articles on the 2002 elections from the independent newspaper *Oslobodjenje* (Liberation). Because reliance on this paper likely underplays extremist messages, I added randomly selected local articles from the U.S. government's World News Service. The World News Service does not publish its selection criteria for articles, but its mandate suggests it focuses on articles whose content appears threatening. The articles focused on the campaign, which I systematically analyzed using NUD*IST (Scolari 1997).

which each party tries to convince its ethnic electorate that only *it* is capable of protecting their ethnic interests. In an example of ethnic outbidding, a prominent religious official supportive of the SDA branded the Social Democratic Party (SDP) a traitor for cracking down on Bošnjak criminals. The hatib of Sarajevo's King Fahd Mosque warned in a sermon that "Bošnjaks are not aware of how they are encircled by enemies; while Bošnjaks look for culprits for all their misfortunes within their own ranks, their neighbors are sharpening their daggers" ("Sarajevo Mosque" 2002). Evoking the threat posed by Serbs, an *Oslobodjenje* journalist ratcheted up tensions by playing up the fact that "leading politicians and the ruling party from the Republika Srpska gave support to [then Serbian President] Vojislav Kostunica's position that the Republika Srpska should be annexed to Serbia" (Dizdarević 2002). These nationalist claims dwell on threats posed by other ethnic groups and those within their own group to propagate fear and to offer a quick fix for them: protection by nationalists. Even leaders of more moderate parties or parties willing to engage in interethnic accommodation like SDP engaged in outbidding when they responded to SDA claims that they failed to protect Bošnjaks. Bosnians of all backgrounds recognize that politicians campaign more on protection of ethnic interests than on socioeconomic issues (UNDP 2004b, 52). A clear majority of Bosnians—73 percent—agreed that politicians obstruct better interethnic relations (UNDP 2005, 69). Even though Bosnians are politically savvy, such rhetoric poisons the environment for minorities and for inclusive statebuilding.

Other political institutions depress grassroots enthusiasm for political parties with utilitarian messages. The rigid rules for balanced representation of ethnic groups and ethnic-based regions that permeate virtually all of the bodies for political representation encourage—even more strongly than in 1990—voters in each group to vote for their nationalist party to balance the anticipated votes by other ethnic group members for their respective nationalist parties. Furthermore, the slow pace of economic reconstruction, the nationalists' entrenched dominance of the economy, continued displacement, raw memories of the war, and slow progress toward reconciliation all help the nationalists dominate political power. Nationalist parties also benefit from party in-fighting and fragmentation, which splinter moderate parties and work against cross-ethnic cooperation.

Though nationalist parties have generally retained their grip over political power in the postwar period, their rhetoric has softened (Bose 2002). In addition, the share of the vote captured by nationalists has gradually but steadily declined (Izborna komisija 2006). Qualitative analyses

(Rhea 2006) assert that a handful of factors contributed to decreasing support for the nationalist parties that came into power in 1990. Increasing distance from the war and poor governance during the postwar period are two prominent ones. And while significant international involvement in Bosnia's political process has not led to the election of parties committed to good governance for all of Bosnia's citizens, efforts by transnational actors appear to have weakened—slightly—the popularity of nationalist parties. International campaigns to uncover corruption, the UN High Representative's use of the Bonn powers to facilitate return, and the engineering of new election rules appear to have slightly dampened enthusiasm for nationalists.[14] In addition, the death of prominent party leaders who had once held together hardline and moderate factions within the nationalist parties led either to their splintering (HDZ) or to their movement toward the center (SDA) (Rhea 2006).

Even so, the results of the 2006 elections demonstrate the continued dominance of parties embracing nationalist rhetoric. Counter to the hopes of transnational actors, SDA's move toward moderation only created an opportunity for SBiH to move to the right during the 2006 campaign, a strategy that voters rewarded by electing SBiH leader Haris Silajdžić as the Bošnjak member of the state presidency. Furthermore, debates over constitutional reform, Montenegro's independence, the negotiations over Kosovo, and competition for the Bosnian Serb vote encouraged the Party of Independent Social Democrats (SNSD), considered by transnational actors to be the leading moderate party for Bosnian Serbs, to move to the right in the 2006 campaign by threatening to hold a referendum on independence for the Republika Srpska. So the SNSD maintained its dominance over politics in the Republika Srpska as well. Only among Croats did the split of HDZ provide electoral openings for more moderate parties.

The difference in the concerns voiced by the electorate and those expressed by political elites helps explain the low levels of *external* efficacy, defined as an individual's belief that his vote will matter for political policy. To be blunt, few Bosnians believe they can influence political policy (UNDP 2004b). To explain this lack of external efficacy, some observers reach back in history to suggest roots in a longstanding political culture that recognizes authority, becomes resigned to it, and learns to cope with it. During a van ride to a local conference in 1999, civic activists in Bihać

14. In a controversial move, the UN High Representative dismissed Republika Srpska President Nikola Poplašen in 1999 and disqualified his Serb Radical Party from the November 2000 elections (see ICG 2002, 2–3). It is not clear that interference with elected officials at such a high level has contributed to moderation.

took pains to emphasize to me that ethnic animosity did not cause the war. The real puzzle of the war, one activist asserted, was that leaders were able to convince the people to fight each other largely along ethnic lines. In response, the Bošnjak seated next to me related a tale I heard several times:[15]

> There is a story about a Muslim during World War II applauding in Foča's town square when the ustaše [Croat fascists] took power. Then he also applauded Tito when he came to Foča and declared the victory of the partisans. When Tito pulled him aside and asked him how it was he could applaud both the fascists and him, he said, "Simple. I respect power [*čijenim vlast*]." I think this helps explain Bosnia now.

Some scholars have argued that this adaptive tradition developed in response to centuries of imperial rule over Bosnia.[16]

Nonetheless, most Bosnians pointed to experiences with politics since the disintegration of Yugoslavia to explain their alienation from politics. Though ordinary citizens throughout the West distrust politicians and dislike politics, Bosnians have an unusually poor opinion that has only become worse in the postwar period. Bosnians have judged existing political parties to be incapable of implementing reforms that would improve the lives of ordinary people (UNDP 2004b, 53). In June 2002, once, as I waited in line at a newsstand in downtown Sarajevo, I overheard the vendor and a customer talking about how important it is to vote, but in the next breath they both bemoaned the self-interested behavior of politicians. When I asked for a local newspaper, the clerk turned to me:

> He's right, isn't he?! For whom to vote?! They [politicians] are all crooks; they only look out for themselves. They don't do anything for the people. They haven't opened new factories so that people can earn a living. My monthly salary is 200 km, but my boss gets 2000 km. During the war, I didn't want to leave; now I do. It just gets worse.

I heard this sort of complaint many times in Bosnia. One common refrain was that politicians enriched themselves at the expense of ordinary people. In another example, my host Jovan said in 1999 that "SDP is the same as SDA, SDS, HDZ. Nationalist." When I asked him to elaborate, Jovan counseled, "Just wait and see what SDP does once it is in power!" He predicted that the opportunities presented by holding political office would

---

15. See also Gordy (1999).

16. Panel discussion, "Transacting Transition: Practices of International Assistance in the Former Yugoslavia" (National Convention of the American Association for the Advancement of Slavic Studies, Salt Lake City, Utah, November 3, 2005).

cause all political parties to seek personal profit, favor co-ethnics, and ignore the well-being of the citizens they represent.

Corruption within the dominant nationalist parties—SDA, SDS, and HDZ—was widely recognized (ICG 2001a), although—perhaps predictably—ordinary Bosnians were more eager to point out the corruption of nationalist parties representing *other* ethnic groups than their own. Opposition activist Avdo explained the popularity of the nationalists as rooted in the benefits they provided their supporters. "Nationalist parties are useful for promoting one's self-interests. During the war, nationalists moved from villages into the cities, upgrading their living situations." Others were disgusted by the sudden wealth that high-level military officials—most of whom were closely tied to nationalists—accumulated during the war. Mirsada bitterly shouted, "These generals had nothing before the war but now they all have villas and drive Mercedes. . . . Meanwhile, soldiers in the Bosnian army and war invalids have nothing!" In addition to benefiting from the war, nationalists profited from flawed privatization (Donias 2005). One evening in 1999 during a TV news segment on privatization, Alija's sister sardonically observed that, given their manipulation by ruling nationalists, the privatization vouchers Bosnians were receiving—*certifikat*—should actually be called "*falsifikat.*"

In 2000, moderate parties took over power at the national level, the only time in the postwar period that that happened. Transnational actors and moderate voters hoped that the victory of the SDP would bring about major reform. Instead, the SDP-led Alliance for Change made only token efforts to bring about reform and appeared most interested in installing its members in high positions in the remaining public companies. This dismal record reinforced the widespread belief that "all politicians are vain, incompetent, corrupt, and unworthy" (ICG 2002, 22) and nearly matched Jovan's prediction. The vast majority of citizens in Bosnia think that "the country is run by a few big interests," with 77 percent of Bošnjaks, 82 percent of Serbs, and 84 percent of Croats agreeing with the premise (European Values 2004). Since the end of the war, corruption has remained among the top concerns of ordinary Bosnians (UNDP 2005). Citizens are so annoyed that they have resorted to "protest voting," designed to boot out incompetent incumbents (Office of the High Representative 2002). Apathy is rampant.

Asking Bosnians to talk about their political views often elicits little more than grunts of disgust. Many blamed the politicians for leading them into war. I was told over and over again, "I'm fed up with politicians!" Or "Politicians lie!" People connected with politics were simply considered "dirty." As a result, Bosnians tried to stay clear of anything connected to politics. My hostess Kristina told me that she did not read the newspaper regularly because "it makes me nervous to read about the politicians' lies." Almost all of my host families chose to watch soap operas and music videos rather than the television news. One of the surest ways to kill a conversation among ordinary Bosnians was to mention politics.

As she tilled the soil in the garden of her home in a hamlet outside Bihać in 1999, Serb returnee Rada explained to me her political philosophy. She described an experience during her recent visit to Serbia, where people asked her how she dared return to Bosnia when another ethnic group ruled the country:

> It isn't important who rules. It's important only that the government leaves me alone to work from and with my own hands. And that there is peace. I came in May and planted and harvested vegetables, so I can survive the winter.

Rada simply wanted the government to ignore her so that she and her husband could get on with rebuilding their lives.

Young people were particularly disgruntled with politicians. Especially in impoverished Bihać, young adults tended to be so disgusted by the lack of political options that they did not vote. A college student active in a multiethnic local NGO in Mostar declared, "Youth need opportunities. Youth are fed up with politics. Politicians only make promises and never implement them." Violeta was interested in becoming more active in a major opposition party, but she had failed to gain a leadership position within the party's youth group. "Everything happens only through connections," she said. "All political parties work the same." Ana tended to agree, expressing the view that political parties would not be capable of working toward real political change until they allowed more young people to take over party leadership.

Of all political institutions, Bosnians hold political parties in the lowest regard (table 5.5), a view that is common across all of Eastern Europe (Baskin and Pickering 2007). The lack of confidence in political parties is so high across the board that those living as minorities are no less likely than those in the majority to distrust them. But minorities express significantly less confidence in the parliament and government than do those living in areas where they are in the majority. This difference is statistically significant at the 0.05 level. One time, Ana laughed heartily out of exasperation when a television news update showed representatives in Bosnia's parliament deadlocked for the umpteenth day over national symbols, an issue she considered trivial: "And we [in the Federation min-

Table 5.5. Lack of confidence in Bosnian political institutions

	Percentage lacking confidence				
Political institution	*Bošnjaks (%)* *(N = 412)*	*Croats (%)* *(N = 88)*	*Serbs (%)* *(N = 176)*	*Those living as minorities (%)* *(N = 93)*	*Those living as majorities (%)* *(N = 592)*
Political parties	84.8	80.7	88.6	81.7	85.9
Parliament	75.8	84.1	86.4	82.6	78.7
Government	64.0	70.6	76.0	76.3	67.3

Source: European Values Study Group and World Values Survey Association 2004.

istry] don't even get paid, because they can't agree on a budget!" Not surprisingly, voter turnout has decreased in Bosnia since the first multiparty elections. It slipped from 80 percent in 1990 to 70 percent in 1998, down to a low of 46.8 percent in the 2004 elections, and then to 54.5 percent in 2006 (Izborna Komisija 2006). Youth, who have expressed the most progressive views, have abstained from voting in larger percentages than older cohorts (OSCE 2004).[17]

As we saw in chapter 1, Bosnia's power-sharing rules have failed to promote either good governance or cross-ethnic cooperation among politicians. The political paralysis of the central government serves only to sap Bosnians' confidence in political institutions even further. Public trust in triethnic national-level political institutions in Bosnia is significantly lower than trust in local political institutions. While Bošnjaks, who support the Bosnian state more than the other groups, trust local political institutions only 1 percent more than central political institutions, Serbs trust local political institutions 19 percent more, and Croats trust local political institutions 31 percent more (UNDP 2004b).[18]

The political power exercised by an unelected UN High Representative has done little to increase popular confidence in Bosnia's political process. Low levels of participation result partly from the general perception that

17. When asked in May 2004 whether they intended to vote in the municipal elections in October 2004, 45.6 percent of respondents in the 18–25 age group said they would not, while only 30.7 percent of the 26–35 age group, 32 percent of the 36–50 age group, and 26 percent of the 51 and older age group said they would not (OSCE 2004).

18. While 52 percent of Bošnjaks express approval of Bosnia's parliamentary assembly, only 42 percent of Croats and 32 percent of Serbs express approval of Bosnia's parliamentary assembly. The approval ratings for the Bosnian presidency are even lower for all groups (UNDP 2004b, 47).

domestic politicians have little power in contrast to the UN High Representative, who can fire them for obstructing implementation of the Dayton Peace Agreement and can decree laws. Of those who did not vote in the 2004 elections, 43 percent explained that they had stayed home because "Bosnia and Herzegovina's politicians cannot change anything," a clear comment on the supreme power of the High Representative (UNDP 2004, 52).

The newsstand vendor mentioned above felt that the High Representative should continue to use his powers to remove corrupt politicians from power. A survey of his co-ethnics in Bošnjak-dominated areas, however, shows that only about a third of them (32 percent) share his view that the High Representative should continue to play this important role in the politics of Bosnia (UNDP 2004, 12). Bošnjaks are split over the powers of the High Representative, with another third believing that his powers should be reduced. In contrast, Serbs in Serb-dominated areas and Croats in Croat-dominated areas overwhelmingly (65 percent and 68 percent, respectively) believe that the powers of the High Representative should be reduced (UNDP 2004, 12). This stems from the perception of Croats and Serbs living as majorities that the High Representative has unfairly singled out their elected officials for removal, in effect overturning the will of the people (IDEA 2001a, 14; 2001b, 13).

I observed that those living in localities where they are in the minority are more supportive of a strong role for transnational actors in Bosnia. In Bihać, Jasna, a journalist who suffered workplace discrimination, asserted in 1999 that ordinary people were refraining from speaking their minds until the international community did something about the nationalists in power. In 2002, Ana applauded the High Representative's removal of Bugojno's SDA mayor, who had been obstructing minority return. In Banja Luka, Darija, who had battled city housing officials for four years before she and her family could reenter their private home from which they had been evicted, yearned for the day that the international community would fire the clerks in the municipal housing office who had obstructed the realization of property rights. That those living in areas where they are in the minority continue to prefer a strong role for transnational actors in the Bosnian peacebuilding process complicates already ambivalent efforts among transnational actors to transfer more authority to indigenous elites. This in turn maintains tensions between transnational actors and domestic politicians, the strongest of whom pursue exclusive statebuilding projects.

Understanding Political "Choices"

Given the range of views I heard ordinary Bosnians express about the configuration of political power in Bosnia, especially their pessimism about their capacity to influence policy, what drives the choices of those ordinary people who bother to go to the polls? The 2001 World Values Survey has some interesting data on how Bosnians' social and political views influence political behavior. In contrast to my investigation of intolerance, which focused on the views of majority group members, this time I include those Bosnians living as minorities.[19] This survey allows us to examine more systematically the views and political behavior of those living as minorities and compare them to those Bosnians living in areas where they are in the majority.[20]

The survey reveals that Bosnians living in areas where they are in the minority were just as likely as those in the majority to vote. As suggested in my interviews and observations, individuals living as minorities were significantly more likely to support moderate political parties than those living as the majority (table 5.6).

For instance, 50 percent of Bošnjaks in the Republika Srpska supported the SDP, in comparison with 28 percent of Bošnjaks in Federation towns where they were in the majority.[21] Serbs in the Federation were also more likely to support moderate parties than Serbs in the Republika Srpska. Granted, Serbs living as minorities have fewer political choices than Bošnjaks in the Republika Srpska because many of the most popular Serb parties—the SDS, the Socialist Party of the Republika Srpska, and the Serb Radical Party of the Republika Srpska—did not run in the Federation until 2004. In this sense, at the time of the survey in 2001, they must vote for moderate parties, represented by SNSD and SDP, virtually by default. If Serbs in the Federation were utterly disgruntled with their op-

19. The sampling design of the World Values Survey is not intended to identify and understand persons living as minorities in their localities. Because the survey reveals only the entities and the settlement sizes—not the municipalities—in which the respondents live, the only minorities I could identify were Bošnjaks living in the Republika Srpska, Serbs and "others" living in the Federation, and Croats living in the most populous cities of the Federation, or those with more than 100,000 inhabitants. Because I could not determine whether the remainder of Croats in the Federation were living as minority or majority, I dropped them from the sample.

20. Among the survey's limitations, however, is that it does not identify returning refugees. In addition, the survey is not designed to predict voting and thus lacks some variables commonly used to predict voting, including past voting record and evaluations of personal or national economic situations (see Lynch 2002).

21. These differences, however, are not statistically significant, probably due to the tiny number of Bošnjaks ($n = 8$) in the Republika Srpska.

Table 5.6. Voting for nationalist parties in 2001, by minority / majority status

Intended vote	Those living as minorities (%) (N = 59)	Those living as majorities (%) (N = 420)
Moderates	61.0	39.3
Nationalists	39.0	61.7

Source: European Studies Group and World Values Survey Association 2004.

Note: I labeled as *nationalist* the following parties that the World Values Survey mentions: SDA, SBiH, HDZ, SDS, SPRS, the Serb Radical Party of the RS (SRS RS), the Serb National Union (SNS), and the Party of Democratic Prosperity (PDP). Parties labeled *moderate* include: SDP, the Party of Independent Social Democrats (SNSD), the Bosnian Party (BOSS), the Democratic National Community (DNZ), the Women's Party, and the Bosnian Party of Rights (BSP), the New Croatian Initiative (NHI), and the Croatian Peasant Party (HSS BiH). Those Bosnians who did not know for whom they would vote or those who did not plan to vote were dropped from the sample.

The different preferences are statistically significant at the 0.05 level.

tions, however, they probably would have been more likely than other respondents to refrain from voting or at least express indecision about their political preferences. Yet the World Values Survey indicates that Serbs in the Federation were not less likely to vote, nor were they likelier to indicate that they could not decide on a party. These data suggest that persons living as minorities do not represent any "fifth column" seeking to undermine the postwar political system.

Quantitative analyses of factors influencing voting in Bosnia have not focused on explaining the political preference of individual Bosnians, particularly those living as minorities. Instead, these analyses have relied on municipal-level, rather than individual-level, data. They have reached somewhat contradictory conclusions about the role of diversity. Two quantitative investigations agree that municipalities in which two ethnic groups compete for demographic dominance see significantly lower support for moderate political parties (Pugh and Cobble 2001; Caspersen 2004). However, in her analysis of the 2000 elections, Nina Caspersen (2004), who labels as "heterogeneous" municipalities dominated by either two or three ethnic groups, argues that heterogeneity generally undermines support for moderate parties. In contrast, in their analysis of the 1997 local elections, Michael Pugh and Margaret Cobble (2001) found that municipalities with both a mix of all three ethnic groups and a higher density were more likely to support moderate parties.[22]

22. Coding of variables affects the findings and comparability of these results. For example, Pugh and Cobble (2001, 37–38) use the 1991 census to measure heterogeneity while Caspersen (2004, 577) relies on "electoral heterogeneity," which she infers from votes cast

As the dispute over the role of heterogeneous localities demonstrates, using municipal-level data to analyze voting has significant limitations. Municipal measures of heterogeneity and density can mask variations within those municipalities and thus confound analysis. First, there is the issue of types of heterogeneity—are there two or three ethnic groups? Furthermore, municipalities are often made up of at least one urban area, some larger villages, and many hamlets. Therefore, investigating voting patterns on the municipal level can tell us virtually nothing about voting in cities, voting in hamlets, and the like. Another obvious limitation of municipal-level data is that they can tell us nothing about individuals (Achen and Shively 1995). For example, there is no way to tell whether income levels of individuals favor any particular type of political party by looking at a municipality's average level of income.

Individual-level data, such as those provided by the World Values Survey, are critical for understanding the factors that influence how Bosnians vote. To analyze data on individual Bosnians, I created a logistic regression model to predict the likelihood that Bosnians would vote for moderate political parties.[23]

This statistical model allows me to assess the individual effect of each possible factor on political preferences. An innovative aspect of my model is that it does not assume that ethnic affiliation is the only factor that can explain a significant amount of variation in political preferences. Instead, it investigates whether self-understandings—whether measured by attachment to ethnicity or to a supraethnic national civic identity—influences voting. Furthermore, distinguishing between individuals who live

for ethnic parties. Electoral heterogeneity fails to provide information about the ethnicity of those in the municipality who refrained from voting. Pugh and Cobble's measurement is more sophisticated, even though it relies on older demographic data. In addition, it is possible that between 1997, when Pugh and Cobble analyzed election results, and 2000, when Caspersen analyzed election results, heterogeneity began to play a more negative role in supporting moderates.

23. Because of the literature's concern about what political parties should be labeled "nationalist," I tested different dependent variables to capture voting for moderates. The dependent variable used here is a dichotomous variable in which I have coded the parties as either moderate or nationalist. That is, nationalist parties include SDA, SBiH, HDZ, SDS, SPRS, SNS, PDP, and the Serb Radical Party of the Republika Srpska (SRS RS). But given discussion of "degrees" of nationalism—moderate to radical (Pugh and Cobble 2001)—I also tested with an ordered logit model a more complex dependent variable with three categories: moderate, moderate nationalist (SBiH and PDP), and radical nationalist (SDA, HDZ, SDS, SPRS, SNS). In that model, the same variables remained statistically significant as in the logit model I display here, except that urban-rural inhabitance crossed the threshold of statistical significance in that model, while it just misses it in the logit model.

Table 5.7. Predicting votes for moderate parties in Bosnia in 2001 ($N = 454$)

Independent Variables	b	$s.e.$
Social capital		
Member NGO (not religious)	.045	.229
Attend religious services	**−.205**	.057
Social identity		
Civic identification of a local minority	**1.624**	.704
Ideology		
Left-right self-placement	**−.245**	.057
Dissatisfaction		
Dissatisfaction with national office holders	.163	.165
Demographics		
Education	.078	.063
Income	−.117	.074
Age cohort	−.074	.074
Gender	−.075	.214
Rural-urban residence	.071	.046
Entity	**.664**	.257
Local minority	−.159	.485
Constant	1.441	.989

Source: European Values Study Group and World Values Survey Association 2004.
Note: See appendix G for coding of the variables used.
Log Likelihood = −269.949
Probability > χ^2 0.001
Percentage of votes correctly predicted: 68 percent

as minorities in their municipality from those who live among the majority allows me to examine how this status interacts with notions of self-understanding. My statistical model also investigates the role of social capital, both potentially bridging (membership in nonreligious NGOs) and bonding (attendance at religious services). Another group of factors it explores is the role of specific political views, such as the ideological preferences of respondents and their opinions about incumbents (dissatisfaction with national office holders). Finally, it considers the influence of demographic and socioeconomic factors. It is only with disaggregated data that I can test how individuals' backgrounds and attitudes affect political behavior in Bosnia (table 5.7).

What jumps out is the power of inclusive social identifications among Bosnians who live in municipalities where they are in the minority. Those minorities who identify first and foremost as citizens of Bosnia-Herzegovina rather than as members of a particular ethnic group are more likely to support moderate political parties. Once we control for other factors, merely living as a local minority is not enough to generate politically moderate choices. This finding reinforces results from my interviews and observation that demographic factors do not alone determine the views and behavior of Bosnians. Instead, subjective factors, such as the attachment that individuals feel toward social groups, have social and political consequences. The effort required for a minority to choose a civic over an ethnic identification is much greater and riskier for minorities than it is for Bošnjaks, who can both choose civic identity and harbor a preference for Bošnjak domination of the state. In other words, majority members do not have to choose between the civic state and their own ethnic group—minorities do.

Religious attendance weakens support for moderation, as in the case of factors influencing tolerance. This reflects not only the inward-looking mission of religious organization and the hierarchical structure of religious institutions but also the nationalist parties' use of religious authorities to mobilize support (Dizdarević 2002; Bougarel 2002).

The influence of ideological views, with those on the left more likely to support political moderates, makes sense in that communist successor parties, such as SDP, continue their heritage of preaching tolerance. It also indicates that citizens distinguish between leftist ideals, such as government responsibility and progressive social values, and rightist ideals, such as individual responsibility and traditional social values (Kitschelt et al. 1999). My analysis demonstrates that residents of the two entities (the Federation of Bosnia-Herzegovina and Republika Srpska) express systematically different views not just about social relations but also about politics. Those living in the Federation are more likely to support political moderates. This suggests not just the influence of geography but also the influence of the legacy of violence, an influx of Western aid, and less exclusivist political rhetoric in comparison to that in the Republika Srpska.

To aid in the interpretation of the statistical results, I created ideal types of respondents. These help illustrate the support that an "average" voter would give to moderate political parties as well as the support granted by "extreme" voters on opposite ends of the scales for factors found to be statistically significant (table 5.8).[24]

Several other factors are associated with support for moderate parties

24. In logistic regression, the effect of a variable depends on where in the logistic curve we are evaluating the effect. In determining the effect of each statistically significant independent variable, I have calculated the effect of each independent variable at the value specified in table 5.8 while also choosing to fix the values of all other independent variables at their means. An "average" respondent would be one with mean scores on *all* independent variables, including those statistically significant. The command in the statistical software Stata 8 is "prvalue."

Table 5.8. Interpreting support for moderate political parties

Ideal type	Probability of voting for moderate political parties
A respondent living as a minority who identifies first with her ethnicity, attends religious services more than once a day, lives in the Republika Srpska, and places herself on the far right end of the ideological spectrum	0.06
An "average" respondent[a]	0.42
A respondent living as a minority who identifies first as a citizen of Bosnia, attends church rarely, lives in the Federation, and places herself on the far left end of the ideological spectrum	0.95

Source: European Values Study Group and World Values Survey 2004.

[a]A respondent with mean scores on all independent variables, including the statistically significant ones, of a minority's self-identification, attendance of religious services, residence in Bosnia's entities, and ideology.

in ways the literature predicts, but these relationships do not reach the threshold of statistical significance. While membership in nonreligious voluntary organizations appears to increase support for moderates, the effect is not statistically significant. This finding is consistent with the results of my qualitative research on the meager influence of civic involvement in building bridges in postwar Bosnian society (see chapter 4). As with the lack of impact of education on religious tolerance, the politicization of education probably undermines its ability to increase support for moderate parties. Similarly fierce economic competition in urban areas probably saps the capacity of urban environments to increase support for moderate parties.[25]

Understanding the political preferences of returnees requires turning to a different survey. In 2001, returnees of all backgrounds to the Federation were more likely than the rest of the population to support more moderate parties, particularly SDP, yet they were also more disaffected than the electorate as a whole (Bell and Smeltz 2001, 1). This pattern does not hold among returnees to the Republika Srpska. Both Serb and, to a lesser extent, Croatian returnees to Republika Srpska in 2001 were more likely to support nationalists.[26] While minority returnees to the Repub-

25. Statistical tests found that including factors such as national minority status, Bošnjak background, and unemployed were insignificant and added nothing to the model. I therefore removed them from the model.

26. Though Bell and Smeltz do not provide data to explain why Serb returnees to the Republika Srpska are more likely to support nationalist parties than are Bošnjak returnees to the Federation, one possibility is that many Serbs fled to Serbia during the war, where

lika Srpska were more likely not to vote than minority returnees to the Federation, Serb returnees to the Republika Srpska were even more engaged than the Serb electorate as a whole (Bell and Smeltz 2001, 2).

Shaping Nationwide Social and Political Aspects of Peacebuilding

Since the signing of the Dayton Peace Agreement, grassroots trends indicate increasing support for coexistence with those who are ethnically different. That these patterns have largely held amid significant levels of minority return should increase the likelihood of sustaining those returns. Views about interethnic contact in Bosnia, as elsewhere, vary according to demographic, social, economic, and political contexts. Increasing support for coexistence among Bosnian Serbs in the Republika Srpska requires concerted efforts by international officials and domestic elites to engage them constructively.

But the Dayton constitution provides few incentives for such efforts. Most Bosnians feel powerless to influence political policy, not because of a supposed innate tendency toward passivity but rather because of their poor experiences with the present-day political institutions imposed at Dayton. This is particularly true for those living as minorities in their municipalities. These convoluted institutions empower transnational actors and, to a lesser extent, a select group of domestic elite (nationalists) over ordinary citizens or moderate political forces. Quantitative analysis indicates that the social identifications of those who live as minorities in a locality spill over and significantly influence choices between nationalist and moderate parties. Minorities with inclusive social identifications that emphasized supraethnic Bosnian identity over ethnic identity support key partners for members of the multilevel network committed to the inclusive statebuilding project in Bosnia—political parties willing to engage in interethnic cooperation. The concluding chapter explores the implications of these findings for grassroots efforts at peacebuilding in other heterogeneous societies in Eurasia.

---

the political atmosphere remained authoritarian and nationalist until the ouster of Milošević at the end of 2000. That Croatia's political system moderated a little earlier may have somewhat lifted nationalist pressure among Bosnian Croat refugees there. Bošnjaks were more likely to have been spread out in European countries and thus had greater exposure to more moderate influences.

6

Implications for Eurasia

A peace process that only involves political elites is unlikely
to bring long-term peace.

Atmar and Goodhand, 2002, 109

I have used field research and a dynamic model to understand the processes of reintegration and peacebuilding after war. What are the theoretical and practical implications raised by the multilevel model? What
do these findings mean for other postconflict areas in Eurasia?

Implications for Peacebuilding

If we want to understand how peacebuilding projects affect people, we
should start with how people react to them. Postconflict institutions need
an honest "buy in" from both elites and non-elites if they are to succeed.
To the extent that either half of that equation feels hoodwinked into ac-
quiescing to the new system, it is likely to fail. Transnational actors, when
they impose top-down approaches to peacebuilding, seem to assume that
ordinary people either obey domestic activists naturally or can be persuaded to follow their programs, thus ignoring the capacity of ordinary
people to rebuild their own lives. Ordinary citizens in postconflict societies often think that elite programs and institutions for reconstruction
are not truly intended to help them address the practical issues they confront in everyday life. This compels them to develop their own strategies
to meet their needs.

The starting point for any project in which transnational and domestic
elites seek to assist peacebuilding must be careful observation of how ordinary people navigate the multilevel network of actors to find the people and mechanisms they need to help them rebuild their lives. No
practitioner believes in a cookie-cutter approach to peacebuilding. Yet
pressure to produce results causes transnational actors to oversimplify

social and political dynamics. Transnational actors who want their peace-building projects to resonate should make fewer assumptions and listen more carefully to common people about what they need to address concerns about security, financial stability, and participation. Paying attention to ordinary people as they go about their everyday lives in real postconflict landscapes—rather than focusing on attention-getting minority activists and local brokers (Brown 2006) who purport to represent the "true" interests of citizens—is a great way to understand the conditions necessary for reconstructing more inclusive urban communities even as their residents put up with displacement, economic scarcity, nationalists, and the slow progress toward reconciliation.

Social identity theory helps to flesh out the concerns of ordinary citizens and how members of the multilevel network model interact to shape those concerns. It uncovers the variation and complexity of self-concepts, social relations, and state-society relations. In designing postconflict programs and institutions in divided societies, transnational actors must realize that they will take root only if they take into account the varied meanings that ordinary people give to ethnic labels, the social divisions that sometimes trump and always complicate ethnic ones, and the concrete needs that common people desperately require new institutions to address. Social network theory anticipates the importance of weak links in allowing minorities to bridge ethnic differences and helping them reintegrate. Such weak ties can be forged in venues that are difficult to opt out of and allow for repeated mutually dependent interaction—such as the workplace.

The multilevel model highlights the potential of forces from the bottom, albeit as part of a dynamic interactive network with other powerful actors—the nationalizing state, national and local-level minority activists, putative homeland leaders, and transnational actors. Grassroots forces are not often given much credence among scholars or practitioners. But for the first time in many postconflict states, political pluralism and the rudimentary building blocks of the rule of law are present, giving ordinary people opportunities to influence political developments. This lack of attention to non-elites risks repeating the flaws of past political systems, so often imposed from above. These systems failed to resonate with citizens, fomenting disillusionment and encouraging reliance on the informal ties that, as with prior generations, helped ordinary people cope with political institutions that do not appear to offer them a better life.

Policy Implications for Bosnia

The time I spent with Bosnians in real-life postconflict settings to flesh out the multilevel network model revealed that ordinary Bosnians—particularly those living as minorities—have reacted in ways that have undermined both the inclusive (multiethnic) and exclusive (partitionist) statebuilding projects. Rather than allowing the nationalizing state, national-level minority activists, or transnational actors to dictate their choices, individuals living as minorities struggled to protect their self-understandings and to make decisions about where to rebuild their lives in a manner consistent with values they considered important. Decisions that are *internally* driven by individuals' self-understandings contradict the prevailing explanation for migration, an interest-based theory that assumes that individuals react mechanistically to incentives determined from on high by elites and institutions.[1] Individual Bosnians' self-understandings helped them interpret job prospects and other critical issues that needed to be met to decide about where home was. That said, Serbs, Croats, and those who resisted ethnic labels living in Bošnjak areas struggled with integration and existed in a state of unsettling "in-betweenness." They are somewhat similar to Arab citizens of Israel, who have become "unduly Palestinian and marginally Israeli in their identity because exclusionary Israel does not let them become full Israelis" (Smooha 2005, 95). If opportunities are not made available to those in Bosnia who live as minorities—particularly young people—they will intensify their efforts to leave Bosnia for areas beyond the Balkans, and peacebuilding efforts will suffer.

In this environment—where elites from the nationalizing state and national-level minority activists perpetuate an exclusionary ideology and transnational actors press on with their single-minded approach to remaking the region and its peoples—ordinary people turn to traditional mechanisms to get by. These traditional strategies feature personal networks, which today serve roughly the same functions they once served during rule by outsiders (various empires) and by unaccountable domestic elites (e.g., Communists). These functions are a defense against and means of coping with the demands of distrusted political institutions and authorities (Smolar 1997, 275).

Perhaps more important, these social networks are also a mechanism for locating trusted members of a community haunted by wartime betrayals of trust. After the war, turning to the norm of reciprocity to help

---

1. Thanks to Martha Feldman for pointing this out.

with reintegration is not just naive optimism. If a gesture is not returned, then minorities abandon efforts to cultivate the relationship. It is also an approach that is rooted in tradition and seems to have at least a partial track record of success. In other words, it is a *practical* approach that is born out of necessity and tied to experience.

Direct encounters with those ethnically different willing to engage in contact in peaceful everyday life offer the most promise for individuals to recognize the importance of personal qualities over ethnic affiliations (Povrzanović 1998, 73). Local realities that require dealing with difference in everyday life are familiar to ordinary Bosnians—albeit to different degrees. Creating a secure environment should allow individuals to exercise choice about where to rebuild their lives and about what kind of interethnic interaction they would feel comfortable pursuing. This suggests that transnational actors should not punish those individuals who prefer to live among co-ethnics. Instead, they should both facilitate the return to prewar homes for those who seek to do so and assist in the construction of alternative accommodations for displaced persons who do not want to return and who lack the resources for a home in an area of relocation. They, too, confront tremendous obstacles to integration.

Developing peacebuilding strategies that accommodate the varied willingness of ordinary individuals to interact with those of different backgrounds is a challenge. Ordinary people tiptoeing around sensitive topics over a shared cup of coffee, plus indigenous leaders refusing to work toward reconciliation, makes for a formula that will never lead to peace.

In a polity run by nationalists who associate any type of heterogeneous links as a threat to their own power, such everyday ties harbor the potential for ordinary people to work together to bring about a local reality that is autonomous and diverges from nationalist dictates. Transnational actors often dismiss these informal ties as remnants of a "backward" legacy to be eradicated. They should not. Indeed, they are important indigenous cooperative networks, whose many positive aspects richly deserve support from above. Identifying and successfully bolstering these well-rooted domestic cooperative practices require that transnational actors invest time and develop approaches to working with locals that are more collaborative, less hierarchical, and less influenced by preconceived ideas of what should work. Nadia Molenaers (2003) found that local and informal horizontal cooperative networks, as in the case of farmers in rural postconflict El Salvador, were more able to generate inclusive social capital than were voluntary associations, which tended to be hierarchical.

Social capital is one of several factors, along with elites and institutions, that shape interethnic relations. Comparative research suggests that in- terethnic cooperation among ordinary people cannot prevent campaigns waged by well-armed groups to destroy ethnic coexistence (Minard 1952; Varshney 2001, 9). More extensive and durable bridging social capital re- quires an interactive process, suggested by John Paul Lederach (1997), in which inclusive grassroots initiatives gain influence and compel domes- tic elites to support them and provide opportunities.

How can transnational actors fertilize this process of more inclusive peacebuilding in Bosnia? By supporting mixed workplaces and mixed civic groups that are responsive to local communities. The most produc- tive approach would encourage nondiscriminatory workplaces as well as expand the economy in general, rather than radically redistribute em- ployment among ethnic groups. This would still be difficult because of the ramifications of challenging nationalist control over patronage. Yet trying to foster economic growth and integration while ignoring nation- alists entrenched in the most profitable enterprises is bound to fail. One lesson a high-level former U.S. policymaker learned from the Bosnian peacebuilding experience was the severe setback for fostering sustainable peace that was created by the unwillingness to break the nationalists' grip over the economy as early as possible.[2] Even in Iraq, U.S. policymakers have recently recognized the essential capacity of jobs in helping ordinary people to provide for themselves and their families and thus make them less susceptible to extremism (White and Witte 2006).

The international community could make a difference by investing in open and heterogeneous small businesses and civic initiatives that build on local talent and seem likely to improve the lives of ordinary people. After that, it is important to monitor how aid is used by employers who are at least initially inclusive and how much of it helps ordinary workers build bridging ties and financial stability.

The sustainability of mixed areas in Bosnia will rest partly on the abil- ity of minorities to find both employment and arenas for reaching beyond ethnicity to establish relationships of reciprocity and inclusive identifica- tions. Scholars of peacebuilding in Afghanistan who urged the impor- tance of "reaching people on the fence," who have not yet chosen between transnational actors' and extremists' visions of peacebuilding (Cole and Bajpai 2006, 1), seem to make an appropriate suggestion for Bosnia. This would also realize the long-overdue priority of supporting *sustainable* returns (Donais 2005), rather than merely repossessing homes. Transna-

---

2. Interview with former senior U.S. policymaker actively engaged in Bosnia, Wash- ington D.C., September 2005.

tional actors from the High Representative and the UN High Commissioner for Refugees (UNHCR) have only focused on the sustainability of returns since the mid-2000s. It also suggests that conflicts within the U.S. assistance community over whether to emphasize development aid or democracy aid (Carothers 1999) are, in Bosnia's case, counterproductive because Bosnians need both kinds of aid. It should be possible to work toward both goals by assisting in the development of small businesses, enterprises, and cooperatives that commit to nondiscriminatory hiring policies and workplace environments.

In light of the variety of views expressed by ordinary people about how best to go about rebuilding their lives, a peacebuilding strategy that constructs political institutions on the assumption that Bosnian society is any one way (cosmopolitan and tolerant or ethnically divided and intolerant) seems destined to failure. Neither a Bosnian state that enshrines demographic and political separation nor a polity based on multiculturalism appears to be a recipe for durable peacebuilding in Bosnia. More specifically, enshrining rules that provide for the viability of only ethnic parties would be as flawed as abolishing ethnic parties (as an ill-fated attempt in Nigeria shows). There must be a way to implement less formal power-sharing rules that can cultivate cooperation at the elite level and confidence and participation at the grassroots level. Some seem to think that elections will automatically jump-start democracy with no thought to the capabilities of domestic institutions or the conditions on the ground. Scholars of postconflict states (Bose 2002; Lyons 2002) demonstrate that these ideas are unlikely to contribute to a stable peace. Listening to the interpretations of ordinary Bosnians about political policies and postconflict institutions should be a key part of efforts for building sustainable peace.

Neither the inclusive nor the exclusive statebuilding project has won out in Bosnia, a reality evident from analysis of elites and institutions (Bose 2002; Bieber 2005; Rhea 2006) and of ordinary citizens presented here. If transnational actors really want to help build a sustainable peace in Bosnia, they must stick around, listen to both domestic elites and ordinary people, adapt and make more collaborative their approaches, and engage in the follow-up activities necessary to create new institutions that resolve conflicts amicably. The Balkans may have been out of the headlines for the past few years, but the challenges to peacebuilding there remain. If ongoing negotiations over the final status of Serbia's province of Kosovo have already destabilized the political situation in Bosnia and Serbia, the negotiation's outcome holds the potential for more serious reverberations in these deeply divided societies. Further afield, the disintegration in mid-2006 of what appeared to be a stable peace in East Timor provides a valuable lesson for peacebuilding. Factors viewed as contributing to the unraveling of peace there include premature withdrawal of UN troops and the failure of indigenous leaders to connect with ordinary people, prevent corruption and discrimination, and build institutions that address grassroots needs (Kurlantzick 2006). Peacebuilding requires long-term, carefully crafted engagement.

Lessons for Eurasia

The multilevel network model should improve our understanding of peacebuilding in other divided postconflict societies in Eurasia. A cross-national study of grassroots approaches to peacebuilding requires significant field research in each society. However, we can begin to explore how my findings tally with peacebuilding elsewhere in the region by looking at research. Applying the model requires investigating the complexity of ethnic and social relations, so I begin by focusing on social relations in these societies. I then examine how members of the multilevel model have contributed to or worked against conflict in each case. The model urges special attention to ordinary people, whose self-conceptions, needs, and customs shape their reactions to postconflict projects and institutions. How well do these new institutions meet those needs and support indigenous practices of cooperation and conflict prevention? Based on my study of Bosnia, we should expect self-conceptions to help minorities interpret the incentives offered by network actors in deciding where to rebuild their homes. We should also anticipate that minorities seek out institutions that allow for repeated horizontal interaction to help them cultivate the bridging ties that provide concrete help. Finally, we should expect that ordinary people, particularly minorities, who get shut out of the design of postconflict institutions will keep their distance from them, which inhibits their ability to gain credibility. The model prioritizes looking at empirical evidence from all levels of society as the basis for policy suggestions for building sustainable peace.

Where shall we apply the multilevel network model? Other areas of the Balkans offer the closest cases for comparison to peacebuilding in Bosnia. The postconflict "near abroad" shares the socialist experience and influence of putative homelands, but its predominant minority—Russians—have shallower roots in the region, and Western-led transnational intervention has been minimal in comparison with the Balkans. Finally, southwest

Asia shares a history of rule by empires and the interference of putative homelands, but Western-led intervention there faces challenges not present in Bosnia, including terrorists and crushing poverty.

Kosovo

Tensions between the two groups that dominate Serbia's province of Kosovo—Albanians (90 percent) and Serbs (7 percent)—boiled over several times even during the Socialist period (1945–1991) (Baskin 1983). Two separate studies conducted in 1990 found that Kosovo's inhabitants expressed the most ethnically intolerant views of any of Yugoslavia's peoples (Pantić 1991, 180; Hodson, Sekulić, and Massey 1994). Though there were exceptions in several urban areas, Kosovo's Albanians and Serbs, whose languages are not mutually comprehensible, have led largely separate lives. In the 1980s, Belgrade suppressed both Kosovar Albanian claims for greater autonomy and Kosovar Serb accusations of Albanian attacks on them.[3] After President Milošević revoked the province's autonomy in 1989, Kosovar Albanians built a parallel community, establishing their own schools and institutions to provide services. During a 1995 visit, a Kosovar Serb human rights activist told me that she and others who engaged in interethnic cooperation were threatened by leaders of their own groups.[4] Ethnic relations disintegrated further after the rural Albanian population finally gave up on a fruitless, decade-long nonviolent resistance movement led by Albanian urban intellectuals. Then Albanian extremists advocating secession attacked Serb police, Serb civilians, and Albanians working for the Serb authorities in Kosovo, drawing reprisals from Serb security forces (OSCE 1999c, 4). During these attacks and the NATO bombing in 1999, half of the Albanian population fled (OSCE 1999c, 1; International Crisis Group [ICG] 2000b).

Transnational actors' peacebuilding plan involved peacekeepers, a UN civilian administration to "oversee the substantial autonomy" for Kosovo, and power-sharing arrangements that guaranteed Serb participation. Shortly after the UN's deployment, however, most Kosovar Albanians returned to their homes, while half of Kosovo's Serb population fled or were compelled to flee (ICG 2000b). War only increased the already significant ethnic distance between the province's Serbs and Albanians.

The policies of the "putative homeland" of Serbia, which still consid-

---

3. Though the extent of these attacks is disputed, evidence indicates that they did occur. A Serb human rights group investigation, however, found that Serb claims of Albanians committing systematic rape against Serb women were erroneous (Ramet 1999, 307). See also Mertus (1999) on the role of myths in sparking conflict in Kosovo.

4. Interviews with local human rights activists in Kosovo, July 1995.

ers Kosovo an integral part of it, and of the Albanian-dominated nationalizing "state" have undermined peacebuilding. Kosovar Albanian authorities and international peacekeepers have further exacerbated the dismal conditions for minorities by failing to provide physical security for Serbs in Kosovo. Of the 200,000 Serbs and other minorities who fled Kosovo in 1999, only 13,000 had returned by the end of 2005 despite efforts by transnational actors ("The Balkans" 2005, 26). Those few Kosovar Serbs remaining in Albanian-majority urban areas have been subjected to a level of systematic violence after the war that minorities in Bosnia were not. As recently as March 2004, thousands of Serbs in Kosovo were expelled and hundreds of buildings and churches were destroyed when some 50,000 Albanians rioted in apparent retaliation for the mysterious deaths of Albanian children in Mitrovica ("The Balkans" 2005). The continuing violence against minorities significantly complicates transnational actors' efforts to build a peace that accommodates both minorities and Albanians.

As in Bosnia, extremists have held power over ethnic groups and have engaged in ethnic engineering after the war to create ethnically dominant areas. With the exceptions of divided Mitrovica and a few Serb-dominated pockets in the province, Serbs in Kosovo have largely abandoned urban areas for Serb-dominated areas in the northern districts of Kosovo—where Serbia maintains a parallel local government and social services ("The Balkans" 2005). The security situation is so poor that they rarely leave these enclaves. Much like in Bosnia, local minority activists have resisted both Belgrade leaders, who want Serbs to relocate to areas of the province where they are in the majority ("Sofia Declaration" 1999, 1; Sell 2001, 7), and Albanian leaders of the nationalizing "state," who want them to leave for Serbia proper.

Psychological attachment to local communities appears to influence those ordinary people who have attempted to rebuild their lives in their original homes in areas where they are in the minority. Those Serbs who stayed in the village of Kosovo Polje have lived there for generations, while those with more shallow roots—say, residents for less than ten years—have fled (OSCE Mission in Kosovo 2000, para. 51). In comparison with Serbs in Bošnjak areas, however, those Serbs who have stayed in Kosovo have less opportunity for choice; most of them appear to be "stuck" due to lack of resources to start over.

Consistent with my findings on the mechanisms minorities use for coping in tense, mixed settings, weak ties and reputation have helped some Serbs find employment in the Albanian-dominated business community (OSCE Mission in Kosovo 2000). Interethnic ties, however, have often not been able to overcome the dense kinship ties among Albanians. The public sector, which represents the primary employer of minorities in Kosovo, employs less than 1 percent of minority communities (OSCE and UNHCR 2003). So far, economic relationships between separate Serb and Albanian communities have been tremendously difficult. Belgrade-funded parallel Serb structures in northern Kosovo have lured Serbs into monoethnic jobs.

As in Bosnia, transnational actors have focused on building civil society by funneling money to voluntary organizations. Julie Mertus (2004) has criticized transnational actors for imposing NGO structures on Kosovo that fail to recognize indigenous mechanisms for development and activism, such as community networks. Conflict resolution projects that the international NGO CARE conducted in thirty multiethnic villages were a productive exception; they may have been the reason that those villages avoided the violence of March 2004 (ICG 2004). The ability of the Mitrovica citywide youth council to include members from both sides of the divided city also illustrates how transnational organizations can support bridging social capital with strong domestic roots, even in such a polarized environment. The international NGO Catholic Relief Services, which has a long track record in the province, initially worked with separate high school youth councils on conflict resolution and community development. When the youth councils from Albanian schools and Serb schools eventually met up, they formed a citywide youth council to work jointly on common practical problems they faced: lack of school equipment, classroom space, good student-teacher interaction, and security (U.S. Institute of Peace [USIP] 2005). As with the multiethnic youth groups in Mostar and Bihać, a youth leader told me one of the keys to developing these bridging relationships: "We believe in this organization because it is not about politics but about concrete things."

The UN has established a protectorate in Kosovo that grants only minimal powers to elected officials. Despite transnational efforts to cultivate local democracy, Albanians and Serbs are extremely disaffected with their political institutions (Baskin 2005). Anne Holohan's (2005, 5) field-based research found that the municipalities most successful in building institutions, cross-ethnic participation, and reconstruction were the ones where transnational actors directly incorporated local organizations and citizens into the process and worked with them in a mutually dependent manner. In an ominous sign for peacebuilding, voter turnout has progressively declined overall, and Serbs boycotted the last elections (UNDP 2004c). The widespread violence in March 2004 drove home the fragility of these new *formal* institutions: "Within hours virtually all the domestic institutions built up . . . with international tutelage and money to act as bulwarks of 'democratization' gave way" (ICG 2004, 24).

Croatia

Croatia, too, challenged dominance by Belgrade during Socialist rule in Yugoslavia, in this case in 1970, when Croatian elites called for additional autonomy, a demand rejected by Tito. Before the war, 500,000 Serbs lived in Croatia. Fewer than half of those lived in localities where they were the dominant group, adjacent to Bosnia (in the Krajina) or Serbia (Eastern Slavonia), with most of the rest dispersed in urban areas of Croatia. Ethnic distance between Croats (mainly Catholic) and Serbs (mainly Orthodox) in Croatia was narrower than that between Serbs and Albanians in Kosovo but wider than existed among the groups in Bosnia just prior to the outbreak of violence (Massey, Hodson, and Sekulić 1999, 683). Intermarriage rates in urban areas of Croatia and Bosnia were similar, from 25 to 35 percent of marriages ethnically mixed (Borba 1991). On the eve of the war, polls found that most Serbs and Croats judged interethnic relations as good (Gagnon 2004, 35–36).

In 1990, the policies of Milošević and newly elected Croatian President Tudjman stoked fear in Croatia's Serbs. Milošević claimed that Serbs could never live as minorities, while Tudjman pushed through a new Croatian Constitution that paved the way for independence and officially relegated Serbs to minority status. Furthermore, the Tudjman-led nationalizing state removed many non-Croats from the police and the judiciary, where they had been overrepresented, as well as resurrected symbols connected with the World War II fascist puppet state of Croatia. Milošević orchestrated the assistance of the putative homeland's Yugoslav army and Serb paramilitary groups to Croatian Serbs living in rural areas of Croatia so that they could wage a war of secession from Croatia (Magaš and Zanić 2001). As an integral part of their strategy for gaining control over territory for an independent state, Croatian Serb extremists practiced ethnic cleansing, in a foretaste of the strategies that Bosnian Serb extremists would employ. During this campaign for independence, Serb rebels killed an estimated 10,000 Croats (Cohen 1997, 104). Some 250,000 Serbs fled or were forced to flee Croatia between the beginning of war in 1991 and the reintegration in 1998 of the last part of Serb-held land; an estimated 900 Serbs were killed in the Croatian offensive against Krajina in 1995 (Amnesty International 1998).

Human rights observers criticized the Croatian government's treatment of minorities throughout the 1990s and beyond. As in the case of Bosnia and Kosovo, this policy of ethnic engineering has taken advantage of the grievances of displaced members of the majority to hamper minority return and interethnic relationships in mixed areas. Only about a third (106,000) of displaced Serbs have returned home since 1990 (OSCE 2004), underscoring the minority status of Serbs. The election of a non-nationalist government in 2000 and its adoption of less-discriminatory policies helped spur minority return (UNHCR 2000). Yet, legislation still favors squatters, who are generally Croat refugees from Bosnia (of which there are some 25,000) or Croats displaced from other areas of Croatia. And the uneven implementation of new property laws still makes it difficult for minority refugees to reclaim their homes and return permanently (Human Rights Watch 2004).

Consistent with my findings on the role of psychological ties on the migration decisions that ordinary people make after war, 65 percent of Croatian Serbs who returned to their homes were motivated by a desire to return to their communities and their neighbors with whom they had shared experiences (Sweeney 2001, 2). On the other hand, a survey of Croatian Serb refugees now living in Serbia who had decided against return found that two-thirds of them felt that they belonged to their current communities rather than their prewar communities (OSCE 2004, 26). Research on persons in mixed marriages in Croatia found that they were more likely to remain in their community if they had built up bridging social networks in their communities before the war (Agger 1995). Survey data suggest that age played an even greater role in influencing minorities to return to Croatia than I found in return to Bošnjak areas in Bosnia. While two-thirds of those minority returnees to Bošnjak areas were of working age, about half of the minorities who returned to Croatia were under 65 (UNHCR 1999). Furthermore, aid workers also reported that many of those 9,000 Serbs who stayed even after the Croatian military recaptured Serb-occupied territory in 1995 were elderly people, who were less willing or able to move (Amnesty International 1998).

Intervention by transnational actors was limited in Croatia to UN peacekeeping missions with weak mandates and, in the case of Eastern Slavonia, temporary civil authority. These efforts failed to convince minorities that they were protected or Croats that their efforts were just. In the end, the transition of these areas under UN protection to the nationalizing state's authorities led to a significant exodus of minorities.

As in Bosnia and Kosovo, the war radicalized opinions about ethnic relations. The hostile views of Croats toward Serbs have discouraged the return and reintegration of minorities. In 1995, 80 percent of Croats rejected having a Serb as a close relative, and 60 percent rejected Serbs as a neighbor or a colleague (Kasapović 2001, 313). A 1996 survey found that those Croats who had experienced property damage and violence during the war were more likely to express both strong affiliation with their ethnicity and less trust of Serbs (Kunovich and Hodson 1999, 655).[5] In other words, these Croats were the most likely both to view their identity in an ethnically exclusive way and to express the highest levels of intolerance toward Serbs. In 2004, most Croats (66 percent) were "not happy" about Serbs returning to their prewar villages, and one-third feared that returning Serbs might start the war over again (OSCE 2004, 56). As elsewhere in the former Yugoslavia, rural-urban differences significantly influenced tolerance, with urban Croats expressing less intolerance than rural Croats before, during, and after the war (Sekulić, Massey, and Hodson 2006).

Most Serbs live in economically depressed rural areas of Croatia, which further limits possibilities for generating bridging ties.[6] Most Croats believe that interethnic relations would normalize if the economy improved (OSCE 2004, 30). In the still-struggling economy, minority returnees are at the bottom of employers' list of desired employees. A colleague in Zagreb observed that once tourism and the local economic situation improved in Plitvica, interethnic relations improved as well. Although the 2002 Constitutional Law on the Rights of National Minorities mandates proportional representation of minorities in the judiciary, police, and administration, Croatian authorities have filled almost none of those slots with Serb *returnees*. This undermines the government's message that they are willing to accept minority return. Serb returnees have found better employment opportunities in private businesses than in state institutions (Human Rights Watch 2004, 13). Though some of these jobs are only seasonal, they assist reintegration by offering salaries and opportunities for interethnic cooperation.

Not surprisingly, transnational actors have focused on cultivating civil society by supporting voluntary organizations. The most successful groups in attracting members and participants have addressed local issues and avoided politics (USAID 2004). Perceptions of widespread corruption in the civil service have recently decreased social capital that ordinary people in Croatia generate (Štulhofer 2004).

---

5. The violence index used in this survey is the sum of affirmative responses to the following questions: "Did you have any of these war-related experiences: forcefully emigrated, life endangered, a relative was in life-threatening danger, a friend was in life-threatening danger, relatives disappeared, friends disappeared, relatives wounded, friends wounded, family member attacked, relatives attacked, friends attacked, relatives captured, friends captured, family forcefully emigrated, relatives forcefully expelled, friends forcefully emigrated, relatives killed, friends killed?" (Kunovich and Hodson 1999, 665).

6. Serbs in urban areas of Croatia deserve further investigation.

Serbs are now guaranteed political representation, with 3 of the 148 seats in the Croatian parliament reserved for Serbs. Turnout among Serbs was low in 2003 elections (OSCE / ODIHR 2003, 18), an indication of dissatisfaction with this political system. The most powerful transnational actor in Croatia is now, through its lure of membership, the European Union (EU). The coveted carrot of EU membership helped convince the Croatian Democratic Community (HDZ), which retook power at the end of 2003, to adopt policies more hospitable to return. In an encouraging gesture of cross-ethnic political cooperation, HDZ leaders in 2004 offered to promote minority return in exchange for Serb politicians' pledge to support the new HDZ-led government (Judah 2004). The practical results of HDZ's overture have been very modest so far.

Macedonia

This highly contentious country, which managed to extricate itself peacefully from a disintegrating Yugoslavia, suffered only a brief conflict between its two predominant groups, Slavic Macedonians (64 percent of the population) and Albanians (25 percent) (Republika Makedonija 2003). Most ethnic Macedonians, who are Orthodox, and Albanians, who are primarily Muslim, live in adjacent communities rather than being intermixed, with most ethnic Macedonians urbanized and many Albanians in rural areas. An estimated half of the Albanian population lives in compact and homogeneous communities in northwest Macedonia that border Albania and Serbia's Albanian-majority province of Kosovo (ICG 2001, 8), a factor that encourages irredentism. In a 1990 survey, citizens of Macedonia expressed the least tolerance toward those ethnically different of all citizens of the former Yugoslavia except for Kosovars (Hodson et al. 1994, 1548). In 1990, only 19 percent of ethnic Macedonians would consider marrying a hypothetical Albanian partner, while 17 percent of Albanians would consider marrying an ethnic Macedonian (Pantić 1991, 180).

Before the initiation of violence by Albanian extremists in 2001, observers of the Balkans considered the regime in Macedonia to be the most adept of all of the former Yugoslav states at managing its minorities (Mickey and Albion 1993). This is despite, or perhaps because of, the serious external and internal threats it faces. The external threats include efforts by extremist Albanians to destabilize Macedonia. They also involve efforts by nationalists in Greece and Bulgaria to weaken it. Macedonia's ethnic Albanians, who even before the 2001 violence resented their minority status and marginalization, pose the most serious internal threat. Though Albanian parties have consistently won seats in parliament, and their politicians have regularly been appointed as government ministers,

Albanians have not been well integrated into the Macedonian state—whether politically, socially, or economically (Perry 1997, 252). In 1990, Albanians won local elections in the towns of Gostivar and Tetovo, but the ethnic Macedonian-dominated government did not allow them to take office. In response, Albanian leaders formed a shadow administration (Mickey and Albion 1993, 77). In the mid-1990s, they claimed that Albanians composed only 3 percent of the country's public officials and professionals (Xhaferi 1998, 5).

As in Kosovo, the languages of the two dominant groups are not mutually comprehensible, a factor that contributes to distance between the two communities. Albanian leaders contended up until 2001 that requiring Albanian students to study in Macedonian strongly discouraged Albanians from gaining a university education (Schmidt 1995, 29; Perry 2007, 259). In 1995 Albanians created an unofficial Albanian-language university in Tetovo that the government forcibly shut down, over the objections of all four Albanian political parties (Brown 2000, 5). The Organization for Security and Cooperation in Europe (OSCE) cobbled together a compromise agreement about the South East European University in Tetovo that allows for teaching in Albanian, Macedonian, and English.

Despite the distance between Macedonians and Albanians, the bulk of both communities support coexistence within the same state. In contrast with the views of Albanians in Kosovo, who overwhelmingly believe that Kosovo should be only for Albanians, just one-third of ethnic Macedonians in 1993 believed that Macedonia should be only for Macedonians (MacIver 1993). Just as important, polls showed that Albanians possessed dual identities—both to their ethnicity and to the state (USIA 2000, 6),[7] a factor that Brewer (2001) thinks should encourage compromise in divided societies. But the violence between Macedonians and Albanians in 2001 strained those attitudes. With the encouragement and assistance of Albanian extremists in Kosovo, Albanian rebels in Macedonia used violence to achieve greater autonomy from the state (ICG 2001, 9; Hislope 2002). Fighting between Macedonian Albanian rebels and Macedonian government forces displaced 150,000 citizens. The restraint exhibited by putative homelands—Serbia and Albania—who were less able and interested in intervening than in the cases of Bosnia, Croatia, and Kosovo, probably helped prevent full-blown war.

7. The Albanian respondents described themselves as: "primarily Albanian, and then a citizen of Macedonia" (50 percent); "only Albanian" (29 percent); "primarily a citizen of Macedonia, then Albanian" (9 percent); "equally Albanian and a citizen of Macedonia" (8 percent); or "only a citizen of Macedonia" (3 percent). The survey was based on a nationally representative sample of 1,007 adults in Macedonia (USIA 2000, 1, 6).

The early and concerted international mediation by EU and U.S. offi-cials in Macedonia gave transnational actors more latitude to forge a framework more suitable for consolidating peace in Ohrid than occurred in Dayton, which had to cater more to nationalists. In interviews I con-ducted with Western policymakers and practitioners, transnational ac-tors seem to have learned key lessons from Bosnia that they tried to apply to Macedonia. These included intervening quickly after the onset of vio-lence, working to facilitate the domestic capacity to build peace rather than injecting itself into regional politics, designing more flexible power-sharing rules, and deploying mixed police forces to communities that suf-fered violence to bolster security for the return of displaced persons.[8]

Despite reasons for pessimism, there is evidence, as in Bosnia, that eth-nically heterogeneous urban areas have been less prone to the interethnic violence (in this case between ethnic Macedonians and Albanians) that has plagued more ethnically homogeneous areas. A local human rights leader has argued that communities with more experience with diversity are less hospitable to extremism (Smith 2001).

Kumanovo, which is two-thirds ethnic Macedonian, one-fifth Alba-nian, and one-tenth Serbian, is an example. Efforts by a municipality gov-ernment commission working with voluntary associations of ethnic Macedonians and Albanians have helped keep the peace. The NGOs in Kumanovo are ethnically homogeneous groups that have been cooperat-ing to prevent interethnic violence, not the multiethnic associations that Varshney advocates for building the kind of bridging social capital that can best preserve peace in divided communities (2001). But the traditions of Macedonian society make it difficult for ethnic Macedonian and Al-banian leaders to spread the word together publicly (Smith 2001). So members of the multiethnic municipal commission worked at lower lev-els by appealing to their respective constituencies, while Albanian com-mission members appealed to voluntary groups of Albanians and local Albanian political activists to work to maintain peace and to refrain from any activities, such as rallies, that might incite violence (Naegele 2001). Despite its weaknesses, this interethnic cooperation in the midst of in-

---

8. Interviews with former U.S. and EU policymakers, Washington, D.C., September 2005. Although the Ohrid Framework Agreement mandated power-sharing arrangements in Macedonia, such as a vital interest veto, raising Albanian to the status of an official lan-guage, an increase in Albanian representation in state institutions, and decentralization, it stopped short of imposing ethnic quotas in parliament and government and ethnic-based federalism (Pearson 2002). Furthermore, its vital interest veto is more clearly and narrowly defined than in Bosnia, creating greater possibilities for effective multiethnic governance in Macedonia (European Commission 2005).

terethnic violence elsewhere shows the power of local voices of interpretation and practice.[9]

Other mixed localities where community leaders have worked together to avoid violence include Cair (Daskalovski 2004) and Gostivar. In the latter case, Albanian youth told me that they credited good leadership and the traditional mixture of the town's neighborhoods, schools, and social life with allowing the town's citizens to "find a common 'language.'"[10] They also acknowledged urban–rural divisions by identifying the composition of the town's Albanian community as another key ingredient in maintaining peace. Macedonians who grew up in Gostivar found communication possible with the town's Albanian inhabitants, the bulk of whom had also grown up there and who shared its urban traditions. In comparison, Macedonians who had been raised in Tetovo found communication difficult with their town's Albanian inhabitants, many of whom consisted of newcomers from surrounding villages and Kosovo, who "do not know how to behave" in town.

Consistent with my findings on the possibilities for economic cooperation in Bosnia are the results of a nationally representative sample survey in Macedonia. This survey, conducted by the UN Development Programme (2003b, 70–71), found that more ethnic Macedonians and Albanians are willing to do business (61 percent) or share a workplace (70 percent) with a person of another ethnicity than they are to share a neighborhood (54 percent). The postconflict constitution provides for proportionality in the police and civil administration, which should increase opportunities for generating bridging ties with colleagues from the workplace, which are otherwise limited by ethnic Macedonians' domination of public institutions and Albanians' concentration in the private sector (Smith 2001).

In a clear sign of the willingness of minorities to engage in new political institutions viewed as more responsive to their needs, Albanians turned out in large numbers in the first elections in Macedonia after the violence. They punished corrupt Albanian officeholders and supported the new party of the former leader of the Albanian rebel movement, who campaigned on implementation of the framework agreement at Ohrid and "integration." Though Albanians distrust state institutions, they express higher trust in the post-Ohrid constitution than in its predecessor (European Values 2004). This is a positive sign for peacebuilding. As was

9. Keith Brown, Balkans Working Group meeting, U.S. Institute of Peace, Washington, D.C., October 1998.
10. Interviews with Albanian young men, Gostivar, July 2006.

the case in Croatia, the EU carrot has encouraged nationalizing state elites to moderate their policies toward minorities. However, poverty, continued ethnic distance and parallelism (Brown 2000), a still unsettled regional neighborhood, and EU enlargement fatigue combine to maintain fragile conditions in Macedonia. Indications of the still-delicate situation include intra-Albanian violence during the 2006 parliamentary election campaign (Božinovska 2006) and the leading Albanian party's monthslong boycott of parliament in 2007 after the election's conservative Macedonian victors formed a government with a less popular Albanian party.

Tajikistan

Unlike minorities in Yugoslavia, Russians in the Central Asian state of Tajikistan are not indigenous to the region and are viewed by Tajiks as unwelcome reminders of empire. After being dispatched by Moscow to Central Asian cities with the import of industrialization between 1926 and 1970, Russians came to constitute an economic elite concentrated in urban areas (Chinn and Kaiser 1996, 213). In 1990, Tajikistan was 63 percent ethnic Tajik (mainly Muslim), 25 percent Uzbek (mainly Muslim), and 8 percent Russian (mainly Orthodox) (Chinn and Kaiser 1996, 209). Partly due to Russia's conquest of Tajikistan, relations between ordinary ethnic Tajiks and Russians have rarely been close. As in Kosovo and Macedonia, the languages of the communities are not mutually comprehensible, which reinforces ethnic distance. Only 30 percent of Tajiks in 1990 claimed fluency in Russian (Olcott 1990, 266).

After the Soviet Union disintegrated in 1991, the citizens of Tajikistan elected a Communist as president in their first multiparty elections. The president could not control various political factions, and the country disintegrated into violence that was not ethnic in nature but rather clanbased (Slim and Hodizoda 2002). Some 40,000 people died in the war, which also displaced nearly a million. However, Russians also got caught up in the violence, particularly as the war dragged on and sentiment against "outsiders" increased and troops from the putative homelands—Russia and Uzbekistan—together with other Central Asian states intervened to back the Communists. The 1997 Moscow peace accord that ended the war created a power-sharing agreement among the warring parties, including the only legal Islamic party in post-Soviet Central Asia (Helsinki Commission 2006). Western-based transnational actors have had little influence on Tajik politics, deferring to Russia's strategic interests in the region. Russia's priority of stability in the region supports the goals of dominant domestic elites in Tajikistan to maintain a political system that restricts political rights.

In general, the influence of Islamic groups in Tajikistan, the war, and widespread poverty has helped convince the Russians in Tajikstan that there is no future for them there. By 1992, one-third of Russian respondents who had remained in the Central Asian republic had firmly decided to leave (Chinn and Kaiser 1996, 233–35).[11] By 2005, the Russian population had dwindled to 1.1 percent of the population (OSCE/ODIHR 2006). The Russians who stayed appear to exhibit some patterns consistent with my findings on minorities in Bosnia. Those Russians who felt, through long-term residence in Central Asia, that they shared some common aspects of culture with the local population were the most likely to stay in the Central Asia states (Olcott 1996, 552).[12] As an indication of how many Russians felt this way, less than a quarter of all Russians in Tajikistan considered Tajikistan to be their "homeland" (Chinn and Kaiser 1996, 234). Even though Tajikistan has experienced interethnic violence, minority activists for those Russians who have decided to stay have pointedly told journalists from Russia that Tajiks are not difficult to live with and that interethnic cooperation is possible (Kolsto 1995, 214).

As a moderating influence, most officials in the putative homeland of Russia consider it strategically useful for Russians to remain in Central Asia (Olcott 1996; Chinn and Kaiser 1996). Furthermore, representatives of the Russian Orthodox Church in Tajikistan have encouraged Russians to stay there by appealing to the perceived cultural differences between Russians from Russia and Russians from Tajikistan (Kolsto 1995, 214). They have warned Russians born in Tajikistan of the cool reception they would likely receive if they decided to return to Russia, implying that they would be viewed more as Tajikistanis than as Russians. Jeff Chinn and Robert Kaiser (1996, 235) found that Russians' decisions to stay in or leave Central Asia depend on

> a complex set of factors including regional economic conditions, the degree to which the state is promoting indigenization, the level of anti-Russian sentiments and nativism, the degree of political stability in the republic, and the degree to which each individual Russian has come to view the Central Asian republic as home.

As with minorities in Bošnjak areas, then, a minority's sense of belonging to Tajikistan interacts with other factors, including economic ones and the opinions of members of the majority, to influence decisions about migration.

11. About one-third of the prewar Russian population of 433,481 had left Tajikistan by 1993 (Chinn and Kaiser 1996), 231.
12. Nadezhda Lebedeva, as quoted in Olcott 1996, 552.

As elsewhere in the region, transnational actors have sought to strengthen civil society through aiding voluntary organizations. The problem is that these organizations have even weaker roots in Central Asian society than in the Balkans and almost no domestic support. As a result, their activities are often driven by donors and not domestic constituents (USAID 2004). One assessment found that these incentives left "local communities at times not reaping much benefit" from projects designed by Western-funded NGOs (Foroughi 2006, 10). Furthermore, these organizations are concentrated in the city and staffed by elite activists who are educated in Russia and "lack real connections" to the local people, particularly in rural areas (Slim and Hodizoda 2002, 180). Civic organizations also have no connections to a traditional local institution in civil society—the *mahalla,* or village council. While this organization is a bonding, monoethnic, and local one that usually excludes women, it is often useful in settling local disputes (Slim and Hodizoda 2002, 179). Several international NGOs have successfully used the *mahalla* in their rural development projects (Foroughi 2006, 2). Transnational actors could benefit from working more with the *mahallas* while encouraging them to be more inclusive.

The authoritarian political system's hostility toward independent social groups further weakens these NGOs. This hostility only increased after civic organizations participated in a largely nonviolent uprising that brought down the authoritarian leader of neighboring Kyrgyzstan in 2005. Due to dominant political elites' opposition to independent groups, NGOs prefer to operate under the radar of tax authorities and criminals, which further limits their activities.

The possibility of workplace ties to facilitate everyday interethnic cooperation in Tajikistan is constrained by the traditional Russian dominance of economically powerful positions. In addition, the increasing number of skilled Russian workers who have emigrated has forced the closing of many Central Asian enterprises, which has ruled out some possibilities for interethnic interaction in the workplace and has led to some anti-Russian sentiment (Chinn and Kaiser 1996, 235). But the workplace and economic life still remain key venues for interethnic cooperation.

Ruling political elites have not fully implemented provisions stipulated in the 1997 peace accord, such as reserving 30 percent of government posts to oppositionists (Foroughi 2006, 6). The concentration of power in the Tajik presidency has facilitated President Emomali Rahmonov's efforts to flout aspects of the peace accord. International observers of the tainted 2005 parliamentary elections in Tajikistan noted low levels of political participation and a reluctance to speak out against the government (OSCE/ODIHR 2005, 8). In the 2006 presidential elections, university students were bussed into—and apparently required to attend—campaign meetings held by the ruling party (OSCE/ODIHR 2006, 7). The postconflict political institutions cater to a desire for stability, but shut out ordinary citizens, whether majority or minority, from meaningful participation. This raises questions about the level of grassroots support for this peacebuilding project.

Afghanistan

The six major ethnic groups that inhabit Afghanistan have suffered decades of war since the Soviets supported a coup there in the 1970s. A multilevel network has been active in stirring up conflict in Afghanistan, with putative homelands—Iran and Pakistan in particular—pursuing their strategic interests in the country through arming their co-communal groups in Afghanistan. The interests of regional actors have resulted in constantly shifting alliances that are the very definition of instability.

As in the Balkans, Afghanistan's society is riven by a complex variety of divisions, in this case between religion, ethnicity, and tribal affiliation. Scholars characterize the recent violence in Afghanistan as mainly the result of political entrepreneurs' and external powers' use of ethnicity to mobilize groups, partly over resources, rather than the result of ethnic grievances naturally bubbling up from below (Atmar and Goodhand 2002, 115; ICG 2003). While the rise of the Taliban has been blamed on international and regional actors (Rubin 2002), these actors capitalized on a vacuum of power and the frustrations of long-repressed rural poor with an unyielding tribal aristocracy (Atmar and Goodhand 2002, 15). Afghanistan is one of the poorest countries in the world; 85 percent of the population lives in rural areas (UNDP 2004d), making the delivery of staples more of a priority for transnational actors engaged in peacebuilding there than in post-Communist societies recovering from war.

Rule by a succession of authoritarian regimes widened a deep gap between governing elites and ordinary Afghans, a legacy similar to that found in post-Communist Eurasia. Successive regimes in Kabul did little to improve the lives of citizens across Afghanistan, perpetuating distrust of formal institutions and encouraging reliance on traditional mechanisms to solve problems (ICG 2003, 11). These indigenous mechanisms—the *shura* (an Islamic consultative council) and *jirga* (a council of Pasthun or Baluchi elders)—have often erected a "mud-curtain" to insulate local communities from an interfering and often repressive state and have helped manage local conflicts among individuals, families, and communities (Atmar and Goodhand 2002, 125–26). Similar to the *mahalla* in neighboring Tajikistan, these informal centuries-old norm-based networks, which are generally bonding and hierarchical, are at the core of Afghanistan's civil society. As in the deeply divided societies of Kosovo, Macedonia, and Tajikistan, where intermarriage is rare, local mechanisms for managing communal conflict are monocommunal. These informal groups organized around bonding social networks have nonetheless sometimes been willing to work constructively with other monocommunal groups.

The conflicts in Afghanistan have generated millions of refugees and displaced persons. Since the U.S.–led coalition intervened to overthrow the Taliban, the UNHCR has assisted the largest return movement in its history, helping more than 3.5 million refugees return to the country. Reasons for return included improved social, economic, and security conditions in Afghanistan (UNHCR 2003b). The lack of job opportunities has presented the largest impediment to reintegration for these refugees and for Afghans who have gone through the UN mission's program for disarmament and demobilization. Many men immediately migrate to urban areas in search of work. This disperses families, whose members are not well integrated into either urban or rural communities. Certain areas still lack security and basic utilities, which obviously impedes return. And disputes over land and access to water have also complicated reintegration. The UN High Commissioner for Refugees (UNHCR 2003b, 36) views three areas as crucial for sustainable reintegration in Afghanistan: security, the development of the rule of law through both customary and judicial dispute settlement mechanisms, and economic development. As some scholars have warned, the stakes of this project are high, since failed reintegration programs perpetuate the cycle of dependency for ordinary people on warlords.[13]

Practitioners and scholars have bemoaned the tendency of transnational actors in Afghanistan to repeat mistakes made in other postconflict societies, especially the implanting of alien NGO structures as a strategy for building civil society. One report found that ordinary Afghans resented that NGOs received money that could have gone directly to communities (Social Impact 2005, 42). Instead, evaluators suggested, donors should adopt a broader view of civil society that encompasses more than just NGOs. This would include developing mechanisms for engaging with less formal groups that hold important influence over rural society while simultaneously working to encourage the traditional mechanisms to become more inclusive (Atmar and Goodhand 2002, 127).

13. Personal communication, Rani Mullen, February 2006.

Shura and *jirga* based at the level of the local community appear to be better at managing conflict than those at the province level, which are often dominated by warlords intent on pursuing their own interests. An external review of USAID assistance for transition initiatives in Afghanistan urged the donor to go further in involving community members in designing their own local projects and monitoring their implementation (Social Impact 2005, 72). One success story of civil society aid was an initiative by Pashtun women in one locality for a women's *shura* to address the practical needs of women in the area. Another case involved a local conflict-regulation organization that worked with villagers near Kandahar to establish a joint *shura* that would include both Pastuns and Hazara; within the *shura*, representatives of the two groups worked together to solve practical problems such as irrigation (ICG 2003, 15).

In general, however, scholars have viewed aid to NGOs in Afghanistan as merely a good short-term Band-Aid rather than an effective strategy for building a lasting capacity for self-help (Mullen 2006). Also, some analysts have rebuked transnational actors for engineering a statebuilding and democratization process that is remote from the realities of ordinary Afghans (Atmar and Goodhand 2002). Remarkably participatory and peaceful elections have not been followed by good governance. President Hamid Karzai has expended much effort in maintaining a government that has the support of key regional and ethnic leaders, and parliament has produced more bickering than legislation among factions that vary from former Islamic militia leaders to feminists (Constable 2007). The inability of transnational actors to make significant progress in jump-starting a process of building local capacity to meet even the most basic needs of ordinary citizens led one group of practitioners to conclude in 2006 that transnational actors and the Afghan government were "losing a battle of confidence" among ordinary Afghans (Cole and Bajpai 2006, 1).

The View from Below

A multilevel network model of peacebuilding helps us understand ongoing peacebuilding projects in deeply divided societies in Eurasia. It calls attention to the interference of putative homeland elites and the often dueling agendas of national-level and local-level minority activists. It highlights persistent problems in other models and practices of peacebuilding. These include oversimplification of social relations and the bases of conflict, shortcomings in the methods used to support the sustainability of refugee returns, and assistance to civil society based more on Western concepts than on an understanding of local mechanisms with strong bases in recovering societies. Most important, attention to the views of grassroots forces on peacebuilding has helped reveal why the roots of postconflict institutions in traumatized societies remain dangerously shallow. Dismissing the enduring informal mechanisms that ordinary people use to help address the everyday aspects of reconstruction in favor of top-down formal institutions may well be a serious impediment to peacebuilding efforts in the region. The importance of listening to and observing ordinary people struggling to cope in postwar societies cannot be overstated.

Appendix A
Methods

Franjo: [a middle-aged Croat from Sarajevo]: You are crazy!

To give the reader a better idea of why Franjo believes I am crazy and of the approach I used to conduct research in a postconflict setting like Bosnia, I delve here into the methods I used to learn how ordinary persons influence peacebuilding. In this appendix, I discuss (1) how I approached Bosnians and built rapport with them and (2) how opportunities and obstacles I encountered in the field influenced my research.

Efforts to Gain Access

I asked a lot from Bosnians. I used intensive interviewing to elicit from Bosnians their stories of struggling to rebuild their lives. In addition, I sought access to the everyday lives of the families with whom I lived because I wanted to participate in their neighborhood communities to learn firsthand about the character of local interethnic relationships. I asked a few families whose lives I had followed for several years to take me on visits to friends and members of their social networks beyond their neighborhoods. Observing behavior is particularly important because people consider questions about interethnic relations to be controversial. In interviews, people try to present themselves in a positive light, but when they act in real life, this is less true.

I interacted with individuals from communities over a significant period of time. I have known some families since January 1996. But it was difficult to penetrate the exceedingly high levels of mistrust that I encountered. Vera tried to persuade me to give up on conducting interviews with minorities. She warned me: "People won't want to talk to you. . . . You should mind your own business." Though 90 percent of those I ap-

Some ideas in the chapter have been published in Pickering 2002.

proached agreed to an interview, there were people I considered approaching but later decided not to in anticipation of rejection.

My primary strategies for gaining access were living with minorities and participating in their everyday lives (for participant observation) and snowball sampling (for intensive interviewing). Conducting surveys on sensitive topics in postwar societies does not make sense. Indeed, there was a strong tendency for minorities to resist answering sensitive survey questions, an obvious indication of the need for me to get creative in thinking about how to gather valid data.[1] I informed Bosnians that I wanted to learn about the perspectives and concerns of ordinary people attempting to rebuild their lives after war.[2] I paid rent to the local families with whom I lived. Rent contributed to increasing Bosnians' precarious financial security. I also offered my hosts a short-term diversion from the boredom and hardship of everyday life.

Living with Bosnians helped me learn about family members, whose trust I attempted to cultivate over repeated, considerate interaction in and around the home. It was only after spending considerable time with neighbors over several months that I believed they would feel comfortable enough to discuss their personal experiences as a minority and be willing to suggest others whom I could approach for anonymous interviews. Because many minorities tended to keep opinions to themselves, I often found participant observation more fruitful than interviews in understanding interethnic interaction. Like Jonathan Rieder (1985, 81) and many other ethnographers, I considered it important in understanding intercommunal relations to observe individuals in their communities rather than to treat them as "lonely atoms." Participant observation helped me understand the dynamics of social relations in real life.

Access was complicated by Bosnians' poverty and interaction with transient foreign aid workers. Many urban Bosnians were understandably cynical of international "interest" and were busy meeting their own everyday needs. Once some of these urbanites realized that I had nothing "concrete," such as money, jobs, or connections to influential people to offer them, while other internationals did, some hesitated to spend time with me rehashing unpleasant experiences. I attempted to address these concerns by being open and by listening.

My attempts to gain access were further confounded in the middle of my research in 1999 by war in neighboring Kosovo. An intensive effort to

1. In a 2001 survey, half of minority returnees to Republika Srpska refused to answer whether they encountered hostility (Sweeney 2001).

2. My research was approved by the University of Michigan's Behavioral Sciences Institutional Review Board, File number 1083.

gain trust over time through repeatedly interacting with minorities took on an added importance then. The NATO bombing and Serb extremist violence heightened anti-Serb sentiment in Sarajevo. Some Serbs expressed anti-American sentiment, but most I knew were mainly pained by the suffering, often of family members, in Serbia. The U.S. embassy temporarily closed off Republika Srpska to Americans, which impeded my interviews in those areas.

In traveling to areas outside of my neighborhoods to talk with minorities, I relied more heavily on local voluntary organizations, transnational organizations, international governmental organizations, and even businessmen, like Hamdo, a real estate broker. It was simply impossible for me to show up in a new town or village and start talking, for example in a café, to people who might or might not have been minorities and to have expected for them to open up to me. To find persons displaced from Bihać and Sarajevo, I asked for suggestions from international refugee officials and locals dealing with leaders of the displaced persons associations. To find minority returnees to villages around Bihać and Sarajevo, I sought out humanitarians involved in reconstruction. To find minorities and relocatees in Banja Luka, I received help from Dayton-implementing organizations and NGOs.

In working with civic activists, I endeavored to make a tiny contribution by volunteering. I translated documents and worked with members on their conversational English. I hoped that these small actions would foster a more reciprocal relationship between me and Bosnians, but I really did too little. To gain access to the clients of one minority NGO, I agreed to an activist's suggestion that I follow closely several cases on which the NGO had provided free legal advice. After consulting with legal experts on the validity of one case alleging ethnic discrimination and at the request of the minority plaintiff, I even agreed to observe a hearing. This provided an intimate look at interaction between a minority members and majority officials, and even helped bring about progress toward the case's resolution.

Bosnians' perceptions of me and my interests had both positive and negative consequences for my research. I knew full well that I could never become a Bosnian,[3] but I also did not want to be an "ugly American." I

---

3. I sometimes identified with Elliot Leibow, who described his understanding of the impact of his identity during an ethnography of low-income blacks in Washington, D.C. Liebow portrayed his relationship with these blacks, as if they had a "chain-link fence" between them (1967, 250–51). "When two people stand up close to the fence on either side . . . they can look through the interstices and forget that they are looking through the fence." I tried to get up as close as possible to the "chain-link fence" between Bosnians and me.

felt that gaining deeper understanding and access demanded that I re-spect Bosnian traditions. I attempted to live up to the identity that that one Bosnian friend gave to me: "part American and part Bosnian."

From my previous work in the Balkans, I knew that my gender (female), marital status (single), and profession (academic) would brand me as an anomaly in Bosnian culture.[4] However, I was surprised to discover that my identity interacted with Bosnians' different levels of vulnerability and wartime experiences to create easier access to some Bosnians and obstacles to others. Women and older persons were more willing to share their experiences than were others.[5]

I attributed this partly to the fact that Bosnians' strategies for coping with the postwar environment were in an important way linked with their wartime experiences. For instance, I found it extremely difficult to gain access to minority men of fighting age, whose wartime experiences had been so controversial and horrifying. On the other hand, men above fighting age were more forthcoming. When I approached one young Croat, Franjo, who had fought on the front lines for the Bošnjak-led army about the possibility of granting me an anonymous interview, he responded: "No way. You are crazy. I hope that you can provide protection to the men who are willing to talk with you." But this rejection could not be explained merely by intimacy with horror because several women told me of their experiences with violence. Instead, I believe Bosnian culture's expectations of women presented serious obstacles to my gaining access to young men. Displaced persons, who often lived in precarious housing situations, were often difficult to approach.

In some cases, my "outsider" identity helped me gain access to Bosnians. While most Bosnians assumed my views were infected by the bias of official U.S. policy, they did not impose on me the prejudices that Bosnians tend to attach to someone with roots in one of Bosnia's ethnic groups. I endeavored to make the most of this relative neutrality by conducting one-on-one interviews in the local language.

---

4. According to Bosnian culture, a woman my age should focus on her family and home.

5. As Susan Eckstein discovered during her field research in Mexico (1977, 241–43), I found my nationality and my sex to be both advantageous and disadvantageous. Eckstein found that being an American woman helped her to avoid local status systems, to appear less threatening than a man, and to gain access through her presumed connection to powerful Americans. At the same time, she found being an American hindered her research by conveying an imbalance in the distribution of power in relationships and in limiting her access to men.

Building Rapport

In building rapport and trust, I tried to convey passion about my research problems and their practical impact on peoples. I attempted to be a good listener, which psychologists emphasize is particularly needed by persons who recently experienced war.[6] Some informants also told me that I demonstrated a commitment to understanding Bosnians by living with local families and acquiring knowledge of the local language. Vera complimented me, "You understand this place really. You live with our people. You live their lives." Nikola echoed Vera's belief that my approach of living with local families and getting "real, first-hand experiences," ensured that I would better be able to understand ordinary Bosnians than if I had studied them from afar, focused instead on elites, or relied only on newspaper reports. Dragan appreciated my knowledge of the Bosnian language, which he believed showed my investment in trying to understand peoples living in Bosnia. Hida, a returnee to Republika Srpska, asked me,

> Where did you learn our language? It's great! When I approach international organizations, I tell them what is necessary for my story, but I am speaking against the nation of the translators. I don't know what they are translating. Sometimes, I've been to an International Organization several times, and they ask me the same questions.

Hida did not believe that the local translators who belonged to the majority were conveying all of her concerns to their international superiors. My language skills increased her confidence that I would understand and convey the details of her agonizing story.

To help meet a few of Bosnians' practical needs, I offered small favors. For instance, I connected Bosnians with international humanitarian organizations that might be able to assist them. In another instance, I offered suggestions on the application of an informant's daughter to a student program for a visit to the United States. On one occasion, I asked my colleague to give an informant a ride to a relative's village that was not serviced by public busses. Also, during a visit to the United States, I carried letters and care packages from Bosnians to relatives and colleagues in the States. And in a moment of luck, my discussion of the dire situation of displaced Bošnjaks, many of whom had been living in garages and garden shacks within Banja Luka for years while trying to reclaim their illegally occupied homes, helped prompt a U.S. official to visit these floaters.

6. Kent Jennings and David Jones reminded me of this.

Often, however, I was not able to help. Some informants thought that I could use my "influence" to improve their situations. One lawyer sought to convert me into an advocate for her clients. A real estate broker in several instances tried to introduce me as an official with a powerful intergovernmental organization in order to pressure majority officials into acting more favorably toward his clients. In another case, a Serb informant wanted me to confront the illegal occupant of his apartment in an effort to convince him to vacate it. In these cases, I reminded Bosnians of my status as scholar. I agonized, however, about difficult situations that Bosnians faced and my privileged status.

I believe my approach of combining participant observation at the neighborhood level and intensive interviewing resulted in the collection of richer data that could not have been extracted through a survey questionnaire. One indication of this was the amount of time—sometimes four hours—that some Bosnians spent with me discussing highly sensitive topics. On a more worrisome note, other signs included the level of emotion that some of my subjects expressed, from sobbing during an interview to breaking out in a rash just after one. One hostess in Sarajevo told me several days after my move that she had to stop cleaning up my former room, and shut its door, because she had "gotten used to" me and was sad to see the room empty. As further signs that I had established trusted relations with former hosts, several different hosts in Sarajevo called me in my new residence in Bihać to say hello and to request that I visit before leaving Bosnia.

My observation and interviewing uncovered a diversity of stories about interethnic relations. Observing behavior is particularly important because people consider questions about interethnic relations to be controversial. In interviews, people try to present themselves in a positive light, but when they act in real life, this is less true. In general, I *observed* more interethnic tension than I heard about. With time, I also noticed a progression in the level of trust and an increase in the opportunities to compare words with unconscious behavior. For example, toward the end of my volunteering stint, a minority NGO official fed up with international officials flitting in and out of Bosnia sought my opinion during a round table where I was the only foreigner present. By the end of one stay, I was frequently invited to family gatherings outside my host's home.[7]

At other times, hosts revealed sensitive information to me that in some

---

7. This brings up the problem that Fenno (1978, 272) confronted of "too much rapport." I tried to keep relationships with those whom I observed from sliding into friendships. In several cases, I was not successful.

cases contradicted earlier testimony only after I had lived with them for several months. Mirsada initially had told me that her mother wanted to reclaim her private property in Banja Luka and return there, even though she would be a minority. But several months later, when Mirsada's sister visited, she talked about their other sister's intention to sell the family home in Banja Luka. Mirsada interpreted my work with returnees as a sign that I believed that minority return was the "correct" choice. As a result, she probably initially voiced opinions she thought I would like to hear. Over time and many interactions that she could not fully control, she revealed more sincere intentions.

Finally, an encounter with Janja, a displaced Serb, and his son demonstrated the hazards of gathering data from minorities during a one-shot visit. Bošnjak activist Hamdo introduced these two Serbs to me after a chance encounter at the Bihać municipality building, where they had just inquired about the return and reconstruction of their property. They told me they both wanted to return and then invited me to accompany Hamdo to their home on the outskirts of Bihać, where they were cleaning up the debris around Janja's burnt-out home. My suspicions about the honesty of the family's testimony were strengthened when, while picking walnuts with Janja, I overheard Hamdo say to Janja's son, "She's not stupid; after all she is getting a doctorate." The tears of joy that Janja shed after a surprise visit by a humanitarian announcing that her agency would reconstruct part of his home suggested the sincerity of his interest in returning. Alone with Hamdo on the ten-minute drive back to the center of town, however, I confronted him, "Janja's son is not genuinely interested in return, is he?" "No, he isn't," replied Hamdo, "he merely seeks to regain his apartment so that he can exchange it for one in Banja Luka." These cases demonstrate why I did not attempt to gauge "interest" in return among those displaced. Instead, I focused on those minorities who were already physically in their homes. These examples also illustrate Bosnians' assumption that I wanted to hear about minority return rather than relocation.[8]

If rapport was difficult even after months of living with individuals, then certainly "cold calling" for a survey about views on sensitive topics would not have been productive. Bosnians expressed concern about the validity of answers provided in a survey. Jovanka warned me, "If you give people questionnaires, people will lie." A local colleague involved in

---

8. These issues point to the importance of avoiding settings and interview questions that generate "saccharin" answers that lack theoretical validity (Kirk and Miller 1986, 26–27).

conducting a mail survey told me some respondents came to his office and wanted to know what the "correct" answers were. Some Bosnians were pessimistic about the validity of the answers that I would receive during intensive interviews. Slavica looked at my question about migration and frowned,

> When you ask people about why they stayed [during the war,] they will lie. In many cases, there wasn't time for thinking over things. And for example, we didn't have money to send our daughter out of Sarajevo.

These warnings helped me become a better listener. Partly as a check against interviewer bias, I contracted one local in Sarajevo and one in Bihać each to conduct five interviews, or if the respondent insisted, to collect questionnaires that the interviewees had filled out. Both colleagues reported difficulty in finding willing respondents. They often heard: "I'm fed up with all these types of things." In comparing those interviews that I conducted with those that I contracted out, I found no significant differences except that contractors elicited shorter answers and slightly more pessimistic views about the future.[9] All these experiences suggested the wisdom of my approach that was centered on my living with different families and conducting intensive interviews.

Ethnographic methods helped me see in Bosnians' stories the dilemmas they faced after war. I took pains to listen to the Bosnians I met and to watch their social behavior in order to find interpretations that arose from Bosnians themselves. As time passed I began to see how these citizens were embedded in particular spatial, social, and temporal contexts. The information I gathered in the field caused me to alter the interpretive frameworks I had started out with.[10]

Confronting Obstacles

Based on my prior field experiences in Bosnia, I had anticipated running up against practical and emotional obstacles to implementing my re-

9. I believe that the shorter answers that my contractors elicited meant that they did not conduct probes. The more pessimistic answers that they gathered may reveal that respondents assumed I wanted to hear positive views about the personal futures and the prospects for multiethnicity, whereas the contractors would not care. I have factored this into my analysis, shifting what had already emerged from my own interviews as a norm of pessimistic views further toward profound pessimism.

10. I extend the grounded theory approach (Glaser and Strauss 1967) by applying theory arising out of my data to new situations (see chapter 6).

search design. To my surprise, I was still quite unprepared for some of the tests that I would face in the field.

I encountered numerous logistic obstacles that mainly resulted from living and working in a postwar country, struggling alongside the Bosnians with disrupted, inadequate public services. Even tracking down people was time-consuming in the times prior to widespread mobile phone use (the bulk of my field research). The phone system was in chaos, partly because of the massive effort to rebuild infrastructure that was intentionally destroyed during the war to sever connections between Bosnians. Contacting minority returnees was often made more difficult by the nationalist authorities' discrimination against minorities seeking to reconnect their phones. Many Bosnians living in rural areas never had phones, and the phone at their village post office—if it was standing—no longer worked. When traveling to villages, I was hostage to public bus schedules and drivers who were often not willing to pick up a passenger at a bus stop at a minority village. One time I had traveled forty-five minutes to a village only to find that my contact was not at home; after the return bus whizzed by me several hours later, I resorted to hitchhiking. In other cases, many of my informants had possessed temporary occupancy that they had changed in the interim. This meant that I often had to call several other contacts to reach ultimately the desired one. Calling Republika Srpska from the Federation was an ordeal because the local post office in 1999 had no information for the "other" entity. This improved by 2002. These experiences gave me a taste of the ordeals that Bosnians faced.

In addition to the difficulty of tracking down people, the cultural practice of arranging meetings just beforehand ate up time. My attempts to arrange a meeting or interview even several days beforehand were virtually always quashed by the typical response, "a meeting would be fine, but call me in the morning in two days and we'll see what we can set up." This often left me to clear most of a day for a meeting that might or might not happen. Invitations to accompany Bosnians on visits were often extended at the last minute. It was hard to anticipate how long visits would last; it was rude to cut short a visit to someone who had opened their home. To prepare for the cancellation or delay of a meeting or bus, I always brought along a prioritized list of additional people to call and alternative projects to work on. I also used long bus rides to meet fellow passengers.

Because I did not take notes during participant observation, I was always searching for a place to write up my notes so that I lost as little information as possible. I constantly struggled over the tradeoff between writing up data at home and participating in the evenings of my host families and their neighbors. Most hosts expected me to spend time with them in common living areas when I was at home, and indeed I wanted to do so. I found it difficult to draw boundaries around opportunities for rich participant observation.[11]

In the process of studying attitudes about interethnic relations and interethnic behavior, I found myself in the uncomfortable situation of participating in ethnicizing people. I was painfully aware of names, which most often bore ethnic markers. While observing social behavior in everyday life, I tried not to ask about the ethnicity of someone if it was not volunteered. I found it uncomfortable to place labels on Bosnians that they themselves often did not use. Nonetheless, I was also aware in an environment where people have been punished for their ethnic background that building sustainable peace would require studying how ethnic diversity was managed in everyday life. In the process of trying to understand identity politics, however, scholars and implementers have sometimes become trapped by ethnicity and have failed to attend to Bosnians' perspectives and the complexity of social relations.

One month into my research, I realized that I had underestimated the day-to-day struggles that ordinary Bosnians faced in meeting basic needs. This hit home after a three-and-one-half-hour meeting with a group of minority returnees, each of whom took a turn excitedly explaining to me his traumatic story of return, experience with discrimination, and torturous attempts to reclaim property and to obtain work. These stories were gut-wrenching. Jelka told me that after she and her husband had paid their rent and utilities and bought a carton of cigarettes and one bottle of liquor, they were left with 50 pfennings a day (enough to buy one loaf of bread) from their monthly pensions. In such dire circumstances, I felt uncomfortable asking questions. In other cases, I became depressed after conversations with Bosnians who spun stories around chauvinistic stereotypes, such as "Bošnjaks are uncultured," "Serbs are hardwired to commit atrocities," or "Croats are Fascists."

Upon Reflection

It was not easy for me to say good-bye to Bosnians, especially my host families. These people let me into their homes and lives even while they

---

11. Also difficult was a misunderstanding I had with one of my hosts about using the kitchen. I moved early.

struggled to rebuild fundamental aspects of their lives. I try to keep up written and phone communication with a core group of Bosnians. And when I return to Bosnia, I always visit them. But my desire is larger than my follow through. These people, their stories, and our joint experiences continue to enrich my scholarship and my life.

Appendix B Pseudonyms and Demographics for Bosnians

INFORMANTS[a]

Pseudonym	Age group[b]	Gender	Profession	Nationality	Minority?[c]	Migration status[d]	Current location	Settlement
Adil	Old	Male	Professional	Multiple	Majority	Stayer	Sarajevo	Urban
Aleksandra	Young	Female	Skilled worker	Mixed minority-majority	Ethnic minority	Relocatee	Sarajevo	Urban
Alen	Young	Male	Skilled worker	Mixed minority-majority	Ethnic minority	Returnee	Sarajevo	Urban
Alija	Middle	Male	Professional	Muslim	Majority	Stayer	Bihać	Urban
Alma	Middle	Female	Agriculture	Serb	Ethnic minority	Returnee	Petrovac hamlet	Rural
Amela	Middle	Female	Skilled worker	Bošnjak	Majority	Returnee	Sarajevo	Urban
Ana	Middle	Female	Admin or technician	Serb	Ethnic minority	Stayer	Sarajevo	Urban
Anica	Young	Female	Professional	Serb	Ethnic minority	Stayer	Sarajevo	Urban
Anisa	Middle	Female	Skilled worker	Bošnjak	Majority	Stayer	Sarajevo	Urban
Armin	Young	Male	Student	Bosnian	Majority	Stayer	Sarajevo	Urban
Azra	Middle	Female	Professional	Mixed minority-majority	Ethnic minority	Stayer	Sarajevo	Urban
Bata	Young	Male	Skilled worker	Serb	Ethnic minority	Returnee	Bihać	Urban
Blagoje	Middle	Male	Skilled worker	Serb	Ethnic minority	Returnee	Petrovac hamlet	Rural
Borka	Middle	Female	Professional	Serb	Majority	Stayer	Belgrade	Urban
Bosko	Middle	Male	Professional	Serb	Ethnic minority	Stayer	Sarajevo	Urban
Branka	Old	Female	Pensioner	Slovene	Ethnic minority	Stayer	Sarajevo	Urban
Brka	Middle	Male	Admin or technician	Serb	Ethnic minority	Relocatee	Banja Luka	Urban
Ceca	Middle	Female	Admn or technician	Serb	Ethnic minority	Relocatee	Bijeljina	Urban
Damir	Young	Male	Professional	Mixed minorities	Ethnic minority	Stayer	Vojvodina	Urban
Danica	Young	Female	Student	Croat	Ethnic minority	Returnee	Sarajevo	Urban
Dobrica	Old	Male	Skilled worker	Serb	Ethnic minority	Returnee	Bihać hamlet	Rural
Dragana	Middle	Female	Professional	Serb	Ethnic minority	Returnee	Sarajevo	Urban

Name	Age	Gender	Occupation	Ethnicity	Status	Movement	Place	Rural/Urban
Dragomir	Old	Male	Skilled worker	Serb	Ethnic minority	Returnee	Bihać hamlet	Rural
Dunja	Old	Female	Housewife	Serb	Ethnic minority	Returnee	Petrovac hamlet	Rural
Dus'an	Old	Male	Admin or technician	Serb	Ethnic minority	Returnee	Bihać hamlet	Rural
Dusko	Old	Male	Pensioner	Serb	Ethnic minority	Relocatee	Banja Luka	Urban
Edhem	Old	Male	Pensioner	Muslim	Ethnic minority	Stayer	Sarajevo suburb	Urban
Edin	Young	Male	Skilled worker	Muslim	Majority	Stayer	Bihać	Urban
Edina	Middle	Female	Skilled worker	Bošnjak	majority	Returnee	Bihać hamlet	Rural
Elizabeta	Middle	Female	Admin or technician	Bošnjak	Ethnic Minority	Relocatee	Sarajevo	Urban
Elvadin	Young	Male	Professional	Bošnjak	Majority	Stayer	Bihać	Urban
Emira	Young	Female	Professional	Muslim	Majority	Stayer	Bihać	Urban
Enver	Old	Male	Pensioner	Bošnjak	Majority	Stayer	Sarajevo	Urban
Fadila	Middle	Female	Admin or technician	Bošnjak	Ethnic minority	Returnee	Prijedor village	Rural
FadilaK	Middle	Female	Skilled worker	Muslim	Ethnic minority	Stayer	Banja Luka	Urban
Fatima	Middle	Female	—	Muslim	Majority	Relocatee	Third Country	Urban
Frane	Middle	Male	Professional	Croat	Ethnic minority	Returnee	Sarajevo	Urban
Franjo	Young	Male	Professional	Croat	Ethnic minority	Stayer	Sarajevo	Urban
Gordon	Middle	Male	Professional	Mixed minority-majority	Ethnic minority	Stayer	Zenica	Urban
Halid	Young	Male	Skilled worker	Bošnjak	Majority	Stayer	Sarajevo	Urban
Hamdo	Old	Male	Professional	Bošnjak	Majority	Relocatee	Third Country	Urban
HamdoI	Old	Male	Skilled worker	Bošnjak	Majority	Stayer	Bihać	Urban
Haris	Young	Malel	Student	Bošnjak	Ethnic minority	Relocatee	Sarajevo	Urban
Hida	Middle	Female	Unskilled worker	Muslim	Ethnic minority	Stayer	Prijedor	Urban
Hrvoje	Young	Male	Unskilled worker	Croat	Ethnic minority	Returnee	Sarajevo	Urban
Inis	Old	Female	Pensioner	Croat	Ethnic minority	Stayer	Vojvodina	Urban
Ivan	Middle	Male	Professional	Croat	Ethnic minority	Stayer	Sarajevo	Urban
Janja	Old	Female	Pensioner	Serb	Ethnic minority	—	Bihać hamlet	Urban
Janko	Old	Male	Skilled worker	Serb	Ethnic minority	Returnee	Bihać hamlet	Rural
Jasmina	Middle	Female	Skilled worker	Bošnjak	Ethnic minority	Relocatee	Sarajevo	Urban
Jasna	Young	Female	Professional	Croat	Ethnic minority	Stayer	Bihać	Urban

(continued)

Appendix B Continued

INFORMANTS[a]

Pseudonym	Age group[b]	Gender	Profession	Nationality	Minority?[c]	Migration status[d]	Current location	Settlement
Jelena	Old	Female	Professional	Serb	Ethnic minority	Returnee	Sarajevo	Urban
Jelka	Old	Female	Pensioner	Serb	Ethnic minority	Stayer	Sarajevo	Urban
Josip	Middle	Male	Skilled worker	Serb	Ethnic minority	DP	Bihać hamlet	Rural
Jovan	Old	Male	Pensioner	Yugoslav	Ethnic minority	Relocatee	Vojvodina	Rural
Jovanka	Middle	Female	Professional	Serb	Ethnic minority	Stayer	sarajevo	Urban
Jovo	Old	Male	Agriculture	Serb	Ethnic minority	Returnee	Petrovac hamlet	Rural
Jozo	Old	Female	Pensioner	Serb	Ethnic minority	Returnee	Sarajevo	Urban
Kasim	Middle	Male	Admin or technician	Bošnjak	Ethnic minority	Relocatee	Zenica	Urban
Katerina	Young	Female	Student	Croat	Ethnic minority	Stayer	Sarajevo	Urban
Kosta	Old	Male	Skilled worker	Serb	Ethnic minority	Returnee	Bihać hamlet	Rural
Kristina	Old	Female	Professional	Yugoslav	Ethnic minority	Stayer	Bihać	Urban
Lazar	Young	Male	Admin or technician	Serb	Ethnic minority	Relocatee	Brcko	Urban
Lidija	Middle	Female	Professional	Mixed minority-majority	Ethnic minority	Returnee	Prijedor village	Rural
Lilac	Middle	Female	Admin or technician	Croat	Ethnic minority	refugee	Belgrade	Urban
Liljana	Old	Female	Agriculture	Bošnjak	Ethnic minority	Returnee	Prijedor village	Rural
Ljubica	Old	Female	Skilled worker	Serb	Ethnic minority	Stayer	Sarajevo	Urban
Ljubinka	Old	Female	Pensioner	Serb	Ethnic minority	Returnee	Grahovo	Rural
Ljubo	Middle	Male	Professional	Serb	Ethnic minority	Returnee	Sarajevo suburb	Urban
Lula	Middle	Female	Skilled worker	Bošnjak	Ethnic minority	Returnee	Prijedor	Urban
Maja	Middle	Female	Skilled worker	Croat	Ethnic minority	Stayer	Sarajevo	Urban
Malik	Young	Male	Professional	Croat	Ethnic minority	Relocatee	Zagreb	Urban
Martin	Middle	Male	Professional	Croat	Ethnic minority	Stayer	Sarajevo	Urban
Milada	Young	Female	Professional	Muslim	Ethnic minority	DP	Vojvodina	Urban

Name								
Milan	Middle	Male	Professional	Serb	Ethnic minority	Relocatee	Srebrenica	Rural
Milena	Old	Female	Pensioner	Serb	Ethnic minority	Relocatee	Petrovac hamlet	Rural
Mima	Old	Female	Skilled worker	Serb	Ethnic minority	Returnee	Bihać hamlet	Rural
Miro	Middle	Male	—	Serb	Ethnic minority	Relocatee	Banja Luka	Urban
Mirsada	Middle	Female	Admin or technician	Muslim	Majority	Stayer	Bihać	Urban
Mladen	Young	Male	Skilled worker	Serb	Ethnic minority	DP	Banja Luka	Urban
Mladin	Middle	Male	Professional	Serb	Ethnic minority	Relocatee	Banja Luka	Urban
Munir	Old	Female	Pensioner	Muslim	Ethnic minority	Returnee	Herzegovina	Rural
Nadezda	Old	Female	Agriculture	Serb	Ethnic minority	Returnee	Petrovac hamlet	Rural
Natasha	Middle	Female	Admin or technician	Serb	Ethnic minority	Relocatee	Srebrenica	Rural
Neda	Middle	Female	Skilled worker	Serb	Ethnic minority	Returnee	Petrovac hamlet	Rural
Nedjo	Middle	Male	—	Serb	Ethnic minority	DP	Prnjavor	Rural
Nela	Middle	Female	Professional	Yugoslav	Ethnic minority	Returnee	Sarajevo	Urban
Nikola	Middle	Male	Professional	Mixed minority-majority	Ethnic minority	DP	Pale	Rural
Nina	Middle	Female	Professional	Croat	Ethnic minority	Stayer	Sarajevo	Urban
Novica	Middle	Female	—	Croat	Ethnic minority	Relocatee	Brcko	Urban
Novka	Old	Female	—	Mixed minority-majority	Ethnic minority	Returnee	Sarajevo	Urban
Olivera	Middle	Female	Professional	Serb	Ethnic minority	Stayer	Sarajevo	Urban
Paulina	Old	Female	Pensioner	Serb	Ethnic minority	Returnee	Petrovac hamlet	Rural
Predrag	Old	Male	Professional	Serb	Ethnic minority	Returnee	Third Country	Urban
Rada	Old	Female	Skilled worker	Yugoslav	Ethnic minority	Returnee	Petrovac hamlet	Rural
Sandra	Middle	Female	Skilled worker	Serb	Ethnic minority	Returnee	Sarajevo	Urban
Seka	Young	Female	Student	Croat	Ethnic minority	Returnee	Sarajevo	Urban
Selma	Middle	Female	Professional	Bošnjak	Ethnic minority	DP	Sarajevo	Urban
Senka	Young	Female	Student	Catholic	Ethnic minority	Returnee	Sarajevo	Urban
Silvana	Middle	Female	Pensioner	Muslim	Ethnic minority	Relocatee	Vojvodina	Urban
Slavenka	Old	Female	Admin or technician	Yugoslav	Ethnic minority	Stayer	Sarajevo	Urban
Slobodan	Middle	Male	Skilled worker	Serb	Ethinic minority	Returnee	Petrovac hamlet	Rural

(continued)

Appendix B Continued

INFORMANTS[a]

Pseudonym	Age group[b]	Gender	Profession	Nationality	Minority?[c]	Migration status[d]	Current location	Settlement
Spomenka	Old	Female	Pensioner	Serb	Ethnic minority	Returnee	Third Country	Urban
Stipe	Middle	Male	Professional	Catholic	Ethnic minority	Stayer	Sarajevo	Urban
Stojanka	Old	Female	Housewife	Serb	Ethnic minority	Returnee	Sarajevo	Urban
Suzana	Young	Female	student	Mixed minority-majority	Ethnic minority	refugee	Belgrade	Urban
Tamara	Old	Female	Admin or technician	Serb	Ethnic minority	refugee	Belgrade	Urban
Tanja	Middle	Female	Unskilled worker	Muslim	Ethnic minority	Stayer	Banja Luka	Urban
Teresa	Old	Female	Skilled worker	Serb	Ethnic minority	Returnee	Bihać' hamlet	Rural
Tomislav	Old	Male	Skilled worker	Croat	Ethnic minority	Stayer	Banja Luka	Urban
Vera	Old	Female	Pensioner	multiple	Ethnic minority	Stayer	Sarajevo	Urban
Veselin	Old	Male	Professional	Serb	Ethnic minority	DP	Bihać	Urban
Vesna	Middle	Female	Unskilled worker	Bošnjak	Ethnic minority	Stayer	Banja Luka	Urban
Vid	Old	Male	Professional	Serb	Ethnic minority	Relocatee	Third Country	Urban
Violeta	Young	Female	Student	Croat	Ethnic minority	Returnee	Sarajevo	Urban
Vuk	Old	Male	Pensioner	Serb	Ethnic minority	Returnee	Petrovac hamlet	Rural
Zdravka	Old	Female	Agriculture	Serb	Ethnic minority	Returnee	Petrovac hamlet	Rural
Zeljko	Old	Male	Skilled worker	Serb	Ethnic minority	Returnee	Bihać hamlet	Rural
Zlata	Old	Female	Pensioner	Serb	Ethnic minority	Temporary returnee	Sarajevo suburb	Urban
Zlata S	Middle	Female	Professional	Serb	Ethnic minority	Stayer	Sarajevo	Urban
Zlatko	Middle	Male	Professional	Serb	Ethnic minority	Stayer	Sarajevo	Urban
Zorica	Middle	Female	Professional	Mixed minorities	Ethnic minority	Returnee	Sarajevo	Urban

RESPONDENTS

Pseudonym	Age group[b]	Gender	Profession	Nationality	Minority?[c]	Migration status[d]	Current location	Settlement
Ahmet	Old	Male	University	Muslim	Political minority	Stayer	Bihać	Urban
Aida	Old	Female	Middle	Muslim	Majority	DP	Bihać	Urban
Amir	Young	Male	Middle	human	Majority	Stayer	Bihac′	Urban
Avdo	Old	Male	University	Bošnjak	Ethnic minority	Stayer	Banja Luka	Urban
Bogdan	Middle	Male	High	Serb	Minority in mixed marriage	Relocatee	Banja Luka	Urban
Darija	Middle	Female	High	Muslim	Minority	Stayer	Banja Luka	Urban
Davor	Old	Male	Middle	Croat & Catholic	Ethnic minority	Stayer	Sarajevo	Urban
Ditka	Middle	Female	Middle	Muslim	Majority in mixed marriage	Returnee	Bihać	Urban
Dragan	Middle	Male	Middle	multiple	Ethnic minority	Returnee	Sarajevo suburb	Urban
Dragica	Old	Female	University	Serb	Ethnic minority	Stayer	Sarajevo	Urban
Emina	Young	Female	University	Muslim	Majority	Stayer	Bihać	Urban
Emsuda	Old	Female	Middle	Bošnjak	Ethnic minority	Returnee	Prijedor village	Rural
Ena	Young	Female	University	Bosnian	Majority	Returnee	Sarajevo	Urban
Esad	Old	Male	University	Bosnian	Political minority	Returnee	Velika Kladusa	Rural
Faruk	Old	Male	University	Muslim	Political minority	Returnee	Cazin	Rural
Goran	Old	Male	High	Serb	Ethnic minority	Returnee	Bihać hamlet	Rural
Gordana	Young	Female	Middle	Serb	Ethnic minority	Returnee	Bihać	Urban
Ismet	Old	Male	University	Bošnjak	Majority	DP	Bihać	Urban
Ivo	Old	Male	University	Croat	Ethnic minority	Stayer	Sarajevo	Urban
Jadranka	Young	Female	High	Muslim	Ethnic minority	Stayer	Banja Luka	Urban
Jelica	Middle	Female	University	Bosnian	Minority in mixed marriage	Returnee	Sarajevo	Urban
Katica	Middle	Female	University	Yugoslav	Minority in mixed marriage	Returnee	Sarajevo	Urban
Marijan	Middle	Male	Middle	Croat	Ethnic minority	Stayer	Velika Kladusa	Rural
Mara	Old	Female	High	Macedonian	Ethnic minority	Returnee	Sarajevo	Urban
Marko	Middle	Male	High	Serb	Ethnic minority	Relocatee	Banja Luka	Urban

(continued)

Appendix B Continued

RESPONDENTS

Pseudonym	Age group[b]	Gender	Profession	Nationality	Minority?[c]	Migration status[d]	Current location	Settlement
Mina	Old	Male	University	Serb	Ethnic minority	Stayer	Sarajevo	Urban
Minka	Old	Female	High	Serb	Ethnic minority	Stayer	Sarajevo	Urban
Mira	Middle	Female	University	Serb	Ethnic minority	Stayer	Sarajevo	Urban
Muharema	Old	Female	Middle	Bosnian	Majority	Stayer	Sarajevo	Urban
Munira	Middle	Female	University	Bošnjak	Majority	Stayer	Bihać	Urban
Mustafa	Middle	Male	University	Bošnjak	Ethnic minority	Relocatee	Sarajevo	Urban
Nada	Old	Female	High	Serb	Ethnic minority	Returnee	Bihać hamlet	Rural
Nijaz	Middle	Male	University	Muslim	Political minority	Stayer	Velika Kladusa	Rural
Nikola	Old	Male	University	Serb	Ethnic minority	Returnee	Bihać	Urban
Novka	Middle	Female	University	Multiple	Ethnic minority	Returnee	Bihać	Urban
Nuna	Old	Female	High	Muslim	Majority	Stayer	Sarajevo	Urban
Petar	Old	Male	University	multiple	Ethnic minority	Stayer	Sarajevo	Urban
Radislav	Old	Male	University	multiple	Ethnic minority	Stayer	Sarajevo	Urban
Radmila	Middle	Female	Middle	Yugoslav	Majority in mixed marriage	Refugee	Belgrade	Urban
Rajko	Middle	Male	Middle	Serb	Ethnic minority	Stayer	Sarajevo	Urban
Renata	Old	Female	University	Croat & Catholic	Ethnic minority	Stayer	Sarajevo	Urban
Sandra	Young	Female	Middle		Majority	Stayer	Sarajevo suburb	Urban
Sanel	Old	Male	High	Muslim	Majority	Stayer	Bihać	Urban
Sanela	Middle	Female	Primary	Bosnian	Majority in mixed marriage	Stayer	Sarajevo suburb	Urban

Name	Age[b]	Gender	Education	Ethnicity	Status	Mobility	Location	Urban/Rural
Sanil	Young	Male	Middle	Muslim	Majority	Stayer	Bihać	Urban
Sladjana	Middle	Female	University	Bosnian	Ethnic minority	Returnee	Sarajevo	Urban
Sofia	Old	Female	University	multiple	Ethnic minority	Returnee	Sarajevo	Urban
Srecko	Middle	Male	University	Croat	Minority in mixed marriage	Stayer	Sarajevo	Urban
Suada	Middle	Female	Middle	Bosnian	Minority in mixed marriage	Stayer	Sarajevo suburb	Urban
Tina	Young	Female	Middle	Bosnian	Ethnic minority	Stayer	Bihać	Urban
Veljko	Middle	Male	University	Serb	Ethnic minority	Stayer	Sarajevo suburb	Urban
Vojo	Old	Male	High	Serb	Minority in mixed marriage	Stayer	Sarajevo suburb	Urban
Zoran	Middle	Male	University	Serb	Minority	Relocatee	Banja Luka	Urban

[a]"Informants" refers to those Bosnians I observed but talked with only informally. "Respondents" refers to those Bosnians I formally interviewed; I also observed a portion of respondents.

[b]Young = up to 21 years of age; Middle = 22 to 59 years of age; Old = 60 years and older

[c]"Political minority" refers to those Bošnjaks affiliated with the political party of Bošnjak autonomist Fikret Abdić

[d]DP refers to displaced person

Appendix C
Structure for Ethnographies

Collect information on minority families in ethnically mixed apartment complexes over a series of interviews with members of at least two different generations:[1]

- Choose "host" with at least one child. Gather background information on:
  - Host
  - All host's siblings
  - Host's spouse, spouse's siblings, and spouse's parents
  - Host's parents and grandparents
  - Host's children and their spouses
  - Two friends of host
- Gather more specific information on:
  - *Patterns* of interaction and *content* of interaction with individuals belonging to a different nation
  - Places lived and school/work experiences at those places
  - Wartime experiences and "lessons" from the war
  - Census nationality
  - Sense of unofficial nationality or identity
  - Sense of native place, if any
  - Conception of out-group
  - Extent to which their decisions regarding interethnic interaction appear calculated vs. culturally driven
  - Work before 1991 and now
- Obtain the following information about households:
  - Nature of talk relating to interethnic relations that is not induced by researcher

1. The structure of this ethnographic design is based on David Laitin's ethnographic work on Russian minorities (see his Methods Appendix, 1998, pp. 394–95).

- Gratuitous comments on other nationality groups as part of everyday conversation
- Newspapers read and frequency
- Radio and TV patterns, particularly time spent watching TV channels originating in areas outside Bošnjak-majority Bosnia (such as from Republika Srpska, Serbia, Croatia, Europe) in comparison with time spent watching TV channels originating from chiefly Muslim Bosnia

Appendix D
Interview Protocol

[Interviewer introduction]

- Pseudonym
- Birthplace
- Birth date
- Sex
- Education
- Profession
- Place during war
- Nationality according to census
- Was your nationality before the war different than now?

1. (For those that stayed during the war in [X place]): Why did you stay?
   - Do you consider you had a choice?
   - What choices did your family members make?
   - Why do you think that others left?
   - (For those that left and then returned)—Why did you return?
   - Why do you continue to stay?
2. Do you consider you had a choice?
   - What choices did your family members make?
   - Do you think about leaving?
   - If you think about leaving, what are the reasons?
   - Where would you go, and why?
3. Where do you consider your home?
4. What everyday steps do you take to increase your feeling of security and well-being during such insecure and difficult times?
5. Some people feel a sense of community with a specific group and others not. If you feel that you have a sense of community with a group, what is that group?

6. For example, some people have a sense of community with their neighborhood. Others don't. What do you think?
   - Did your relations with your closest neighbors change when the war began?
   - How are your relations with your new neighbors?
7. Do you consider that the activities of local or international organizations help you in everyday survival and sense of security?
   - If yes, who helps you?
   - Are you a member or participant in any organization?
8. What source of information do you most trust?
9. How do you feel about education? Should all children study under the same program, or should each ethnic group study under its own?
10. What do you think about your future in Bosnia-Herzegovina?

Appendix E
Predicting the Return of Minorities to Prewar Homes

Coding of variables used in the model

Variable	Coding
Returned to an area where respondent is in the minority	0 = no; 1 = yes
Experience of a family tragedy	0 if no; 1 = yes if respondent has had a family member disappear or be killed
Desire to return	0 = negative (mention of only expiry of permit, imminent deportation, accommodation available, incentive package, and/or employment); 1 = positive (any mention of "wish to return" and/or "family reunification")
Age group	0 = to 20 years; 1 = 21–30 years; 2 = 31–40 years; 3 = 41–60 years; 4 = 61 and over
Education	0 =no formal schooling; 1 = primary school; 2 = secondary school; 3 = high school or university
Serb background	0 = no; 1= yes
Unemployed	0 = no; 1 = yes
Pensioner	0 = no; 1 = yes
Worked abroad	0 = no; 1 = yes
Income	0 = respondent can cover 0% of living costs; 1 = can cover 25% of living costs; 2 = can cover 50% of living costs; 3 = can cover 75% of living costs; 4 = can cover 100% of living costs
Property owner	0 = no; 1 = yes (land, home, apartment, and/or shop)
Gender	0 = male; 1 = female
Percentage of non-nationalists in local legislature	A continuous variable indicating the percentage of votes in the municipality that non-nationalist political parties won in the 1997 elections. The strongest non-nationalist parties were SDP and the Independent Social Democrats.
Percentage of municipality's minorities cleansed	Percentage of prewar minority inhabitants that is not present in a municipality in 1998

Variable	Coding
Compliance of municipality with property legislation	Property Legislation Implementation Plan: the total number of cases closed (the number of properties that have been vacated and/or sealed and/or repossessed and/or the occupancy rightholder or owner was notified that she can repossess), divided by the total number of claims (the number of properties on which a claim and/or request for enforcement of a commission on real property claims decision was filed with municipal housing authorities, May 2000
Municipality's population density	The population estimate of municipalities (UNHCR 1997)
Percentage of municipality that is Croat	Percentage of the municipality's population that is Croat based on UNHCR 1997 data
Entity of prewar home	0 = Republika Srpska, 1 = Federation
Urbanism	A continuous variable indicating the population of the locality of a respondent's prewar home

Appendix F
Explaining Religious Intolerance

Coding of variables used in the model

Variable	Coding
Religious intolerance	1 = if respondent mentioned unwillingness to live next to a neighbor of a different religion; 0 = if respondent did not mention an unwillingness to live next to someone of a different religion
Member of an NGO (not religious)	1 = if respondent reported membership in one or more of the following voluntary organizations: political parties, sports, arts, labor unions, environmental, heath, professional, youth, service for elderly, charity, local, human rights, peace, other; 0 = if respondent did not belong to one of the above voluntary organizations
Attend religious services	1 = never, 2 = rarely, 3 = on holy days, 4 = once a month, 5 = once a week, 6 = more than once a week
View of the communist system	A scale of views of the former communist political system: Ranges from very bad = 1 to very good = 10
Supraethnic identification	1 = if described self as foremost a citizen of Bosnia-Herzegovina; 0 = if described self as foremost a member of a particular ethnic group
Age cohort	1 = if between 18–24; 2 = if 25–34; 3 = 35–44; 4 = 45–54; 5 = 55–64; 6 = if . 65 years
Rural urban residence	1 = if resident in a town with population , 2,000; 2 = between 2,000–5,000; 3 = 5–10,000; 4 = 10–20,000; 5 = 20–50,000; 6 = 50–100,000; 7 = 100–500,000
Education	1 = no formal schooling; 2 5 incomplete primary; 3 = complete primary; 4 = incomplete secondary technical; 5 = complete secondary technical; 6 = incomplete secondary university-prep; 7 = complete secondary university prep; 8 = some university education; 9 = complete university degree
Income	Increasing scale of monthly income before taxes
Unemployed	1 = if respondent is unemployed; 0 = if not
Gender	1 = if male; 0 = if female

Appendix G
Predicting Votes for Moderate Parties in Bosnia in 2001

Coding of variables used in the model

Variable	Coding
Vote for moderate parties	1 − if intend to vote for one of the following: 1 = Social Democratic Party (SDP), the Party of Independent Social Democrats (SNSD), the Bosnian Party (BOSS), the Democratic National Community (DNZ), the Women's Party (SBiH), and the Bosnian Party of Rights (BSP), the New Croatian Initiative (NHI), and the Croatian Peasant Party (HSS BiH); 0 = "national-ist": SDA, SBiH, HDZ, SDS, SPRS, the Serb Radical Party of the Republika Srpska (SRS RS), the Serb National Union (SNS), and the Party of Democratic Progress (PDP)
Member of an NGO (not religious)	1 = if respondent was a member in at least one of the following voluntary organizations: political parties, sports, arts, labor unions, environmental, heath, professional, youth, service, charity, local, human rights, peace, other; 0 = if respondent did not belong to a voluntary organization
Attend religious services	1 = never; 2 = , once a year; 3 = once a year; 4 = special holy days; 5 = once a month; 6 = once a week; 7 = > once a week
Civic identity of a local minority	1 = if respondent is a local minority who described self as foremost a citizen of Bosnia-Herzegovina; 0 = if a local minority described self as foremost a member of a particular ethnic group
Left–right placement	Self-placement of political views on a scale of 1 = left to 10 = right
Dissatisfaction with national office holders	Extent satisfied that those holding national offices are handling the country's affairs: 1 = very satisfied to 4 = very dissatisfied
Education	1 = no formal schooling; 2 = some primary; 3 = complete primary; 4 = some secondary technical; 5 = complete secondary technical; 6 = some secondary university-prep; 7 = complete secondary university prep; 8 = some university education; 9 = completed university

(*continued*)

Variable	Coding
Income	Increasing scale of monthly income before taxes
Age cohort	1 = if between 18–24; 2 = 25–34; 3 = 35–44; 4 = 45–54; 5 = 55–64; 6 = if > 65 years
Gender	0 = if female; 1 = if male
Rural-urban residence	1 = if resident in a town with population , 2,000; 2 = 2,000–5,000; 3 = 5–10,000; 4 = 10–20,000; 5 = 20–50,000; 6 = 50–100,000; 7 = 100–500,000; 8 5 . 500,000

References

Achen, Christopher, and W. Phillips Shively. 1995. *Cross-level Inference.* Chicago: University of Chicago Press.

Afghanistan Research and Evaluation Unit. 2006. "Afghans in Quetta: Settlements, Livelihoods, Support Networks and Cross-Border Linkages." http://www.areu.org.af/index.php?option=com_content&task=viewBid=41Itemid=86 (accessed May 14, 2007).

Agger, Inger. 1995. *Mixed Marriages: Marriage and Ethnicity in a Context of Ethnic Cleansing.* Zagreb: European Community Humanitarian Office and the World Health Organization.

Almond, Gabriel, and Sidney Verba. 1978. *The Civic Culture.* Princeton: Princeton University Press.

Amnesty International. 1998. "Report—EUR 64/04/98, Croatia: Impunity for Killings After 'Storm.'" Amnesty International USA. http://www.amnestyusa.org/documentphD?lang=e&id=BFB8256B84757144802569000006930B5 (accessed May 15, 2007).

Andrić, Ivo. 1990. Translated by Zelimir B. Juricic and John F. Loud. *The Development of Spiritual Life in Bosnia under the Influence of Turkish Rule.* Durham: Duke University Press.

Arnautović, Suad. 1996. *Izbori u Bosni i Hercegovini 1990.* Sarajevo: Promocult.

Atmar, Haneef Mohammed, and Jonathan Goodhand. 2002. "Afghanistan: The Challenge of 'Winning the Peace.'" In *Searching for Peace in Central and South Asia,* ed. Monique Mekenkamp, Paul van Tongeren, and Hans van de Veen, 168–87. Boulder: Lynne Rienner.

Axelrod, Robert. 1981. *The Evolution of Cooperation.* New York: Basic Books.

Baćević, Bjiljana, Stefica Bahtijarevic, Vladimir Goati, Goran Miles, Milan Miljevic, Dimitar Mircev, Dragomir Pantić, Nikola Poplašen, Niko Tos, and Marjana Vasović. 1991. *Jugoslavija na kriznoj prekretnici.* Beograd: Institut Drustvenih Nauka.

"The Balkans: After the War Was Over." 2005. *Refugees* 3:1–31.

Banac, Ivo. 1984. *The National Question in Yugoslavia.* Ithaca: Cornell University Press.

Barrington, Lowell. 2001. "Russian-speakers in Ukraine and Kazakhstan: 'Nationality,' population, or neither?" *Post-Soviet Affairs* 17:129–58.

Baskin, Mark. 1983. "Crisis in Kosovo." *Problems of Communism* 32:61–74.

——. 1984. "Nationalist in Form, Nationalist in Content: Some Consequences of Consociationalism in Yugoslavia." Paper presented at the annual meeting of the American Political Science Association, August 30–September 2.

———. 2005. *Developing Local Democracy in Kosovo*. Stockholm: International Institute for Democracy and Electoral Assistance. http://www.idea.int/publications/dem_kosovo/index.cfm.

Baskin, Mark, and Paula M. Pickering. Forthcoming. "Former Yugoslavia and Its Successors." In *Democracy, the Market and Back to Europe: Post-Communist Europe*, ed. Sharon L. Wolchik and Jane L. Curry. Lanham: Rowman & Littlefield.

Baubock, Rainer, and John Rundell, eds. 1998. *Blurred Boundaries: Migration, Ethnicity, Citizenship*. Aldershot Hants: Ashgate.

Bejdić, Dika. 1995. "Dobro jutro, komšija!" *Unsko-Sansko Novine*. July 30, 5.

Bell, Daniel. 1975. "Ethnicity and Social Change." In *Ethnicity: Theory and Experience*, ed. Nathan Glazer and Daniel Moynihan. Cambridge: Harvard University Press.

Bell, Janice. 2001a. "HDZ Hangs onto Bosnian Croat Support," Washington, D.C.: Department of State, Office of Research, June 4.

———. 2001b. "PDP Gains Bosnian Serbs' Confidence, But SDS Still Maintains Lead," Washington, D.C.: Department of State, Office of Research, June 14.

———. 2001c. "One in Three Bosniaks Supports SDP," Washington, D.C.: Department of State, Office of Research, July 6.

Bell, Janice, and Dina Smeltz. 2001 "Returned Bosnian Refugees Accept Dayton," Washington D.C.: Department of State, Office of Research.

Bell, Pamela. 2005. "Collective Identity and Personal Trauma: The Impact on Mental Health and Well-Being." Paper presented at the workshop, "Accommodating Difference in Bosnia-Herzegovina Ten Years After Dayton." Bergen, Norway, May 8.

Berry, John A., and Carol Pott Berry, eds. 1995. *Genocide in Rwanda: A Collective Memory*. London: Care, UK.

Bertsch, Gart K. 1976. *Values and Community in Multi-national Yugoslavia*. Boulder: East European Quarterly

Bieber, Florian. 2000. "Bosnia-Herzegovina and Lebanon: Historical Lessons of Two Multireligious States." *Third World Quarterly* 21: 269–82.

———. 2001. "Croat Self-Government in Bosnia—A Challenge for Dayton?" European Centre for Minority Issues (ECMI), Brief 5.

———. 2005. "Local Institutional Engineering: A Tale of Two Cities, Mostar and Brčko." *International Peacekeeping*. 12:420–33.

Bose, Sumantra. 2002. *Bosnia after Dayton: Nationalist Partition and International Intervention*. Oxford: Oxford University Press.

Bougarel, Xavier. 2003. "Islam and Politics in the Post-Communist Balkans." In *New Approaches to Balkan Studies*, ed. Dimitris Keridis, Ellen Elias-Bursac, and Nicholas Yatromanolakis, 345–61. Dulles, Va.: Brassey's.

———. 1996. "Bosnia and Hercegovina—State and Communitarianism." In *Yugoslavia and After*, ed. David Dyker and Ivan Vejvoda. 67–115. London: Longman.

Božinovska, Žana. 2006. "VIP nastava vo priroda." *Dnevnik*, s. 1. 28 Juni.

Brewer, Marilynn. 2001. "The Many Faces of Social Identity: Implications for Political Psychology." *Political Psychology* 22:115–25.

Bringa, Tone. 1993. "Nationality Categories, National Identification and Identity Formation in 'Multinational' Bosnia." *Anthropology of East Europe Review* 11:69–76.

———. 1995. *Being Muslim the Bosnian Way*. Princeton: Princeton University Press.

Bringa, Tone, and Peter Loizos. 2001. *Returning Home: The Revival of a Bosnian Village* (documentary film). Sarajevo: Saga Film and Video.

Brown, Keith. 2000. "Macedonia: Prevention Can Work." *Special Report 58*. Washington, D.C.: U.S. Institute of Peace, March 27.

——. 2006. "The New Ugly Americans? Making Sense of Democracy Promotion in the Former Yugoslavia." In *Transacting Transition: The Micropolitics of Democracy Assistance in the Former Yugoslavia,* ed. Keith Brown. 1–22. Bloomfield: Kumarian Press.

Broz, Svetlana. 1999. *Dobri ljudi u vremenu zla.* Banja Luka: Media Centar Prelom.

Brubaker, Rogers. 1995. "National Minorities, Nationalizing States, and External National Homelands in the New Europe." *Daedlaus* 124:107–32.

Brubaker, Rogers, and Frederick Cooper. 2000. "Beyond Identity." *Theory and Society* 29:1–47.

Bugajski, Jansz. 1993. "The Fate of Minorities in Eastern Europe." *Journal of Democracy* 4:85–99.

Bukvić, Nedim. 1998. *Economic Brief for Bosnia and Hercegovina.* Sarajevo: Resident Mission of the World Bank in Sarajevo.

Bunce, Valerie. 1999. *Subversive Institutions: The Design and the Destruction of Socialism and the State.* Cambridge: Cambridge University Press.

——. 2005. "Promoting Democracy in Divided Societies." Manuscript prepared for the American Political Science Association task force on difference and inequality in the developing world.

"Bura zbog izjave Vojislava Kostunice." 2002. Oslobodjenje. Septembar 13.

Burg, Steven L. 1983. *Conflict and Cohesion in Socialist Yugoslavia.* Princeton: Princeton University Press.

——. 1997. "Bosnia-Hercegovina: A case of failed democratization." In *Politics, Power, and the Struggle for Democracy in South-Eastern Europe,* ed. Karen Dawisha and Bruce Parrott, 122–45. Cambridge: Cambridge University Press.

Burg, Steven L., and Michael L. Berbaum. 1989. "Community, Integration, and Stability in Multinational Yugoslavia." *American Political Science Review* 83:535–55.

Burg, Steven L., and Paul S. Shoup. 1999. *The War in Bosnia-Herzegovina.* Armonk: M.E. Sharpe.

Burt, Ronald S. 1997. "A Note on Social Capital and Network Content." *Social Networks* 19:355–73.

Campbell, Angus, Philip E. Converse, Warren E. Miller, and Donald E. Stokes. 1960. *The American Voter.* Chicago: University of Chicago Press.

Caplan, Richard. 2004. "International Authority and State Building: The Case of Bosnia and Herzegovina." *Global Governance* 10:53–65.

Carothers, Thomas. 1999. *Aiding Democracy Abroad.* Washington, D.C.: Carnegie Endowment for International Peace.

Caspersen, Nina. 2004. "Good Fences Make Good Neighbors? A Comparison of Conflict-Regulation Strategies in Postwar Bosnia." *Journal of Peace Research* 41:569–88.

Chandler, David. 2000. *Faking Democracy after Dayton.* London: Pluto Press.

Chandra, Kanchan, ed. 2001. "Cumulative Findings in the Study of Ethnic Politics." Symposium: *American Political Science Association—Comparative Politics newsletter.* 7–25.

Chinn, Jeff, and Robert Kaiser. 1996. *Russians as the New Minority.* Boulder: Westview Press.

Christie, Debbie, and Tone Bringa, directors. 1993. *We Are All Neighbours* (documentary film). Disappearing World: War Trilogy, Granada Television.

Cockburn, Cynthia. 1998. *The Space Between Us: Negotiating Gender and National Identities in Conflict.* London: Zed Books.

Cohen, Lenard J. 1995. *Broken Bonds.* 2nd ed. Boulder: Westview.

Cole, Beth Ellen, and Kiya Bajpai. 2006. "Afghanistan Five Years Later: What Can the United States Do to Help?" *USIPeaceBriefing*. Washington D.C.: US Institute of Peace, November 9. http: /// usip.org / pubs / usippeace_briefings / 2006 / 1109_ afghanistan_taliban.html (accessed May 14, 2007).

Colletta, Nat, and Michelle Cullen, eds. 2000. *Violent Conflict and the Transformation of Social Capital: Lessons from Cambodia, Rwanda, Guatemala, and Somalia*. Washington D.C.: World Bank.

Comisso, Ellen. 1979. *Workers' Control Under Plan and Market*. New Haven: Yale University Press.

Constable, Pamela. 2007. "A Wake-Up Call in Afghanistan." *Journal of Democracy* 18:84–99.

"Constitution of Bosnia and Hercegovina." 1995. In *The General Framework Agreement*. Dayton: Proximity Peace Talks, November.

"Constitution of the Federation of Bosnia and Hercegovina." 1994. Washington D.C.: U.S. Department of State, March.

"Constitution of the Serbian Republic of Bosnia-Hercegovina," 1992.

Cousins, Elizabeth, and Charles Cater. 2001. *Toward Peace in Bosnia: implementing the Dayton Accords*. Boulder: Lynne Rienner.

Cox, Marcus, 1997. "Return, Relocation and Property Rights: A Discussion Paper." Sarajevo: Commission for Real Property Claims of Displaced Persons and Refugees and UNHCR, December.

——. 1998. *Strategic Approaches to International Intervention in Bosnia and Herzegovina*. Sarajevo: Centre for Applied Studies in International Negotiations.

Cushman, Thomas. 1998. "Patterns of Trust and Mistrust in Post-War Bosnian Society." Paper presented at the International Conference, "Bosnia Paradigm," Sarajevo, Bosnia and Hercegovina. November 18–21.

Dahl, Robert. 1989. *Democracy and Its Critics*. New Haven: Yale University Press.

Dahlman, Carl, and Gearoid O Tuathail. 2005. "The Legacy of Ethnic Cleansing: The International Community and the Returns Process in Post-Dayton Bosnia-Herzegovina." *Political Geography*. 24:569–99.

Dani, Anis, Mirsada Muzur, Sarah Forster, Dino Dijipa, Paula Lytle, and Patrizia Poggi. 1999. "A Social Assessment of Bosnia and Hercegovina." Washington, D.C.: The World Bank, Europe and Central Asia Region, Environmentally and Socially Sustainable Development Unit.

Das, Hans. 2004. "Restoring Property Rights in the Aftermath of War." *ICLQ* 53:4.

Daskalovski, Židas. 2004. "Minority Political Participation and Education in the Municipality of Cair." In *Managing Hatred and Distrust: The Prognosis for Post-Conflict Settlement in Multiethnic Communities in the Former Yugoslavia*, ed. Nenad Demetrijević and Petra Kovacs, 125–36. Budapest: Open Society Institute.

"Decisions on Property Laws." 1999. Sarajevo: Office of the High Representative Press Release, April 14.

Delalić, E. 1999. "Refugee Women as Minorities." Paper presented at the annual convention of The Institute for Strengthening Democracy, Konjic, Bosnia-Herzegovina, July.

Demeri, Mary. 2001. "Bosnian Views on Ethnic Relations Show Some Improvement, But Serbs remain Negative Overall." Washington, D.C.: Department of State, Office of Research, August 29.

Demichelis, Julia. 1998. *NGOs and Peacebuilding in Bosnia's Ethnically Divided Cities*. Washington, D.C.: U.S. Institute of Peace.

Denitch, Bogdan. 1973. "Mobility and Recruitment of Yugoslav Leadership: The Role of the League of Socialists," In *Opinion-Making Elites in Yugoslavia*, ed. Allen H. Barton, Bogdan Denitch, and Charles Kadushin, 95–119. New York: Praeger.

———. 1976. "Violence and Social Change in the Yugoslav Revolution." *Comparative Politics* 8:465–78.

Dewalt, Kathleen M., and Billie R. Dewalt. 1998. "Participant Observation." In *Handbook of Methods in Cultural Anthropology*, ed. Russel H. Bernard. Walnut Creek, Calif.: Sage.

Diener, Alexander C. 2005. "Problematic Integration of Mongolian-Kazakh Return Migrants in Kazakhstan." *Eurasian Geography and Economics* 46:465–78.

Dizdarević, Zija. 1998. "Srbi i Sarajevo," *Oslobodjenje*. 2.XII., s. 1.

———. 2002. "Zov mrtvačke glave." *Oslobodjenje*. 17.IX.

Djipa, Dino, Mirsada Muzur, Paula Lytle, and Paula Franklin. 1999. *Consultations with the Poor: National Synthesis Report, Bosnia-Herzegovina*. Washington, D.C.: World Bank.

Donia, Robert J. 2000. "The Quest for Tolerance in Sarajevo's Textbooks." *Human Rights Review* 1:38–55.

Donia, Robert, and John V. A. Fine. 1994. *Bosnia and Hercegovina: A Tradition Betrayed*. New York: Columbia University Press.

Doughten, Lisa. 1998. "Bosnia and Hercegovina: Property Rights and the Right to Return." Unpublished ms.

Dowley, Kathleen M., and Brian D. Silver. 2002. "Social Capital, Ethnicity and Support for Democracy in the Post-Socialist States." *Europe-Asia Studies* 54:505–28.

Drakulić, Slavenka. 1993a. *How We Survived Communism and Even Laughed*. New York: Harper Perennial.

———. 1993b. *Balkan Express: Fragments from the Other Side of War*. New York: W.W. Norton.

Eckstein, Harry. 1975. "Case Study and Theory in Political Science." In *Handbook of Political Science*, ed. Fred I. Greenstein and Nelson W. Polsby. Reading, Mass.: Addison-Wesley.

Eckstein, Susan. 1977. *The Poverty of Revolution*. Princeton: Princeton University Press.

Edwards, Alica. 2000. "Daunting Prospects: Minority Women: Obstacles to Their Return and Reintegration." Sarajevo: UN High Commissioner for Refugees.

Emerson, Robert M., Rachel Fretz, and Linda Shaw. 1995. *Writing Ethnographic Fieldnotes*. Chicago: University of Chicago Press.

Erlanger, Steven. 2001. "The Balkan Disease Isn't Cured Yet." *New York Times*, April 15, 6.

European Commission for Democracy Through Law. 2005. "Opinion on the Constitutional Situation in Bosnia and Herzegovina and the Powers of the High Representative." http://www.venice.coe.int/SITE/DYNAMICS/N_RECENT_EF.ASP?L=E&TITLE1=62ND%20PLENARY%20SESSION&TITLE2=62E%20SESSION%20PLÉENIÈRE (accessed May 15, 2007).

European Security Initiative (ESI). 1999. "Interim Evaluation of the Reconstruction and Return Task Force: Minority Return Programs in 1999." Sarajevo, September 14. http://www.esiweb.org/pdf/esi_document_id_2.pdf (accessed December 2006).

European Values Study Group and World Values Survey Association. 2004. *European and World Values Surveys Integrated Data File*, 1999–2002, Release 1 [Computer file]. 2nd ICPSR version.

Fearon, James, and David Laitin. 1996. "Explaining Inter-ethnic Cooperation," *American Political Science Review* 90:715–35.

Federation Ombudsmen. 1997. *Annual Report on the Situation of Human Rights for 1996.* Sarajevo: Office of the Ombudsmen of the Federation of Bosnia and Hercegovina, March.

———. 1999. *Annual Report on the Situation of Human Rights for 1998.* Sarajevo: Office of the Ombudsmen of the Federation of Bosnia and Hercegovina, March.

Feldman, Martha. 1995. *Strategies for Interpreting Qualitative Data.* Qualitative Research Methods Series, 33. Thousand Oaks: Sage.

Fenno, Richard. 1978. *Home Style: House Members in Their Districts.* Boston: Little, Brown, and Co.

Fetterman, David M. 1989. *Ethnography: Step by Step.* Applied Social Research Methods Series, 17. Newbury Park: Sage.

Filandra, Šaćir. 1998. *Bošnjačka politika u XX. stoljeću.* Sarajevo: Sejtarija.

Fine, John V.A. 1975. *The Bosnian Church: A New Interpretation.* Boulder and New York: East European Monographs, distributed by Columbia University Press.

Finifter, Ada W. 1974. "The Friendship Group as a Protective Environment for Political Deviants." *American Political Science Review* 68:607–25.

Foroughi, Payam. 2006. "Tajikistan." In *Nations in Transit.* New York: Freedom House. http://www.freedomhouse.hu/pdfdocs/tajikistan2006.pdf.

Fox, Jon E. 2003. "National Identities on the Move: Transylvanian Labour Migrants in Hungary." *Journal of Ethnic and Migration Studies* 29:449–67.

Friedman, Francine. 2004. *Bosnia and Herzegovina: A Polity On the Brink.* New York: Taylor & Francis.

Gagnon, V. P., Jr. 2002. "International NGOs in Bosnia-Herzegovina: Attempting to Build Civil Society." In *The Power and Limits of NGOs,* ed. Sarah E. Mendelson and John K. Glenn, 207–51. New York: Columbia University Press.

———. 2004. *The Myth of Ethnic War: Serbia and Croatia in the 1990s.* Ithaca: Cornell University Press.

Geddes, Barbara. 1990. "How the Cases You Choose Affect the Answers You Get: Selection Bias in Comparative Politics." *Political Analysis* 2:131–50.

Gellner, Ernest. 1983. *Nations and Nationalism.* Ithaca: Cornell University Press.

Ghodsee, Kristen. 2003. "International Organizations, Women and Civil Society in post-socialist Bulgaria." In *New Approaches to Balkan Studies,* ed. Dimitris Keridis, Ellen Elias-Bursac, and Nicholas Yatromanolakis, 234–54. Dulles, Va.: Brassey's.

Gibson, James L., and Amanda Gouws. 2000. "Social Identities and Political Intolerance: Linkages Within the South African Mass Public." *American Journal of Political Science* 44:272–86.

———. 2003. *Overcoming Intolerance in South Africa.* Cambridge: Cambridge University Press.

Gitelman, Zvi. 1983. "Are Nations Merging in the USSR?" *Problems of Communism* 32:35–47.

Gjelten, Tom. 1995. *Sarajevo Daily, A City and Its Newspaper Under Siege.* New York: HarperCollins.

Glaser, Barney G., and Anselm L. Strauss. 1967. *The Discovery of Grounded Theory.* New York: Aldine de Gruyter.

Gordy, Eric. 1999. *The Culture of Power in Serbia.* University Park: Pennsylvania State University Press.

Granovetter, Mark S. 1973 "The Strength of Weak Ties." *American Journal of Sociology* 78:1360–80.

Green, Donald, and Ian Shapiro. 1994. *Pathologies of Rational Choice Theory.* New Haven: Yale University Press.

Hadžijahić, Muhamed, 1974. *Od tradicije do identiteta: geneza nacijonalnog pitanja Bosanskih Muslimana.* Sarajevo: Sjetlost.

Hayden, Robert M. 1993. *Constitutional Nationalism in the Formerly Yugoslav Republics.* Washington, D.C.: National Council for Soviet and East European Research. March 11.

———. 1996. "Imagined Communities and Real Victims: Self-Determination and Ethnic Cleansing in Yugoslavia." *American Ethnologist* 23:783–801.

———. 1999. *Blueprints for a House Divided.* Ann Arbor: University of Michigan Press.

Hedges, Chris. 1997. "In Bosnia's Schools, 3 Ways Never to Learn from History." *New York Times*, A1, A4.

Helms, Elissa. 1997. "Understandings of National Identity Among Bosnian Muslim Refugees in Pittsburgh." Unpublished ms. University of Pittsburgh.

———. 2003. "The Nation-ing of Gender?" Paper presented at the Research Network for Post-Communist Cultural Studies (SOYUZ) Conference, Amherst, Mass.

Helsinki Commission. 2006. "Tajikistan's Presidential Election Fall Short." *Helsinki Commission Digest* 39:1–4, December 13.

Helsinki Committee for Human Rights. 2001. "Report on Activities of the Legal Services of the Helsinki Committee for Human Rights in BiH in rendering free legal assistance to citizens." Sarajevo: Helsinki Committee for Human Rights in BiH.

Hislope, Robert. 2002. "Organized Crime in a Disorganized State: How Corruption Contributed to Macedonia's Mini-War." *Problems of Post-Communism* 49:33–41.

Hodson, Randy, Duško Sekulić, and Garth Massey. 1994. "National Tolerance in the Former Yugoslavia." *American Journal of Sociology* 99:1534–58.

Holbrooke, Richard. 1998. *To End a War.* New York: Random House.

Holohan, Anne. 2005. *Networks of Democracy: Lessons from Kosovo for Afghanistan, Iraq, and Beyond.* Stanford: Stanford University Press.

Hooghe, Marc. 2003. "Voluntary Associations and Democratic Attitudes: Value Congruence as a Causal Mechanism." In *Generating Social Capital: Civil Society and Institutions in Comparative Perspective*, ed. Marc Hooghe and Dietlind Stolle, 89–113. New York: Palgrave McMillan.

Horowitz, Donald. 1985. *Ethnic Groups in Conflict.* Berkeley: University of California Press.

Huckfeldt, R. Robert. 1983. "Social Contexts, Social Networks, and Urban Neighborhoods: Environmental Constraints on Friendship Choice." *American Journal of Sociology* 39:651–83.

Hugo, Graeme J. 1981. "Village-Community Ties, Village Norms and Ethnic and Social Networks: A Review of Evidence from the Third World." In *Migration Decision-Making*, ed. Gordon F. De Jong and Robert Gardner, 186–224. New York: Pergamon Press.

Human Rights Department. 1999. "Employment Discrimination in Bosnia and Hercegovina." Sarajevo: OSCE Mission to Bosnia and Hercegovina, June.

Human Rights Ombudsperson for Bosnia and Herzegovina. 1997. *First Annual Report.* Sarajevo: Office of the Human Rights Ombudsperson.

Human Rights Watch / Helsinki. 1997. "Bosnia and Hercegovina: Politics of Revenge, The Misuse of Authority in Bihać, Cazin, and Velika Kladuša," New York: Human Rights Watch / Helsinki.

———. 2004. "Croatia Returns Update." *Human Rights Watch Briefing Paper.* New York: Human Rights Watch, May 13.

Hundley, Tom. 2000. "Thousands of Serb Refugees Returning Home to Croatia," *Chicago Tribune*, April 27.

Hurlbert, Jeanne S., Valerie A. Haines, and John J. Beggs. 2000. "Core Networks and Tie Activation: What Kinds of Routine Networks Allocate Resources in Nonroutine Situations?" *American Sociological Review* 65:598–618.

Internal Displacement Monitoring Centre. 2006. *Croatia: Reforms Come Too Late for Most Remaining Ethnic Serb IDPs.* Geneva: Norwegian Refugee Council. http://www.internal-displacement.org (accessed May 1, 2007).

International Council of Voluntary Agencies. 2000. *ICVA Directory of Humanitarian Development Agencies in Bosnia-Herzegovina.* Sarajevo: Sarajevo International Council of Voluntary Agencies.

International Criminal Tribunal for former Yugoslavia (ICTY). 2001. "Krstić IT-98–33 Srebrenica." Judgment. http://www.un.org/icty/cases_e/index-e.htm (accessed May 11, 2007).

International Crisis Group (ICG). 1998. "Changing Course? Implication of the Divide in Bosnian Croat Politics." Sarajevo: Sarajevo Office of ICG, August 13.

——. 2000. "Kosovo Report Card," Pristina/Brussels: ICG Balkans Report No. 100.

——. 2001a. "Bosnia's Precarious Economy: Still Not Open for Business." Europe Report No. 115, August 7.

——. 2001b. "Macedonia: Still Standing," Balkans Briefing. Skopje/Brussels, July 27.

——. 2002. "Bosnia's Alliance for (Smallish) Change." Balkans Report No. 132, August 2. http://www.crisisgroup.org/home/index.cfm?id=1499&l=1 (accessed January 2, 2007).

——. 2003. "Peacebuilding in Afghanistan." Asia Report No. 64. September 29. http://www.crisisgroup.org/home/index.cfm?id=2293&l=1 (accessed January 10, 2007).

——. 2004. "Collapse in Kosovo." Europe Report No. 155, April 22. http://www.crisisgroup.org/home/index.cfm?id=2627&l=1.

International Institute for Democracy and Electoral Assistance (IDEA). 2001. *South-Eastern Europe and the Stability Pact: New Means for Regional Analysis, Focus Group Studies: Federation of Bosnia-Hercegovina and Republic of Srpska.* http://archive.idea.int/balkans/research.htm.

——. 2002. *South Eastern Europe: New Means for Regional Analysis: Survey Results.* http://archive.idea.int/balkans/results.htm.

International Organization for Migration (IOM). 1999. *IOM Returnee Dataset.* Sarajevo: IOM Mission in Bosnia and Hercegovina.

Isaković, Alija, ed. 1990. *O "nacionaliziranju" Muslimana.* Zagreb: Globus.

Isaković, Relidija, and Alija Isaković. 1994. *Istorija, II Razred gimnazija.* Sarajevo: Republika Bosna i Hercegovina, Ministarstvo obrazovanja.

"The Islamic Declaration: A Programme for the Islamicization of Moslems and Moslem Peoples." 1983. *South Slav Journal* 6:1–16.

Izborna Komicija Bosne i Hercegovine. 2006. "Statistika." http://www.izbori.ba/.

Jelavich, Charles, and Barbara Jelavich. 1977. *The Establishment of the Balkan National States, 1804–1920.* Seattle: University of Washington Press.

Jennings, M. Kent, and Richard Niemi. 1981. *Generations and Politics.* Princeton: Princeton University Press.

Judah, Tim. 2004. "Half-Empty or Half-Full Towns?" *Transitions Online,* February 5. http://www.toi-c2/look/TOL/article.tpl?IDLanguage=1&IDPublication=9&NrIssue=1&NrSection=4&NrArticle=11547&search=search&keywords=Judah&searchmode=on&searchlevel=o (accessed May 14, 2007).

Kaiser, Robert, and Elena Nikiforova. 2006. "Borderland Spaces of Identification and

Dis/location: Multiscalar Narratives and Enactments of Seto Identity and Place in the Estonian-Russian Borderlands." *Ethnic and Racial Studies* 29:928–58.

Kaplan, Robert D. 1993. *Balkan Ghosts.* New York: St. Martin's Press.

Kasapović, Marjana. 2001. *Hrvatska politika 1990–2000.* Zagreb: Biblioteka *Politička misao.*

Key, V. O. 1950. *Southern Politics in State and Nation,* New York: Alfred A. Knopf.

Kinder, Donald R., and Nicholas Winter. 2001. "Exploring the Racial Divide: Blacks, Whites, and Opinion on National Policy." *American Journal of Political Science* 45: 439–56.

Kirk, Jerome, and Marc Miller. 1986. *Reliability and Validity in Qualitative Research.* Thousand Oaks: Sage.

Knaus, Gerald, and Felix Martin. 2003. "Travails of the European Raj." *Journal of Democracy* 14:60–74.

Kollind, Torsten. 2005. "Post-War Identifications and Counterdiscursive Practices in a Herzegovinian Town." Paper presented at the workshop, "Accommodating Difference in Bosnia-Herzegovina: Ten Years After Dayton," Bergen, Norway, May 5–8.

Kolsto, Pal. 1995. *Russians in the Former Soviet Republics.* Bloomington: Indiana University Press.

Kolsto, Pal, ed. 2002. *National Integration and Violent Conflict in Post-Soviet Societies: The Cases of Estonia and Moldova.* Lanham, Md: Rowman & Littlefield Publishers, Inc.

Koser, Khalid, and Richard Black. 1999. "Limits to Harmonization: The Temporary Protection of Refugees in the European Union." *International Migration* 37:521–43.

Križan, Mojmir. 1989. "Civil Society: The New Paradigm in the Yugoslav Theoretical Discussion." *Praxis International* 9:152–63.

Kukič, Slavko. 1998. Position of the Citizen and the Nation in Bosnia and Herzegovina. Sarajevo: Centre for Protection of Minorities Rights Sarajevo.

Kunovich, Robert M., and Randy Hodson. 1999. "Conflict, Religious identity, and Ethnic Intolerance in Croatia," *Social Forces* 78:643–68.

Kurlantzick, Joshua. 2006. "The U.N. Success Story That Wasn't." *Washington Post,* June 4, B04.

Laitin, David. 1998. *Identity in Formation: The Russian-Speaking Populations in the Near Abroad.* Ithaca: Cornell University Press.

Laumann, Edward O. 1973. *Bonds of Pluralism: The Form and Substance of Urban Social Networks.* New York: John Wiley and Sons.

Lederach, John Paul. 1997. *Building Peace: Sustainable Reconciliation In Divided Societies,* Washington, D.C.: U.S. Institute of Peace.

Liebow, Elliot. 1967. *Tally's Corner.* Boston: Little, Brown and Co.

Lijphart, Arend. 1968–69. "Consociational Democracy." *World Politics* 21:207–25.

———. 1971. "Comparative Politics and the Comparative Method." *American Political Science Review* 65:682–93.

Lin, Nan. 2001. "Building a Network Theory of Social Capital." In *Social Capital: Theory and Research,* ed. Nan Lin, Karen Cook, and Ronald Burt, 3–29. New York: Aldine de Gruyter.

Lippman, Peter. 1999–2000. *Journal.*

Lipset, Seymour M., and Stein Rokkan. 1967. *Party Systems and Voter Alignments: Cross-National Perspectives.* New York: Free Press.

Lockwood, William G. 1975. *European Muslims: Economy and Ethnicity in Western Bosnia.* New York: Academic Press.

Longo, Matthew. 2006. "The HDZ's Embattled Mandate." *Problems of Post-Communism* 53:36–43.

Lynch, G. Patrick. 2002. "Midterm Elections and Economic Fluctuations. The Response of the Rational Voter over Time." *Legislative Studies Quarterly* 27:265–94.

Lyons, Terrence. 2002. "The Role of Postsettlement Elections." In *Ending Civil Wars: The Implementation of Peace Agreements,* ed. Stephen John Stedman, Donald Rothchild, and Elizabeth M. Cousens, 215–36. Boulder: Lynn Rienner.

MacIver, Martha. 1993. "Roundup of Public Opinion in Macedonia." USIA Opinion Research Memorandum. Washington, D.C.: Office of Research, USIA.

Magaš, Branka, and Ivo Zanić. 2001. *The War in Croatia and Bosnia-Herzegovina 1991–1995.* London: Frank Cass.

Malkki, Lissa. 1995a. *Purity and Exile: Violence, Memory, and National Cosmology among Hutu Refugees in Tanzania.* Chicago: University of Chicago Press.

———. 1995b. "Refugees and Exile: From 'Refugee Studies' to the National Order of Things." *Annual Review of Anthropology* 24:495–523.

Marsden, Peter. 1990. "Network Data and Measurement." *Annual Review of Sociology* 16:435–63.

Massey, Garth, Randy Hodson, and Duško Sekulić. 1999. "Ethnic Enclaves and Intolerance: The Case of Yugoslavia." *Social Forces* 78:669–91.

Mazower, Mark. 2002. *The Balkans: A Short History.* New York: The Modern Library.

McAdam, Doug. 1982. *Political Process and the Development of Black Insurgency, 1930–1970.* Chicago: University of Chicago Press.

McGarry, John, and Brendan O'Leary, eds. 1993. *The Politics of Ethnic Conflict Regulation.* London: Routledge.

Medjunarodni Forum Bosna. 1999. *Povratak prognanih i raseljenih kao uvjet opstanka Bosne i Hercegovine.* Sarajevo.

Mertus, Julie. 1999. *Kosovo: How Myths and Truths Started a War.* Berkeley: University of California Press.

———. 2000. "National Minorities Under the Dayton Peace Accords." In *Neighbors at War: Anthropological Perspectives on Yugoslavia, Ethnicity, Culture and History,* ed. Joel Halpern and David Kideckel. University Park: Pennsylvania State University Press.

———. 2004. "Improving International Peacebuilding Efforts: The Example of Human Rights Culture in Kosovo." *Global Governance* 10:333–47.

Mickey, Robert W., and Adam Smith Albion. 1993. "Success in the Balkans? A Case Study of Ethnic Relations in the Republic of Macedonia." In *Minorities: The New Europe's Old Issue,* ed. Ian M. Cuthbertson and Jane Leibowitz, 53–98. Prague: Institute for EastWest Studies.

Milinković, Branislav, ed. 1995. *Novi ustavi na tlu bivše Jugoslavije.* Beograd: "Medjnarodna Politika" Pravni Fakultet, Fakultet Političkih Nauka.

Milivojević, Zdenka. 1994. "National Identity as Political Ideology." *Refuge.* 14:15–22.

Miller, Steven, and David O. Sears. 1986. "Stability and Change in Social Tolerance: A Test of the Persistence Hypothesis." *American Journal of Political Science* 30:214–36.

Minard, Ralph. 1952. "Race Relations in the Pocahontas Coal Fields." *Journal of Social Issues* 8:29–44.

Mondak, Jeffery, and Diann Mutz. 2001. "Involuntary Association: How the Workplace Contributes to American Civic Life." Paper presented to the Midwest Political Science Association, Chicago, April.

Molenaers, Nadia. 2003. "Associations or Informal Networks? Social Capital and Local Development Practices." In *Generating Social Capital: Civil Society and Institutions in Comparative Perspective*, ed. Marc Hooghe and Dietlind Stolle, 113–32. New York: Palgrave McMillan.

Mrkić, Jelena. 1997. "Nit me čekaj, niti mi se nadaj!" *Slobodna Bosna* 15 Juni: 24–25.

Naegele, Jolyon. 2001. "How Macedonia's Kumanovo Has Avoided Inter-ethnic Conflict," *Radio Free Europe/Radio Liberty Newsline*. May 5, 21.

National Republican Institute for International Affairs. 1991. *The 1990 Elections in the Republics of Yugoslavia*. Washington, D.C.: National Republic Institute for International Affairs.

Nordlinger, Eric. 1972. *Conflict Regulation in Divided Societies*. Cambridge, Mass.: Center for International Affairs, Occasional Paper 29.

Oberschall, Anthony. 2000. "The Manipulation of Ethnicity: From Ethnic Cooperation to Violence and War in Yugoslavia." *Ethnic and Racial Studies* 23:982–1001.

Olcott, Martha Brill. 1990. "Central Asia: The Reformers Challenge a Traditional Society." In *The Nationalities Factor in Soviet Politics and Society*, ed. Mark Beissinger and Lubomyr Hajda, 253–80. Boulder: Westview.

——. 1996. "Demographic Upheavals in Central Asia." *Orbis* 40:537–56.

Oliver, Eric, and Tali Mendelberg. 2000. "Reconsidering the Environmental Determinants of White Racial Attitudes." *American Journal of Political Science* 44:574–89.

Olzak, Susan. 1992. *The Dynamics of Ethnic Competition and Conflict*. Stanford: Stanford University Press.

Ombudsmen of the Federation of Bosnia and Hercegovina. 1999. "Annual Report on the Situation of Human Rights for 1998, Sarajevo." Sarajevo: Office of the Ombudsmen of the Federation of Bosnia and Hercegovina.

Organization for Security and Cooperation in Europe (OSCE). 1999a. "PC.DEC/305." Vienna: Permanent Council, 237th Plenary Meeting.

——. 1999b. "Employment Discrimination in Bosnia and Hercegovina," Sarajevo: Mission to Bosnia and Hercegovina.

——. 1999c. "Kosovo/Kosova as Seen as Told: An Analysis of the Human Rights Findings of the OSCE Kosovo Verification Mission from October 1998 to October 1999." Warsaw: OSCE Office for Democratic Institutions and Human Rights, December.

——. 2004. *Public Opinion Research, September 2004: Croatia's Refugee Challenge.*" Mission to Bosnia and Herzegovina, Democratization Department. http://www.oscebih.org/documents/740-eng.pdf (accessed May 14, 2007).

OSCE Mission in Kosovo and UNHCR Mission in Kosovo. 2000. "Assessment of the Situation of Ethnic Minorities in Kosovo: Period Covering November 1999 though January 2000." Vienna: OSCE Conflict Prevention Centre, February 17.

——. 2003. "Tenth Assessment of the Situation of Ethnic Minorities in Kosovo: Period Covering May 2002 to December 2002." Pristina: OSCE Mission in Kosovo and UNHCR Mission in Kosovo, March.

OSCE/Office for Democratic Institutions and Human Rights (ODIHR). 2003. "Republic of Croatia: Parliamentary Elections: 2003, OSCE/ODIHR Election Observation Mission Final Report. http://www.osce.org/documents/odihr/2004/01/1897_en.pdf (accessed January 2, 2007).

——. 2005. "Republic of Tajikistan: Parliamentary Elections 2005, OSCE/ODIHR Election Observation Mission Final Report. http://www.osce.org/documents/odihr/2005/05/14852_en.pdf (accessed December 24, 2006).

——. 2006. "Presidential Election: Republic of Tajikistan, 6 November 2006." OSCE/ODIHR Statement of Preliminary Findings.

Orwell, George. 1968. *The Collected Essays, Journals, and Letters of George Orwell.* Vol. 4. New York: Harcourt, Brace, and World.

O'Shea, Brendan. 1998. *Crisis at Bihac.* Pheonix Mill: Sutton Publishing.

Pantić, Dragomir. 1991. "Nacionalna distanca gradjana Jugoslavije." In L. Bacevic et al., *Jugoslavia na kriznoj prekretnici.* Beograd: Institut Drustvenih Nauka.

Paris, Roland. 2004. *At War's End: Building Peace After Civil Conflict.* Cambridge: Cambridge University Press.

Pearson, Brenda. 2002. "Putting Peace into Practice: Can Macedonia's New Government Meet the Challenge?" *Special Report 96.* Washington, D.C.: U.S. Institute of Peace.

Perry, Duncan. 1997. "The Republic of Macedonia: Finding Its Way." In *Politics, Power, and the Struggle for Democracy in South-East Europe,* ed. Karen Dawisha and Bruce Parrott, 226–81. Cambridge: Cambridge University Press.

Pettigrew, Thomas. 1998. "Intergroup Contact Theory." *Annual Review of Psychology:* 49:65–86.

Pickering, Paula M. 2003. "Courting Minorities in Postwar Bosnia." In *Gaining Access: The Inside Story,* ed. Martha Feldman, Jeannine Bell, and Michele Berger, 68–74. Lanham, Md.: Altimira Press.

——. 2006. "Generating Social Capital for Bridging Ethnic Divisions in the Balkans: Case Studies of Two Bošnjak Cities." *Ethnic and Racial Studies* 29:79–103.

Pickering, Paula M., and the Centre for Research and Policymaking. 2006. *Post-Election Survey in the Republic of Macedonia.* Dataset.

Pickering, Paula M., and Craig Jenness. 1996. *Musical Chairs: Property Problems in Bosnia and Hercegovina.* Sarajevo: Organization for Security and Cooperation in Europe, Mission to Bosnia and Hercegovina.

Pickering, Paula M., and Lee R. Schwartz. 1998. "Bosnian Elections: Nationalism Reinforced?" Paper Presented at the annual convention of the Association of American Geographers. Boston, March.

Poggi, Patrizia, Mirsada Muzur, Dino Djipa, Snjezana Kojic-Hasanagic, and Xavier Bougarel. 2002. *Bosnia and Herzegovina: Local Level Institutions and Social Capital Study.* Washington D.C.: World Bank, Environmentally and Socially Sustainable Development (ECSSD).

"Politika" 1992. March 28, 1992, 6 in *FBIS-EEU-92-069,* April 9.

Poppe, Edwin, and Lou Haggedorn. 2001. "Types of Identification among Russians in the 'Near Abroad.'" *Europe-Asia Studies* 53:57–71.

Portes, Alejandro. 1998. "Social Capital: Its Origins and Applications in Modern Sociology." *Annual Review of Sociology* 24:1–24.

Povrzanović, Maja. 1998. "Practice and Discourse about Practice: Returning Home to the Croatian Danube Basin." *Anthropology of East Europe Review* 16:69–74.

Pugh, Michael, and Margaret Cobble. 2001. "Non-Nationalist Voting in Bosnian Municipal Elections: Implications for Democracy and Peacebuilding." *Journal of Peace Research* 38:27–47.

Putnam, Robert D. 2000. *Bowling Alone: The Collapse and Revival of American Community.* New York: Simon and Schuster.

Radio Beograd Network. 1992. 0900 GMT, March 2, 1992, in *FBIS-EEU-92-041,* March 2.

Rajić, Zlata. 1999. "Pismo Broj: 08-36-28/99 do UNHCR-a Mostar." Konjic: Bosna i Hercegovina, Federacija Bosne i Hercegovine, Hercegovacko-Neretvanski Kanton, Općina Konjic sekretarijat za raseljena lica, rad i socijalnu zaštitu. 25.06.

Ramet, Sabrina. 1992. *Nationalism and Federalism in Yugoslavia.* 2nd ed. Bloomington: Indiana University Press.

———. 1999. *Balkan Babel: The Disintegration of Yugoslavia from the Death of Tito to the War for Kosovo.* Boulder, Colo.: Westview Press.

"Report of the Secretary-General pursuant to General Assembly Resolution 53/35: The Fall of Srebrenica." New York: UN General Assembly, November 15, 1999.

Republika Bosna i Hercegovina, Federacija BiH, državni zavod za statistiku. 1994. "Porodice u Republici Bosni I Hercegovini: popis stanovništva, domaćinstava, stanova i poljoprivrednih gazdinstava 1991 godine." Sarajevo: *Statistički bilten* 236, August.

Republika Makedonija drzavni zavod za statistika. 2003. *Popis 2002.* Skopje. http://www.stat.gov.mk/pdf/10-2003/2.1.3.30.pdf (accessed May 1, 2007).

Rhea, Daniel. 2006. "The 2006 Bosnian National Election: Tipping Point Toward Democracy or Dissolution?" Paper Presented at the annual convention of the American Association for the Advancement of Slavic Studies. Washington, D.C., November.

Richter, James. 2002. "Russian Women's Organizations." In *The Power and Limits of NGOs,* ed. Sarah E. Mendelson and John K. Glenn, 54–90. New York: Columbia University Press.

Rieder, Jonathan. 1985. *Canarsie: The Jews and Italians of Brooklyn against Liberalism.* Cambridge: Harvard University Press.

"Rising from the Ashes? 1999—A Year of Decision in the Balkans." 1999. *Refugees Magazine* 114.

Roeder, Philip G., and Donald Rothchild, eds. 2005. *Sustainable Peace: Power and Democracy after Civil Wars.* Ithaca: Cornell University Press.

Romann, Michael, and Alex Weingrod. 1991. *Living Together Separately: Arabs and Jews in Contemporary Jerusalem.* Princeton: Princeton University Press.

Rosand, Eric. 1998. "The Right to Return under International Law following Mass Dislocation: The Bosnia Precedent?" Unpublished ms.

Rose, Richard, Christian Haerpfer, and William Mishler. 1997. "Social Capital in Civic and Stressful Societies." *Studies in Comparative International Development* 31: 85–111.

Ross, Marc Howard. 2001. "Psychocultural Interpretations and Dramas: Identity Dynamics in Ethnic Conflict." *Political Psychology* 22:157–78.

Rothschild, Joseph A., and Nancy Wingfield. 2000. *Return to Diversity: A Political History of East Central Europe since World War Two.* 3rd ed. New York: Oxford University Press.

Rubin, Barnett R. 2002. *The Fragmentation of Afghanistan.* 2nd ed. New Haven: Yale University Press.

Rundell, John. 1998. "Tensions of Citizenship in an Age of Diversity: Reflections on Territoriality, Cosmopolitanism and Symmetrical Reciprocity." In *Blurred Boundaries: Migration, Ethnicity, Citizenship,* ed. Rainer Baubock Rainer and John Rundell, 320–40. Aldershot Hants, England: Ashgate, 1998.

Sali-Terzić, Sevima. 2001. "Civil Society." In *Policies of International Support to South-Eastern European Countries: Lessons (not) Learnt from Bosnia and Herzegovina,* ed. Žarko Papić, 138–59. Sarajevo: Open Society Institute.

Sampson, Steven. 1996. "The Social Life of Projects: Importing Civil Society to Albania." In *Civil Society: Challenging Western Models,* ed. Chris Hann and Elizabeth Dunn, 121–42. London: Routledge.

"Sarajevo Mosque Preacher Questions Work of FOSS, Criticizes FRY's Kostunica." 2002. FBIS Report in Serbo-Croatian, September 13.

Schlozman, Kay L., Nancy Burns, and Sidney Verba. 1994. "Gender and the Pathways to Participation: The Role of Resources." *Journal of Politics* 56:963–90.

Schmidt, Fabian. 1995. "Macedonia: From National Consensus to Pluralism." *Transition* 1:26–30.

Schnell, Izhak. 1994. *Perceptions of Israeli Arabs: Territoriality and Identity.* Aldershot: Avebury.

Schuman, Howard, Charlotte Steeh, Lawrence Bobo, and Maria Krysan. 1997. *Racial Attitudes in America.* Cambridge: Harvard University Press.

Scolari. 1997. QSR NUD*IST 4. Thousand Oaks: Sage Publications Software.

Sekulić, Dusko, Garth Massey, and Randy Hodson. 1994. "Who Were the Yugoslavs? Failed Sources of a Common Identity in the Former Yugoslavia." *American Sociological Review* 59:83–97.

——. 2006. "Ethnic Intolerance and Ethnic Conflict in the Disintegration of Yugoslavia." *Ethnic and Racial Studies* 29:797–827

Seligman, Adam. 1997. *The Problem of Trust.* Princeton: Princeton University Press.

Sell, Louis. 2000. "The Serb Flight from Sarajevo: Dayton's First Failure." *East European Politics and Society* Winter: 179–202.

——. 2001. "A Blueprint for Next Steps in Kosovo." Washington D.C.: Public International Law and Policy Group.

Shingles, Richard D. 1992. "Minority Consciousness and Political Action: a Comparative Approach." In *Ethnic and Racial Minorities in Advanced Industrial Democracies,* ed. Anthony M. Messina et al. New York: Greenwood Press.

Shoup, Paul. 1968. *Communism and the Yugoslav Nationalist Question.* New York: Columbia University Press.

Šiber, Ivan. 1992. "The Impact of Nationalism, Values, and Ideological Orientations on Multi-Party Elections in Croatia." In *The Tragedy of Yugoslavia: The Failure of Democratic Transformation,* ed. Jim Seroka and Vukasin Pavlovic, 141–71. Armonk: M.E. Sharpe.

Sieber, Joan E. 1992. *Planning Ethically Responsible Research.* Applied Social Research Methods Series, 31. Newbury Park: Sage.

Sigelman, Lee, Timothy Bledsoe, Susan Welch, and Michael Combs. 1996. "Making Contact? Black-White Social Interaction in an Urban Setting." *American Journal of Sociology* 101:306–32.

Slack, Andrew, and Roy Doyan. 2001. "Population Dynamics and Susceptibility for Ethnic Conflict: The Case of Bosnia and Herzegovina." *Journal of Peace Research.* 38:139–61.

Slatina, Senad. 1998. "Predstavnici RS očekuju da će u Sarajevu pronaći tijela od 400 do 8000 ubijenih srba!?" *Slobodna Bosna* IV:28.Novembra.

Slim, Randa, and Faredun Hodizoda. 2002. In *Searching for Peace in Central and South Asia,* ed. Monique Mekenkamp, Paul van Tongeren, and Hans van de Veen, 109–40. Boulder: Lynne Rienner.

Smith, Anthony D. 1981. *National Identity.* London: Penguin.

Smith, Graham. 1999. "Transnational Politics and the Politics of the Russian Diaspora." *Ethnic and Racial Studies* 22:500–23.

Smith, Jeffrey. 2001. "Ethnic Leaders Try to Persuade Compatriots to Get Along." *Washington Post,* May 15, A12.

Smith, Rogers. 2004. "Identities, Interests, and the Future of Political Science." *Perspectives on Politics* 2:301–12.

Smolar, Alexander. 1997. "From Opposition to Atomization." In *Consolidating the Third Wave Democracies,* ed. Larry Diamond et al., 263–77. Baltimore: John Hopkins University Press.

Smooha, Sammy. 2005. *A Minority-Majority Relations Index in Deeply Divide Societies and Its Application to Arab-Jewish Relations in Israel*. Final Research Report submitted to Israel Foundations Trustees.

Snow, David A., Burke Rochford Jr., Steven Worden, and Robert Benford. 1986. "Frame Alignment Processes, Micromobilization, and Movement Participation," *American Sociological Review* 51:464–81.

Sociajalisticka Republika Bosna i Hercegovina. 1990. *Statistički godišnjak*. Sarajevo: Republicki zavod za statistiku.

Social Impact, Inc. 2005. "USAID/OTI Afghanistan Program: Final Evaluation." http://pdf.usaid.gov/pdf_docs/PDACF383.pdf (accessed April 20, 2007).

"Sofia Declaration," 1999. Serb National Council.

Somers, Margaret. 1994. "Narratives and the Constitution of Identity, A Relational and Network Approach." *Theory and Society* 23:605–50.

Srpsko Grandjansko Vijece. 1998. Rezultati: Ankete srpskih domacinstava i domacinstava mjesovitih brakova na podrucju Unsko Sanskog Kantona. Bihać: Biro za zastitu ljudskih prava.

——. 2002. "Rezultati:Ankete imovina." Bihac: Srpsko Gradjansko Vijece, Biro za zastitu ljudskih prava.

"Statistički godišnjak SR Bosne i Hercegovine 1990." 1991. Sarajevo: Sociajalisticka Republika Bosna i Hercegovina, Republički zavod za statistiku.

Stefansson, Anders H. 2004. "Sarajevo Suffering: Homecoming and the Hierarchy of Homeland Hardship." In *Homecomings: Unsettling Paths of Return*, ed. Fran Markowitz and Anders H. Stefansson. Lanham, Md.: Lexington Books.

Stojanov, Dragoljub. 2002. "Bosnia-Herzegovina Since 1995: Transition and Reconstruction of the Economy." In *Policies of International Support to South-Eastern European Countries: Lessons (not)Learnt from Bosnia and Herzegovina*, edited by Žarko Papić, 138–59. Sarajevo: Open Society Institute.

Stojanovska, Suncica. 2005. "Tetovo Most Desirable Trophy." *Vreme* 18, January 1–2.

Stokes, Gale. 1993. *The Walls Came Tumbling Down: The Collapse of Communism in Eastern Europe*. New York: Oxford University Press.

Stuart, Jennifer, ed. 2003. *The 2002 NGO Sustainability Index*. Washington, D.C.: US Agency for International Development. http://www.usaid.gov/locations/europe _eurasia/dem_gov/ngoindex/2002/index.htm (accessed May 1, 2007).

Stubbs, Paul. 2001. "'Social Sector' or the Diminution of Social Policy? Regulating Welfare Regimes in Contemporary Bosnia-Herzegovina." In *Policies of International Support to South-Eastern European Countries: Lessons (not) Learnt from Bosnia and Herzegovina*, ed. Žarko Papić, 95–107. Sarajevo: Open Society Institute.

Štulhofer, Aleksandar. 2004. "The Perception of Corruption and the Erosion of Social Capital in Croatia 1995–2003." *Političko Misao* 41:74–86.

Sudetic, Chuck. 1998. *Blood and Vengeance*. New York: Penguin.

Sumka, Howard. 2003. "Message from the Mission Director." U.S. Agency for International Development, Mission in Bosnia and Herzegovina. http://www.usaid.ba.

Šupek, Rudi. 1975. "The Sociology of Workers' Self-management." In *Self-governing Socialism* 2, ed. Branko Horvat, Mihailo Marković, and Rudi Šupek, 3–13. White Plains, N.Y.: International Arts and Sciences Press.

Sweeney, Anna. 2000. "Kosovo Albanians Say Too Much Damage Done to Live with Serbs." Washington D.C.: Department of State, Office of Research.

——. 2001. "Community Bonds Lead Refugees Home to Bosnia and Croatia." Washington D.C.: Department of State, Office of Research.

Tajfel, Henri. 1978. "Social Categorization, Social Identity and Social Comparison." In *Differentiation between Social Groups: Studies in the Social Psychology of Intergroup Relations*, ed. Henri Tajfel, 61–76. New York: Academic Press.

———, ed., 1982. *Social Identity and Intergroup Relations*. Cambridge: Cambridge University Press.

Tanjug. 1992. 2008 GMT, April 8, 1992 in *FBIS-EEU*-92-069, April 9, 1992.

Taylor, Michael. 1988. "Rationality and Collective Action." In *Rationality and Revolution*, ed. Michael Taylor. New York: Cambridge University Press.

Thompson, Mark. 1994. *Forging War: The Media in Serbia, Croatia, and Bosnia-Hercegovina*. Avon: Article 19 / The Bath Press.

Tilly, Charles. 2002. *Stories, Identities, and Political Change*. Lanham, Md.: Rowman & Littlefield.

Tocqueville, Alexis De. 1994. *Democracy in America*. New York: A. Knopf.

Toft, Monica Duffy. 2003. *The Geography of Ethnic Violence: Identity, Interests, and the Indivisibility of Territory*. Princeton: Princeton University Press.

Tull, Stephen. 1994. "Ethnic Conflict and Cooperation During Radical Political Transformation: A Theory of Ethnic Mobilization." Paper Presented at the Woodrow Wilson Center / ACLS East European Studies' Junior Scholars Training Seminar, Aspen Institute / Wye Woods, August 25–28.

Turner, John C. 1982. "Towards a Cognitive Redefinition of the Social Group." In *Social Identity and Intergroup Relations*, ed. Henri Tajfel, 15–39. Cambridge: Cambridge University Press.

UN Development Programme (UNDP). 2000. *Early Warning System in Bosnia and Herzegovina: Base Line Report*. Sarajevo: UN Development Programme.

———. 2001. *National Human Development Report 2001: Bosnia and Herzegovina*. http:// www.undp.ba / index.aspx?PID=14 (accessed April 21, 2007).

———. 2002. *Early Warning System: Bosnia and Herzegovina, Annual Report*. http:// www .undp.ba / index.aspx?PID=14 (accessed April 21, 2007).

———. 2003a. *Early Warning Report: Bosnia and Herzegovina*, No. IV, Sarajevo. http:// www.undp.ba / index.aspx?PID=14 (accessed April 21, 2007).

———. 2003b. *Early Warning Report: FYR Macedonia*, No. I. Skopje. http:// www.undp .org.mk / datacenter / publications / documents / ewr / pdf (accessed May 16, 2007).

———. 2004a. *Consolidated Report of the Municipality assessments in Bosnia and Herzegovina: Rights-based Municipal Assessment and Planning Project*. Sarajevo, April.

———. 2004b. *EarlyWarning System in Bosnia-Herzegovina, IV 52*. http:// www.undp .ba / index.aspx?PID=14 (accessed April 30, 2007).

———. 2004c. *Human Development Report Kosovo 2004, The Rise of the Citizen: Challenges and Choices*. Pristina: UNDP.

———. 2004d. *Afghanistan: National Human Development Report*. http:// www.undp .org.af / nhdr_04 / NHDR04.htm (accessed April 27, 2007).

———. 2005. *Early Warning System in Bosnia-Herzegovina, Quarterly Report, January– March 2005*. http:// www.undp.ba / index.aspx?PID=14 (accessed April 21, 2007).

UN High Commissioner for Refugees (UNHCR). 1997a. "Population Structure." Sarajevo: Office of the Special Envoy.

———. 1997b. "UNHCR 'Open Cities' Initiative." Sarajevo: UNHCR, Office of the Special Envoy, August 31.

———. 1998a. "A Regional Strategy for Sustainable Return of Those Displaced by the Conflict in the Former Yugoslavia." Paper presented to the Humanitarian Issues Working Group, Geneva: UNHCR, June 26.

——. 1998b. "Progress in and Prospects for Sustainable Return and Solutions in the former Yugoslavia." Geneva: Humanitarian Issues Working Group, November 20.
——. 2000. "Refugees and Others of Concern to UNHCR: Statistical Overview—First Quarter 2000." Geneva: Registration and Statistics Unit, Programme Coordination Section.
——. 1998–2005. "Statistics Package." Sarajevo: UNHCR Mission to Bosnia and Hercegovina. (Statistics are updated monthly, http:// www.unhcr.ba.)
——. 2003a. "Framework for Durable Solutions for Refugees and Persons of Concern." Geneva: Core Group On Durable Solutions. http:// www.unhcr.ch/cgi-bin/texis/vtx/home/+owwBmeWlwhCwwwwnwwwwwwwmFqwnFqwh Fqo7E2RN02ItFqopwGBDnG5AFqo7E2RN02IcFqEeJhxxpwBGowBodDaeJl3mB ntGwBodDMzmwwwwwwwwDzmxwwwwwww1FqmRbZVFqn-uPPiFqw/opendoc.pdf (accessed September 2004).
——. 2003b. "UNHCR Returnee Monitoring Report: Afghanistan Repatriation, January 2002–March 2003. http:// www.unhcr.org/cgi-bin/texis/vtx/home/open doc.pdf?tbl−SUBSITES&id=3f1cf64f4 (accessed May 15, 2007).
——. 2004. "One Millionth Returnee Goes Home in Bosnia and Herzegovina." Geneva, September 21. http:// www.unhcr.ba/press/2004pr/210904.htm (accessed May 5, 2007).
——. 2005. "Update on Conditions for Return to Bosnia and Herzegovina." Sarajevo, January. http:// www.unhcr.ba/publications/B&HRET0105.pdf.
UN Secretary General (UNSYG) S/23900, 1992. "Further Report of the Secretary-General Pursuant to Security Council Resolution 749, May 12.
UNSYG A/54/549. 1999. "Report of the Secretary-General pursuant to General Assembly Resolution 53/35: The Fall of Srebrenica," November 15.
UN Economic and Social Council. 1993. Document E/CN.4/1993/50, February 1993.
U.S. Agency for International Development (USAID). 2004. "The 2004 NGO Sustainability Index: Central and Eastern Europe and Eurasia." http:// www.usaid.gov/locations/europe_eurasia/dem_gov/ngoindex/2004/index.htm (accessed February 1, 2007).
U.S. Department of State. 2001. "Bosnian and Croatian Returnees Feel Safe in their Communities," Washington, D.C.: Office of Research, February 15.
U.S. Information Agency (USIA). 1994. *Public Opinion in Croatia, A Special Report.* Washington D.C.: Office of Research and Media Reaction.
——. 1997. *Public Opinion in Bosnia and Hercegovina*, Vol. IV. Washington D.C.: Office of Research and Media Reaction.
——. 1998. *Public Opinion in Bosnia and Hercegovina*, Vol. V. Washington D.C.: Office of Research and Media Reaction.
——. 2000. *Macedonian Albanians' Political Influence Gives Them Reason for Optimism.*, Washington D.C.: Office of Research and Media Reaction.
U.S. Institute of Peace (USIP). 2005. "Mitrovica's Future: Is Reconciliation Possible?" Public event presented by the U.S. Institute of Peace, the Search for Common Ground, and the Washington Network on Children of Armed Conflict, Washington, D.C., September 23.
Ustav Socjalističke Federativne Republike Jugoslavije. 1991. Beorad: Službeni List.
Varshney, Ashutosh. 2002. *Ethnic Conflict and Civic Life: Hindus and Muslims in India.* New Haven: Yale University Press.
Verdery, Katherine. 1993. "Nationalism and National Sentiment in Post-Socialist Romania." *Slavic Review* 52:179–203.

Verkuyten, Maykel. 1991. "Self-definition and Intergroup Formation Among Ethnic Minorities in the Netherlands." *Social Psychology Quarterly* 54:280–86.

Walsh, Katherine Cramer. 2004. *Talking About Politics: Informal Groups and Social Identity in American Life*. Chicago: Chicago University Press.

Walsh, Martha. 1997. "Results and Analysis of a Socio-economic survey of Project Return Beneficiaries." Bihać: Care International.

Wedel, Janine. 2001. *Collision and Collusion: the Strange Case of Western Aid to Eastern Europe*. New York: Palgrave.

White, Josh, and Griff Witte. 2006. "To Stem Iraqi Violence, U.S. Aims to Create Jobs." *Washington Post*, December 12, A01.

Wilmer, Franke. 2002. *Social Construction of Man, State, and War: Identity, Conflict, and Violence in the Former Yugoslavia*. New York: Routledge.

Woodward, Susan. 1995a. *A Balkan Tragedy*. Washington, D.C.: Brookings Institution.

——. 1995b. *Socialist Unemployment*. Princeton: Princeton University Press.

——. 1999. "Bosnia After Dayton." In *After the Peace: Resistance and Reconciliation*, ed. Robert Rothstein, 139–66. Boulder: Lynne Rienner.

Xhaferi, Arben. 1998. "Challenges to Democracy in Multiethnic States." Paper presented at the U.S. Institute of Peace, Washington, D.C., October 1.

Yin, Robert. 1994. *Case Study Research*. 2nd ed. Thousand Oaks: Sage.

Zagreb Radio. 1991. 1800 GMT, November 18, 1991, in *FBIS-EEU-91-223*, November 19.

Zavod za zapošljavanje Bosne i Hercegovine. 1999. "Zapošljavanje i nezaposlenost u Bosni i Hercegovini." *Statistički bilten broj 3*. Sarajevo.

Zimmermann, Warren. 1996. *Origins of a Catastrophe*. New York: Times Books.

Zimmerman, William. 1992. "Social and Economic Change: The Transformation of the Balkans, and the Disintegration of Yugoslavia." Paper presented in Stuttgart, Germany, September.

Živković, Rajko. 1999. "Nacija u raljama politike." *Oslobodjenje*. Mart 22:2.

Županov, Josip. 1975. "Participation and Influence." In *Self-governing Socialism* 2, ed. Branko Horvat, Mihailo Markovic, and Rudi Šupek, 76–87. White Plains, N.Y.: International Arts and Sciences Press.

Index